Dedicated with Much Gratitude

**To All of the Horses and Animals
Throughout My Life**

Copyright 2019

ABOUT THE AUTHOR

Jessamy Rouson left her home in New York City at fourteen years of age to ride horses professionally. She has had a lifetime of success within the International sphere of showjumping and has found it to be a passport to the world.

Jessamy has ridden, trained, developed and sold some of the most famous horses in the world, including some Hall of Fame horses. She has also trained with the United States Equestrian Team and has written for the well-respected Barron's financial paper regarding the syndication of showjumpers. This book contains a lifetime of stories which span the globe. In addition, Jessamy has also been deeply involved in the world of animal rescue. Her all-encompassing love and understanding of animals is a constant throughout the book and extremely moving. Jessamy teaches us the wonder and reward of understanding our horses and our animals.

Jessamy began the career of the world famous showjumper "Philco". Philco came off of a New Jersey racetrack as a severely abused and extremely neurotic animal. He was purchased for a mere $1,200. With Jessamy's kind touch, compassion, understanding, empathy and skill, Philco eventually became one of the top ten showjumpers of all time with Britain's legendary showjumping rider, David Broome. Philco is just one of Jessamy's success stories with horses.

There are many more, including "Dreamy Sam" who came from a racetrack in Ohio for $600 and became a winning Grand Prix horse with Jessamy. There was also the nearly savage German mare "Matadora", who became a Grand Prix winner and the greatest horse of Jessamy's career.

This captivating story also has harrowing tales of riding horses professionally in Northern Ireland during "The Troubles", amidst constant gunfire, bombing and the threat of a brutal death – all while Jessamy was seventeen years old. She then went on to ride in England for Britain's great showjumping rider David Broome. She also rode in Wales, before coming back to America and starting her own very successful business in Virginia.

This is an engaging story about an inspirational life in the International World of Showjumping. The book has tales from all across America and Europe, as well as Russia, Northern Ireland, Britain, Wales, Germany, Switzerland, Sweden, Belgium, Poland, France, New Zealand, Mexico, Puerto Rico and Bermuda. This book reads like a page turning novel, but the most amazing thing is that the stories are truly real and extremely captivating.   Enjoy!

FROM WHERE MY STRENGTH LIES
THE LIFE OF A HORSE WHISPERER

CONTENTS

PART ONE

THE EARLY YEARS
LIFE LESSONS FROM THE HACK STABLE
THE HACK STABLE
MIKE COHEN
BENNY O'MEARA
PHILCO (ON DANCER)
MY SHORTLIVED EQUITATION CAREER ON NEW ETTA
DREAMY SAM
SANBAR'S SAMANTHA
JUNIOR OLYMPIC TOUR PUERTO RICO and MEXICO
HARRISBURG GRAND PRIX
MY DREAM
NORTHERN IRELAND
CROSSMAGLEN
RIDING IN CROSSMAGLEN NORTHERN IRELAND
RIDING IN WALES FOR BRITAIN'S DAVID BROOME
MY TIME IN WALES WITH THE JOHNSEY FAMI
WALES AND PARIS
BACK TO AMERICA

PART TWO

THE START OF MY OWN BUSINESS
PREPARING THE STABLE AT BRIDLESPUR FOR MY NEW BUSINESS
THE EARLY DAYS OF SHOWSTOCK STABLES
THE FABULOUS GUCCI
THE WONDERFUL TOSS THE COIN
THE LOVELY COOL FELLOW
FLIP THE COIN
WHISPER WHY
MY COWBOY DAYS
THE SENSATIONAL SPORTIF
RIDING ROGUES IN TEXAS
BUYING MY OWN FARM
BUYING HORSES AT THE RACETRACKS ACROSS THE COUNTRY
I'M AN EAGLE
BEING SELECTED TO TRAIN AT THE USET HEADQUARTERS
KEEP THE CHANGE
THE OFFICER
THE WONDERFUL WORLD OF NEW ZEALAND

PART THREE

MY NEW INVESTOR
LOOKING FOR TALENTED PROSPECTS IN AMSTERDAM
GOING TO PAUL SCHOCKEMOHLE'S IN GERMANY
THE DISCOVERY OF MATADORA
THE HORSES ARRIVE IN AMERICA
MY NEW CLIENT OUT OF FLORIDA
MY NEW TRACTOR TRAILER
THE FABULOUS CHANEL
CHANEL'S WONDERFUL OFFSPRING
MATADORA
CHIEF de EQUIPE
ALL THE GOLD
THE SILVER BARON
THE SILVER BARON'S EXCEPTIONAL OFFSPRING
SHAREEF & CAPTIVA
THE SILVER CARD
SAMBUCCA
THE SILVER FROST
SOMETHING SPECIAL
LIONNE D'AIR
THE TALENTED
EUROPE BOUND WITH A PLANE LOAD OF HORSES
ANISETTE
TUXEDO
THE SILVER PRINCE
BOYSIE II
GLORIOUS TRIP TO RUSSIA
ANIMAL HAVEN
TURNING AROUND THE HORRIFIC

HELPING HUNTING DOGS
WHAT DOES IT ALL MEAN?
ACKNOWLEDGEMENTS TO PHOTOGRAPHERS

FROM WHERE MY STRENGTH LIES

THE LIFE OF A HORSE WHISPERER

THE MAGNIFICENT WORLD OF SHOW JUMPING
A PASSPORT TO THE WORLD

Jessamy and The Officer in a Grand Prix

I learned quite early in my career that being successful in the magnificent sphere of International Showjumping is a passport to the world. Should one succeed in this difficult and technical sport, they shall inevitably meet VIPs, royalty, dignitaries, celebrities, movie stars and the enormously wealthy. National and International doors open when one shines in this world.

Being successful in the sphere of showjumping enabled me to travel to places which I never would have had the opportunity to see otherwise. With endless thanks to the horses, I have traveled across this country from coast to coast. I have also traveled across Europe, Germany, Holland, Switzerland, Sweden, Belgium, Great Britain, Ireland, France, Poland, Russia, New Zealand, Mexico, Puerto Rico and Bermuda.

To succeed in the showjumping world, one needs to be partnered with a special horse - or perhaps several horses in a string of talent. The partnership between horse and rider needs to be a unique bond with every horse that one rides. Each horse is an individual. A rider and true horse person must be able to feel and study the horse's personality, thus adapting their style and training techniques to each individual horse.

I find the process of becoming a friend and partner to each horse absolutely fascinating. I think the great William Steinkraus, our United States Equestrian Team Captain and Olympic champion for many years, said it beautifully when he said the following:

"Taking things for granted is all too easy. But we must never forget, every time we sit on a horse, what an extraordinary privilege it is to be able to unite one's body with that of another sentient being - one that is stronger, faster, and more agile by far than we are, and at the same time, brave, generous, and uncommonly forgiving."
Epilogue of "Reflections on Riding and Jumping",
By William Steinkraus.

My story is about the understanding of horses and life. This includes all of the national and international ventures along the way.

When a rider is able to get on a vast variety of different horses and understand them, relate to them with empathy, compassion and sympathy, and guide the horse to perform willingly to the best of their ability, one becomes a Horse Whisperer.

It is not the horse's responsibility to understand us.
It is our responsibility to understand the horse.

This book is a compilation of my life stories in the vast international world of showjumping. It involves understanding many different horses - several of which began as extremely difficult horses or rejects from other horsemen in the racing sphere or the world of show horses.

Over and over, what may have been an extremely difficult or misunderstood horse became my friend and my competition partner on the highest level. Many of these horses became nationally and internationally famous. A few of them became Hall of Fame horses.

My hope is that this book shall inspire many other horsemen and horsewomen to view each horse as an individual. Put aside other people's comments or opinions on a horse which may be misunderstood. Find a bond with that horse.

With understanding, compassion, empathy and correct training techniques, the greatly misunderstood and unwanted horse could become a Champion.

Every horse can have a career doing something, as there are so many different disciplines and jobs within the horse industry. Not every horse will make a top showjumper. They must have the innate talent, scope, quality, courage, personality and heart for showjumping. There are horses who have these wonderful traits, but have been rejected because they were misunderstood or because they presented as difficult.

This is a book of stories about some of those misunderstood and rejected horses, and how they accomplished great things once they were finally understood.

This is a book about how I became a Horse Whisperer.

Matadora and Jessamy winning a Grand Prix

PART ONE

THE EARLY YEARS

John Henry Rouson with Jessamy and Cocoa at Clove Lake Stables

It all began in New York City before I could walk. I'd climb on the family dog - a loving rescue from the local animal shelter of indiscriminate breeding. His name was "Bogey". He was my best friend and my first "ride".

Bogey

When I was an infant, Bogey guarded my crib and would only allow my parents to enter the room. When I was out of the crib, Bogey carried me around on his back. Bogey was a patient and wise old soul who I remember lovingly to this day.

I had tried out the family cat, "Pinky", which didn't go well at all. I have permanent scars over my eyebrows and across my eyelids which remind me of this unfortunate venture every time I look in the mirror. I quickly learned that you shouldn't wake sleeping kitties up by rubbing your face on the soft fur of their bellies. Good to know when you're an infant exploring the world, but a tough lesson for me.

Most parents would have taken their child to the hospital, as the scratches around my eyes were significantly deep and bleeding badly, but parents just put iodine on my wounds and called it a day.

Pinky after the attack

At three years of age, I was outgrowing Bogey and was looking to advance my riding career. My father took me to the local riding stable - Clove Lake Stables on Staten Island, New York.

There I met Cocoa, a furry gray and white Shetland pony who was significantly older than I was and had a great deal more experience. I adored Cocoa and was convinced that he was the most wonderful pony in the world. Cocoa and I would go for a walk about whenever I could convince my father to take me.

My love for horses and the nagging instinct to be with them continued throughout my childhood and indeed throughout my life. When I was in kindergarten there was a nice little girl who owned a mule. I made sure that we were the very best of friends so that she would invite me out to ride her mule. I have loved mules and donkeys ever since and have rescued several from Kill Pens. They are incredibly intelligent, kind and generous animals.

My father, John Henry Rouson, was a cartoonist with four internationally syndicated comic strips – "Little Sport", "Little Eve", "Ladies Day" and "Boy and Girl." John Henry Rouson was also an extremely skilled equine artist and recognized as one of the best in the world. He painted the Canadian Horse of the Year and the Queen's plate winner for the Canadian Jockey Club each year for over a decade. Once a year, starting at four years of age, I would accompany my father on his drive to Canada to watch the Queen's Plate and photograph the winner for the next year's painting. I even had the honor of watching the great Northern Dancer win the Queen's Plate. I then had the wonderful opportunity to see Northern Dancer again a year or so later at EP Taylor's beautiful Windfields farm, where Northern Dancer was standing for stud duty.

My father had friends in Canada who had a large breeding operation for racehorses of the highest quality. These people had a boy about my age named Greg and we instantly became great friends. Greg and I used to walk down the lane between the pastures of horses and go to the huge back field where the barren mares were kept. These were mares which had not as yet been bred.

Greg and I used to each catch a mare by the halter, lead them beside the water trough, and climb on – no bridle or saddle - not even a lead rope. We would grab a big handful of mane and hang on like spider monkeys as the mares would take off across the fields at racing speed. These mares would gallop flat out to the end of the field, with all of the other mares joining in one big pack.

"Though he be but little, he is fierce" – Shakespeare (paraphrased)

**Oil Painting of Northern Dancer by John Henry Rouson.
Displayed at Woodbine Racetrack in Toronto[1]**

It was like riding in an actual race except that we had no control whatsoever. We flew like the wind until we reached the other side of the field. Then we'd turn them around by pushing and patting them on the neck and race back to where we started. Of course, this was our secret. Such behavior would be unacceptable to the adults. These were horses meant to breed and produce foal's worth in the high six figures or more. It was definitely forbidden to ride any of these horses. Greg and I got away with this activity because it had not occurred to the adults that four year olds would want to ride virtually untamed horses. It was our secret forever, until this very day.

---

[1] Works by John Henry Rouson can be found at equineartofdistinction.com

The Great Northern Dancer – The Pride of Canada

This thrilling experience taught me a great deal about balance, as well as the ultimate feel of a horse in motion. I was instantly addicted. I was able to sense what the mare I was riding was going to do just by feeling her movements and watching her eyes and ears – basically reading the horse's mind. We always rode different mares every time we raced. This began the creation of a terrific frame of reference for me into the individual personalities and movements of many different horses - something I cherished and which served me well in the years to come.

Northern Dancer's Grave and Memorial in Canada

I read everything that I could get my hands on pertaining to horses and studied for hours on end – particularly veterinary books and books on horsemanship. My parents divorced when I was quite young, so I would visit my mother in Manhattan every weekend. Whenever my mother and I saw a NYC mounted police horse, we'd go up and ask the officer if I may pet his horse. One time when I was about six years old, I examined the teeth of a policeman's horse and told the officer the horse's age. It turned out that I was correct. The kind officer was impressed and allowed me to ride his wonderful bay horse around the basement of a New York City indoor parking garage – a thrill I shall never forget.

There was a professional dog trainer in Greenwich Village named Barney. He was a jovial man who became a good friend. Barney had about eight ponies that he kept in a warehouse which he had converted into a small stable.

Barney had built a corral on the lot where the warehouse and ponies were stabled. He wanted the neighborhood kids to ride and enjoy the ponies, as well as learn to love and care for animals. A group of neighborhood kids soon made up Barney's team of exceedingly loyal pony care specialists. Needless to say, I was one of them. These were kids of many different ethnicities and backgrounds, as well as from very low-income households. We all became great friends.

Jessamy and a favorite horse, Pee Wee

Barney believed that if these kids learned to groom and care for the ponies, as well as ride and drive them, it would keep them out of trouble and teach them to appreciate animals. Barney had several little carts for the ponies and the kids would drive the ponies harnessed to these small carts.

Once we had proven to Barney that we were capable of driving and controlling the ponies in the corral, he would allow us to drive them on the streets and down by the waterfront. There was very little traffic on the waterfront and a good deal of open space. We learned to navigate our pony and cart through the small amount of traffic on the way there, as well as learning to respect and adhere to the rules of the road. This entire experience was a fabulous lesson in responsibility and management, plus it was a great deal of fun.

As a point of social interest, I would like to mention that Barney was correct about involving these kids with a consuming love for animals. These kids were never in trouble. Their lives were totally focused on loving and caring for the ponies, as well as each other. I never heard about any interest in drugs, alcohol, crime, or any other negative influence with these young kids. Though negative influences ran rampant in New York City among adults and children alike, these kids cared only about the ponies, their friends and their respected leader Barney.

Jessamy on a Cherished Ride at a Hack Stable

LIFE LESSONS FROM THE HACK STABLE AND BUNCHY GRANT'S AUCTION

CLOVE LAKE STABLES

After this un-orthodox start, my life became all about working at Clove Lake Stables – the local hack barn on Staten Island. There was a group of little kids who hung around and worked for free, just to be around horses. I was one of those kids. The stable was a hack stable, meaning it rented horses out to the public by the hour.

I was one of the kids who took large groups of people out for an hour walk around the park, after first stopping traffic on horseback and crossing a very busy road. This entire experience taught me tremendous management skills and responsibility, like nothing else ever could. We were literally responsible for the lives and welfare of the horses, as well as the public who was riding them and the safety of the people in the vehicles on the road.

These were seldom groups of quiet, respectful or polite people. I would usually guide groups of teenagers and rowdy young people. They were often partying, drinking, hollering and generally a very rough bunch of characters to control.

Bittersweet and Jessamy preparing to take a group out to Clove Lake Park

We'd get the slick, macho, Fonzey types out of Staten Island, Brooklyn, Queens or the Bronx - with their girlfriends in tow. These gals were particularly tricky to manage, as they often wore high heels and screamed every time the horse moved a hair. The wise old hack horses knew exactly what they were dealing with and immediately took the opportunity to put their heads down and eat grass.

This was a major life crisis for these gals and many just slipped pathetically down their horse's neck - high heels in the air and screaming at the top of their very capable lungs. This scenario entailed a loose horse and a screaming, hysterical woman – in other words a total nightmare, but a management learning opportunity.

The ordeal required getting off my horse, catching the loose horse, convincing the high heeled lady to stop screaming and helping her to get back onto the horse. Usually these ladies flat out refused to get back on the horse UNTIL I told them that they would have to walk all the way back to the stables in high heels.

Figuring out exactly how to get these ladies remounted was not an easy task either. It involved leading the horse up to a fence or a big rock, so the gals could fumble their way on from there. We were not dealing with athletes here. These women were straight out of the wild side of the streets. Add horses to the mix and you have a tough situation to control and manage.

The horses at this hack stable deserve a sincerely honorable mention here. Most of them were not only amazingly patience, kind, generous and forgiving creatures - they were also a big part of my foundation as a rider and a horsewoman. I think of them and thank each and every one daily for their patience, kindness and wise lessons. I remember their names over fifty years later.

All of these horses came out of Bunchy Grant's auction in Metuchen, New Jersey. Bunchy's was a really rough place with hundreds of horses in feedlots and many cigar smoking, tobacco chewing, rough, tough, rowdy cowboys. There were all kinds of horses of every possible breed and quite often, no specific breed at all. Some were gentle horses, some were wild, and there was everything in between. There were draft horses, ponies, minis, donkeys and mules - everything which could remotely qualify within the equine category.

Bunchy's auction had a wide selection of humans as well - everyone from hack stable owners, to riding camp directors, to private owners looking for horses, to the Kill Buyers - who I abhor to this day. Sometimes there would be professional horsemen there looking for a diamond in the rough. Many a Champion has had his or her humble beginning at Bunchy's due to no fault of their own.

Everyone walked around the lots assessing the horses and then took their place in the tiny, cigar smoke filled area where the auction was held. When the auction began, the frenzied atmosphere was electric and hectic. The auction and the horses were held entirely within one huge indoor building.

The auction area was a very narrow dirt and sawdust aisle, with the auctioneer up high in a podium on one side of the aisle, shouting at the top of his lungs. All of the potential bidders were on the other side behind a rope, pushing and shoving each other on the bleachers in order to get a better view. The horses came in one huge door on one side of the auctioneer. The cowboys would gallop the horses up and down the lane, spinning them around at the end of the aisle for effect while they were being auctioned.

Once they had been sold, the horses would go out another door on the other side of the auctioneer as the next horse came into the sales area. Bunchy used to stand in the middle of the aisle with his cane. If Bunchy, in his infinite wisdom, felt that a horse was a jumper type, Bunchy would hold his cane across the aisle and make the sales rider jump the cane for the crowd. That is where I came in.

Bunchy's Auction was my first professional riding gig. The cowboys would throw me on a horse and send me in the auction area one right after the other. They felt the horses sold better with a young girl riding. I'd gallop the horses up and down the aisle, spinning them around at the ends just as I was told to do.

I could be in a western saddle or an English saddle – quite often I didn't get any saddle at all. If Bunchy felt that a horse could jump, he'd hold up his cane across the aisle and have me jump it – whether the horse had ever jumped before or not. I rode every conceivable kind of horse, pony, mule and donkey imaginable - including some really tough rogues. I learned something vital from each and every one of them. I think of the Bunchy livestock I rode and thank them to this day for the many valuable lessons they had taught me.

THE HACK STABLE
CLOVE LAKE STABLES

EMOTIONALLY WINNING THE HENRY BERGH CLASS ON PLAYBOY WEARING MY NEW TWEED JACKET.
GRACE FRANZREB IN THE BLUE JACKET, WITH HER MOTHER ADELE PRESENTING THE RIBBON.

While working at Clove Lake Stables, I was always assigned the new horses straight out of Bunchy's auction. If they were quiet enough to rent out to the public, I was given another horse whose temperament was yet unknown. I was the guinea pig rider. It may not sound like an impressive title, but it was a title and a start.

Every single horse which was safe enough to rent to the public, had to be rented to the public. A horse which could bring in money could not be wasted on a lead rider. Hence I rode everything with hair on it which was not suitable to rent to the inexperienced riders of the public. These were horses who reared or bucked, or barn sour horses who would spin around and try to run home, as well as any horses with too much energy or personality for public use. Basically any horse deemed unsafe or unsuitable for the public was my ride for the day.

I worked all day every day at the hack stable, grooming horses endlessly and cleaning the old, thick military bridles they used. These old war bridles had big brass buckles. I worked diligently on those buckles until they shined enough to pass a military barracks inspection. I'd take the public bus after school to the stable and work until dark. Then I'd take the bus home, have a little dinner and do my homework. I'd also bring those old war bridles home, clean them thoroughly and polish the brass – all alone in the damp basement.

Clove Lake Stables was owned by the Franzreb family. Grace Franzreb was the idol and instructor for all of the little kids at the barn, including me. She had a fabulous Standardbred horse named "Percolator". Grace would do the most amazing things on Percolator and further our devotion to her. She'd jump in and out of the ring fence, which was about 4'6" high.

Grace would jump hay wagons and any other obstacle which she deemed worth jumping. Grace would even jump another human, held up very high in the air horizontally by two people. (In those days, people obviously didn't worry about lawsuits.) Often Grace would take Percolator's bridle off in the ring and insist that we did the same with our horses. There were a bunch of horses with kids on them running around the ring with no bridles. This was a great lesson in learning balance and anticipating the horse's movement. Grace was, hands down, our Hero and Fearless Leader. She and the horses taught us how to ride.

Grace held a summer contest at the stables which entailed keeping two horses in immaculate condition, as well as the bridles and saddles belonging to each individual horse. She would judge the horses and equipment at the end of each week and write her comments, criticisms and weekly scores on a big board in the barn.

Each kid was judged and rated in regard to their level of care, attention to detail and work ethic. This contest went on throughout the entire summer when the kids were at the stable all day.

The winning prize at the end of this contest was to be a brand-new black Melton riding jacket. Back then the jacket probably cost around thirty dollars. This was quite a brilliant plan by Grace. She had all of her hack horses extremely well cared for and groomed, as well as their equipment, all summer long for only thirty dollars. It was pure genius. I really, really, really wanted that jacket. I wanted so badly to look like the other kids. They all had nice new riding clothes from the small local tack shop, Montanti's, and they wore their outfits at the stable's little horse shows.

My "riding jacket" was a bright red blazer which my father had bought at a thrift shop. In fact, that's where ALL my clothes came from – school clothes, riding clothes, work clothes, church clothes, everything. My father was a big customer at the local Thrift Store. He brought the word frugal to a new level. My father, John Henry Rouson, was born and raised in England during the Great Depression. He had been a true hero in WWII.

My father's work for the British Navy during WW II involved defusing bombs and mines, which the Germans and Japanese had dropped on land or on ships – sometimes these mines were on the bottom of the ocean. These were bombs and mines which had not yet gone off, but needed to be defused in order to render the area safe.

His team was named the Death and Glory Boys. Most of them were killed doing this work when a bomb went off unexpectedly as they were working on it.

Greystone and Jessamy at Clove Lake Stables

For this courageous work, my father was honored with the George Medal, the Order of the British Empire and Member of the British Empire. He was a brilliant, amazing man and tough to the core.

Apparently no one had ever told my father that the Great Depression had ended decades ago. We were forever in the Depression, according to my father.

As per my father's colorful British outlook, I believed that Winston Churchill was the President and King of the entire World throughout early childhood. My father loved Churchill, the man he fought for in WWII. He had a huge bookcase dedicated to works solely on Churchill.

My father always wanted me to earn my keep. I remember placing green stamps in little books, licking them until my tongue was green. One needed hundreds of these damn green stamp books, just to trade for a set of sheets or towels at the Green Stamp Store. I hated those green stamps.

Back to the red blazer and the contest at hand. Not only did I feel like a complete idiot in this red blazer, it also made me stand out like a sore thumb. Not one other kid wore a red jacket. I was convinced that I looked like a fool and to this day, I believe I was right.

My Father, Lieutenant Commander John Henry Rouson British Navy WWII

So, I desperately wanted that brand new black Melton jacket. I scrubbed and brushed and shined my two contest horses, better than anyone ever had in their entire lives. I labored endlessly over the ancient equipment assigned to me – equipment which literally had barely survived the Great Depression.

When I won that black Melton jacket at the end of the summer, I cried like a baby. It was my first piece of brand-new clothing and I treasured that jacket.

A little later, after my parents had divorced, my mother took me to Kauffman & Sons - a very fancy saddlery in Manhattan. I was in heaven. Upon entering Kaufman's Saddlery, one was hit with the wonderful smell of fresh leather bridles and saddles.

My wonderful mother bought me a tweed riding jacket and new breeches for my birthday. She had saved up for over a year, working long hours at various jobs.

Finally I could now feel proud about my outfits. That is what my loving and beautiful mother had strived and toiled for – building my self-esteem and confidence. May God Bless my mother always. I was an extremely shy kid to begin with, so I believe my riding improved after I was no longer self-conscious about my attire. I had gained some confidence and pride - new emotions for me at that age. At the next show I won the coveted Henry Bergh Equitation class wearing my new tweed jacket. Once again, I cried
.like a baby.

Jessamy and Bittersweet with the Newly Won Black Melton Jacket

My Father - Lieutenant Commander British Navy, WWII

My Beautiful, Loving Mother – Jolita Rouson
An Artist and a Writer

MIKE COHEN
HOW HE CHANGED MY LIFE

Mike Cohen

I resented school because I wanted to be with the horses all the time. With that said, I was smart enough to realize that I needed to do extra well in school in order to graduate early and get out. I was a top honor student with a score of 100% on two New York Math Regents exams, and I was skipped two years. I graduated from high school when I was fourteen years old.

LSD and Jessamy, in a show at Clove Lake Stables

There was a nice gentleman at the hack stable named Phil, who had a wonderful, young appaloosa gelding named LSD. (Remember this was the late 1960s - early 1970's) Phil often let me ride LSD and teach him to jump. Phil and his terrific girlfriend Arlene were very supportive of my riding career. They were wonderful people and dear friends.

One day Arlene asked me if I would like to meet a friend of hers from Brooklyn who had just started a new horse business in Spring Valley, New York. She said that her friend had several horses and was looking for a rider. I was very excited and said that I would love to try and be the rider for her friend's new business.

One day we took a road trip. Phil, Arlene and I drove up to Spring Valley, which was a little over an hour out of New York City. We pulled into a lovely little place called Lotus Farm. This is when I met the one and only Mike Cohen. My life was forever changed with this meeting. I was only fourteen years old, but I wanted to be a showjumping rider so badly. Mike made all of that possible.

Arlene introduced me to Mike Cohen – a disheveled, bow legged man of medium height, with ruffled blonde/brown hair and a Tareyton hanging out of his mouth. The pleasantries were brief, as Mike was one to cut to the chase.

Mike wanted to see if this fourteen-year-old girl could ride or not. He didn't seem the least bit impressed as Arlene raved on and on about what a great rider I was at Clove Lake Stables. Instead he walked to the stable, pulled out a big, strong, impressive young bay horse and began to put the tack on him.

Mike spoke with Arlene while he was tacking up the horse. He acted as though I was not even there. Mike told Arlene that this horse was a really tough rogue and had quickly gotten rid of everyone he had tried to put on him. Mike said that this horse would stand up on his hind legs and walk like a man - cocky as hell. If the rider was still on him, he said this horse would then lunge forward and buck like a bull. Mike told Arlene that the horse was relentless in his determination to terrify and lose any rider as quickly as possible. Mike wanted to sort out the riders from the non-riders in short order, so this was the horse he retrieved for me.

Mike said he had a barn full of extremely green Thoroughbred horses which he had just purchased at the smaller racetracks out west. Those horses needed riding and training in order to be sold well and support Mike's new business.

Mike made it very clear that he needed a "Real Rider". I listened intently to every single word Mike said to Arlene regarding this horse. I knew exactly what I had to do. I may have been the guinea pig rider once again, but this was not my first rodeo.

With his trademark Tareyton cigarette hanging out of his mouth, Mike brought the horse out of the barn and said, "Hop on." Mike gave me a leg up and I immediately pulled that horse's head around to my knee and began slowly turning him in very tight circles. All of this horse's charades were nothing that I hadn't dealt with while riding horses at Bunchy Grant's auction for one dollar a ride - or riding the outlaws at the hack stable.

I asked everyone to please stand back and let me get to know my new friend, because we needed to talk. I kept the horse's head pinned to my knee and locked my hand and the rein behind my thigh. This is what I do for a rogue who rears, because a strong horse will jerk the reins right out of your hands. Then the horse is in control and you're really in trouble. So a rider needs to be quick about it and ahead of the horse's next move to rear or bolt sideways.

One has to read the horse and act, before the horse has a chance to do his stunts. I slowly turned the horse in tight circles until he began to lose his equilibrium. Nothing earns a horse's respect more than taking away some of their equilibrium. The wonderful thing about this technique is that it does not hurt the horse in any way whatsoever. I always turned them in the tight circles slowly, so the horse would not whack his other leg with his hoof and break a splint bone. It's a fairly passive technique, but an amazingly effective one.

I have found that horses are extremely intelligent and able to come to an entirely new level of respect for their rider without ever raising a hand or a whip to them. After I turned the horse in tight circles for about one minute, I leaned back, gave him his head and assertively kicked him forward. I immediately praised him for going forward - earning his trust and beginning to form a bond. I had also earned the horse's respect, as well as his understanding that I would be the one calling the shots from now on. This began what became a very respectable and pleasant ride, because it was based on mutual understanding.

We were now friends and I fussed over him with praise each time he tried to do the right thing. The horse did try his tricks one more time, but with much less enthusiasm. I felt it early and immediately pulled him into a slow spin, with his head locked by my knee. That was it. Our big tough guy decided it was much better to do things my way and garner all the praise and attention – something he didn't realize that he enjoyed until now. The horse was a lovely ride after that. I rode him around, made a big fuss over him, and gave him back to Mike as a happy horse.

Mike was grinning from ear to ear and almost lost his Tareyton. He said, "You are MY rider from now on!"

Then he turned and walked away with the horse – just two happy guys going back to the barn. Mike was so happy that he lit up a joint while he was working on the horse. I quickly learned that the one thing Mike liked perhaps better than his Tareyton cigarettes, was his marijuana. Hence the name Lotus Farm. (Remember this was the early 1970's.)

I was now the Official Rider for Lotus Farm. To be clear, this new impressive title of "Rider" did not come with any money or salary attached at all. However I could ride horses from sun up until after dark, one after the other, every single day and seven days a week. What more could a gal want?

I was in heaven. I was so happy that I could barely sit still in the car on the way back to the City. Phil and Arlene were quite proud of themselves too for discovering this exciting new talent for Mike. Before we left, Arlene had made sure to say to Mike, "I told you so!" It was a joyful ride home.

Mike Cohen pictured here with the famous boxer
Marvin Haggler

Anyone who knew our time together would understand. I left home at fourteen years old to ride for Mike Cohen. At that time, Mike had two big gray Thoroughbred horses off the racetrack which he felt were special. These horses were the beginning of a wonderful career for both of us.

It was also the beginning of going through many rough financial times together, but Mike was always cool about it and took everything life threw at him in stride. Sometimes this was just downright irresponsible, but that was Mike.

The first time Mike and I went to the big Florida Circuit with our gray horses, we lived on ten dollars per day for the both of us - but we believed in our horses and we believed in each other. We were very excited to be there and filled with hope and joy.

We were right to feel that way. I shall discuss this more in the coming chapters, but we had two of the best horses around - Philco became one of the top ten showjumpers in the World for ALL time – a $1,200 purchase off a New Jersey racetrack.

Rodney Jenkins and Mike Cohen

Dreamy Sam was $600 off an Ohio track and became one of the best horses in the country. They were our main horses, but there were at least hundred more really nice ones which came later. I miss those times; I miss those horses and I miss Mike.

BENNY O'MEARA

MY EARLY IDOL

I never had the opportunity to meet Benny O'Meara before his early, traumatic death in the crash of his own plane. He was only twenty-eight years old. Benny apparently liked to fly his own small plane everywhere, which added to his aura.

When I left home at fourteen years old to ride horses for Mike Cohen, all Mike talked about was Benny. Mike had worked for Benny. There were photos of Benny everywhere on the farm and I would gaze at them in awe. I even watched some very old, grainy tapes of Benny schooling horses. I watched them over and over, hundreds of times, until I had finally worn them out.

I tried my heart out every single day to emulate Benny O'Meara, because that is what Mike preached. I'd ride from sunrise until well after sunset and until there were no more horses left to ride. I rode hundreds of horses straight off the racetracks, as well as many problem horses and rogues which people had sent to be straightened out. The word quickly spread that Mike had a girl who could ride the toughest of the tough, and horses arrived regularly from some of the very best professional trainers in the country.

I rode each and every horse until I had figured them out, worked out their problems and taught them what they needed to know in order to be sold as show horses. I never wore a watch and I never thought about time. For me, the horse designates the time necessary for each ride. Some take more time than others, but I made each horse a willing and happy participant in the work, gaining the respect of the East Coast's best horsemen.

As I had mentioned, Mike also had the two big gray Thoroughbreds which he felt were special. One was Dreamy Sam and the other was On Dancer. We trained these horses and showed them very successfully at the smaller shows. Dreamy Sam had been a $600 purchase from a racetrack in Ohio – Beulah Park to be exact.

On Dancer, (later the World famous "Philco"), was a big gray thoroughbred which had been purchased for $1,200 from the New Jersey Monmouth racetrack. On Dancer had been horribly abused and was a completely neurotic horse when he arrived.

We also had a small gray Quarter Horse mare named Sanbar's Samantha - a pretty mare who was too green for the nice lady who owned her. The lady's name was Maria Lull and she had bought Sanbar's Samantha from an ad in the local newspaper for $900. I won a lot in the junior jumpers with Sanbar's Samantha and she became quite respected within that division. Mike and I had three fabulous gray Superstars.

We had no money, but we were very proud of our horses. In 1973, Mike and I showed up on the huge Florida Circuit for the first time with our two gray Thoroughbreds from the racetrack and our gray Quarter Horse mare purchased out of the newspaper. We won right off the bat against the top professionals. Dreamy Sam was always super and a big winner, despite having been heel nerved several times so that he did not feel any pain within his hoof. On Dancer, (Philco), was an extremely difficult horse in the beginning, but I shall cover that later. On Dancer, aka Philco, deserves his own chapter, as does Dreamy Sam.

On Dancer became so sensational that he was literally the talk of the show. Rodney Jenkins, America's winningest rider, bought him virtually right away with his great sponsor, Harry Gill. Harry and Rodney then sold On Dancer almost immediately to England's legendary David Broome – a rider of tremendous International fame. Philco went on to become one of the top ten show jumpers in the World for ALL time.

During the Florida shows, Mike was standing around with a group of top trainers and they were complimenting him on his horses. One of them said, "That girl rides just like Benny." The others agreed. Mike was beaming with pride and so was I. That may have been the most moving and significant compliment that I have ever received.

PHILCO (ON DANCER)

ABUSED, MISUNDERSTOOD, REJECTED
HOW HE BECAME ONE OF THE
TOP TEN SHOWJUMPERS FOR ALL TIME

Philco and Jessamy competing in Florida in 1973

This is another tale about turning a troubled horse around with love, understanding, empathy, compassion, correct training techniques and endless patience.

I started Philco straight off the racetrack after he had been horribly abused. He was beautifully bred - by "On and On", out of a "Native Dancer" mare. Some inferior racehorse trainers had him and expected him to run and to run fast. They used every trick in the book to get this big, lovely gray Thoroughbred to run, from whipping him down the track, to electric shocks, to injecting him with various drugs.

Philco's papered name on the track was "On Dancer" and he had a dismal racing career. In fact, at that point he had a dismal life and was totally neurotic. As On Dancer later became world famous and known as Philco, I shall refer to him as Philco for the purpose of this story. By the time the racehorse trainers had given up on Philco at the racetrack, he was a mercilessly abused and totally neurotic animal - wild eyed, climbing the walls and swinging his head back and forth frantically – a nervous habit called weaving. Philco would weave so uncontrollably that he would work himself into a complete lather and dig a trench in his stall.

The racehorse people were disgusted with this horse and we bought him for $1,200. Philco also had swollen and inflamed ankles, which are called osselets. His ankles had been pin fired and he was sore all over. Pin firing, also known as thermocautery, is a barbaric procedure which is seldom used nowadays. Pin firing involves using a hot iron and literally burning small holes in the horse's inflamed and injured legs – usually the horse's ankles, shins or tendons. Sometimes racetrack people douse the horse's legs with acid or caustic chemicals which is called blistering, because it literally blisters the skin.

In theory these primitive procedures are supposed to induce a counter-irritation and hasten healing. As I said, these are brutally barbaric and unnecessary procedures which are outdated and seldom used nowadays. Philco ankles were covered with burns and scars from where he had been pin fired and blistered. This was just another example of the abuse which Philco had suffered at the racetrack.

I was fifteen years old by this time and I used to sit in Philco's stall for endless hours, attempting to comfort and soothe him. I would talk to him and with great care, I would set up his legs in poultice, standing wraps and bandages until the inflammation in his ankles finally dissipated. I'd feed Philco treats in an effort to stop - or at least slow down - his weaving.

On our first ride, Philco ran me straight through the ring fence – fence rails flying everywhere. Once I regained control, I turned him right around and jumped back into the ring over the broken fence. I spent endless hours on Philco - just walking and talking to him.

I'd take him in the woods in an effort to relax his neurotic mind. Philco was an extremely nervous horse, but he finally got to the point that he would school well at home and perform well at the smaller shows.

PHILCO
TB g 1967

ON-AND-ON	*NASRULLAH	NEARCO	PHAROS
			NOGARA
		MUMTAZ BEGUM	*BLENHEIM II
			MUMTAZ MAHAL
	TWO LEA	BULL LEA	*BULL DOG
			ROSE LEAVES
		TWO BOB	THE PORTER
			BLESSINGS
ISLAND SINGING	NATIVE DANCER	POLYNESIAN	UNBREAKABLE
			BLACK POLLY
		GEISHA	DISCOVERY
			MIYAKO
	SIS LEA	BULL LEA	*BULL DOG
			ROSE LEAVES
		OUR TREAT	STIMULUS
			RISK

PEDIGREE NOTES
   Philco is by ON-AND-ON, the sire of United States Equestrian Team jumper COACH STOP (described earlier in this book). On-and-On is a full brother to PIED D'OR, sire of the hunter LONESOME WAY and the jumper BARNABAS.
   On the dam's side, Philco descends from NATIVE DANCER, who is in the pedigree of NATIVE SURF (described earlier herein). Philco descends from *TEDDY on his dam's side, again through *BULL DOG and BULL LEA, as he does on his sire's side. RISK is by *SIR GALLAHAD III and out of RISKY. Risky is the third dam of KESWICK, an Open Jumper Champion. Risky also appears in the pedigrees of ENCORE and BLACK MARKET as second dam of POLISHED STEEL.

SHOW RECORD
1977 — Rated in top 10 Jumpers in the world.
   — Grand Prix winner in Europe at Dublin and Olympia.
   — Won King George V Gold Cup and John Player Trophy.
   — On Great Britain Equestrian Team.
   — Runner-up at European Jumping Championships, Vienna.

From Dr. Birdsall's book "Bloodlines of Hunters & Jumpers"

Philco took an absolutely dead quiet, compassionate, sensitive ride and a great deal of empathy, understanding and patience. As Philco's rider, I could not make any unexpected moves whatsoever, or Philco would take off so fast that I would get windburn. I had to be very soft and easy, slow and extremely quiet while riding him, as well as managing him on the ground.

Philco was also an extremely strong horse and there really was no bit to put in his mouth which could contain him. I decided to put what is called a rubber Pelham, (the bit in the photos), so that Philco could hold onto the rubber and feel secure – just like a pacifier. I controlled Philco through mutual trust, understanding and communication – not strength. But Philco responded and we became a team. We were Champion at several of the smaller shows.

Philco and Jessamy at the Beginning of his Jumper Career

It was now time to find out what we really had by competing against the top horses at the big horse shows. Mike and I made the decision to show Philco and Dreamy Sam on the Florida circuit in 1973. We were extremely excited and filled with hope. We believed in our horses and we believed in each other.

The first show was at Jacksonville, which was on a racetrack. Philco literally lost his mind. He was climbing the walls in a total lather - wild eyed and weaving so hard and fast that it was unfathomable.

He dug another big trench in his stall by incessantly weaving back and forth. Philco was so wild, it was impossible to even lead him, so I got on him very early the next morning. Philco was dripping with sweat and in a total lather. He was trembling all over - completely frantic and wild eyed.

Slowly we began making our way up to the ring. The ring was on the racetrack, which terrified Philco due to his history of abuse at the track. I walked big sweeping circles with Philco the entire way to the ring, so that his eye was not always on the racetrack far ahead. I could feel Philco's heart pounding beneath my leg. It took hours and hours and hours of walking and talking to him, all in endless sweeping circles towards the ring.

It was dusk by the time we got to the ring at the racetrack. I just sat still on Philco allowing him to look all around for at least another hour – rubbing his neck and speaking to him the entire time. Philco finally calmed down enough to dry off and take a deep breath. I sat on him quietly for at least another hour, until he totally relaxed and became settled and at peace with his environment. Then we walked slowly back to the barn.

It was dark by the time Philco and I arrived back at the barn and I was finally able to get off of him. I never even asked Philco to trot that day and I never, ever lost my patience. I truly believe that this was the day which enabled Philco to become a World Champion – more so than any other event.

Philco and I had formed a bond of mutual trust, respect and understanding – all due to compassion and empathy expressed over many consecutive hours. Philco now knew that he had someone who understood him and that there was another way to behave. He learned to become my friend through his trust in me and his gratitude for my kindness. The next day Philco walked to the ring and was relatively relaxed. As I said, I honestly believe that the long day before had made his entire career possible from that point forward.

When Philco finally showed, his jump was so sensational that he was literally the talk of the horse show. Everyone would stop to watch him jump. Philco was an amazing athlete and one of the best horses to ever break out on the horse show scene. Philco and I formed an incredible partnership – all because he trusted me and allowed me to be his best friend. We trusted and believed in each other.

After competing Philco in Florida for a few weeks and wowing everyone, America's winningest showjumping rider, the great Rodney Jenkins, approached Mike about Philco. Rodney purchased Philco with the backing of his sponsor Harry Gill, who owned many of Rodney's top horses and was also a superb horseman. Both Harry and Rodney knew that Philco was something special, but I don't believe they realized how complex he was until they actually owned him. Rodney was overheard saying several times, "I cannot believe that little girl rode this horse." It began a nice level of respect from Rodney which I enjoyed, because Rodney was indisputably the best in the country.

It broke my heart to part with Philco - this friend whom I loved so deeply. But that's the horse business. Mike and I had to train and sell horses in order to survive. It is too lofty and expensive a sport for the working person to be able to hang onto their good horses. If a person has a really good horse, someone with enormous wealth will buy it. That's the business.

Philco was supposedly the most expensive preliminary jumper ever sold up to that time. I didn't see any of the money and I didn't care. I just missed my horse.

I believe Rodney and Harry were surprised at how difficult Philco actually was, because they had watched him go around with me - just a kid - as smoothly and beautifully as one could want. Almost immediately, they sold Philco to England's legendary showjumping rider, David Broome. One of David Broome's top sponsors, Phil Harris, purchased Philco for David. (Hence the name change from On Dancer to Philco.) The rest is history. Philco became one of the greatest horses in the World for all time and is in all of the history books.

Shortly after David Broome had purchased Philco, he asked me to ride for him in England. David knew that I had started Philco and developed him into the talent that he had become at that point. David recognized that he had a super talent in Philco, but he also knew that Philco could potentially be an extremely difficult horse in the wrong hands.

David gave me a lot of credit for the early training of Philco and he appreciated me as a rider. He used to call Philco "The Cranky Yankee", which made me laugh. I did fly to England and ride for David the next year. No was allowed to ride Philco except for David, but sometimes David would have me warm Philco up for him at a show. These warm up rides on Philco apparently made me an instant star in the eyes of Britain's public. Because Philco and David trusted me, they liked me too. The British people loved David Broome and they loved Philco. Incredibly, I was actually asked to sign autographs after just riding Philco around a little and warming him up in the schooling area. He was now England's showjumping pride and joy, along with his phenomenal, world class rider David Broome.

This is just a little story to show that even the most difficult of horses can be turned around with love, understanding, patience and proper training. This story also shows how much amazing Thoroughbred talent is available at small racetracks, in auctions and even in Kill Pens, all across the country. I hope that this story inspires anyone who is able and willing, to go out and save a future Champion. Give a horse a second chance with a new career and develop a fabulous show horse. The horses shall reward you tenfold, as Philco rewarded us.

ON DANCER HITS STRIDE

By Julia Longland

What makes a runner — run faster, a jumper — jump higher or a boxer — out box his rivals?

Is it strength, muscle, breeding, mental ability, skill - or a sheer mad flair that is only bequeathed by the Gods to the chosen few?

These problems cause 1,000 sleepless nights for the athletes and horse trainers of the world. But, batter their brains as they may, and have done for probably 3,000 years, the answer will never come. Perhaps, as Robert Louis Stevenson puts it: "To travel hopefully is a better thing than to arrive."

Who knows. But that faith in fate is what causes a man to throw his life's earnings into the horse-sale ring, to buy an untried colt that could, if it can, win him the Kentucky Derby.

It might, of course, do no such thing. The animal might end up in a $10 rent-a-horse stables in the suburbs of some small town, and the owner might turn away knowing that he could just as surely have dug a hole in the garden and buried his $50,000 for the worms to feed on.

This is the story of a horse who was bred to run in such classics as the Kentucky Derby. He was sold as a yearling for a substantial sum, but he did not achieve his owner's ambition on the American racetrack and, inevitably, became something of a drop-out. But then his life suddenly took a different twist. Instead of carrying on the downward trail, to end up as a nobody with only the memory of his colourful past to dream about, he met a man who fell in love with his brains.

After changing hands several times when he left the racetrack, the horse had been spotted in the show jumping ring on the Sunshine circuit in Florida in February 1973. While boarding an airplane home to England, the British Olympic show jumper David Broome was suddenly seized with a conviction. He turned back, asked the officials to hold the plane, and hurried away to buy an attractive flea-bitten grey of 6 years old, called On Dancer. The decision was to change the lives of both man and horse.

David Broome was born in 1940, on March 1 - St. David's day - in Cardiff, the capitol city of Wales. He lives at Caldicot, near the famous Chepstow racecourse, just across the River Severn bridge in South Wales, and helps to run his family's hay and straw and farming business, as well as holding the post of Joint-Master with his father Fred, of the Curre Foxhounds.

In 15 years of international competition as a showjumper, he has achieved a

British equestrian David Broome and his horse - hopeful, Philco, formerly On Dancer.
(Daily Express Photo)

fame throughout the world for his unflappable temperament and his brilliant touch in the saddle, which has won him two Olympic Bronze medals (one at the age of 20), a World Championship, a World Professional Championship, three European Championships and three King George V Gold Cups - that most coveted and historic of all individual trophies competed for at London's Royal International Horse Show.

On Dancer was foaled in Kentucky in 1967, the son of On and On, out of a mare called Island Singing, by Native Dancer. On and On, by the legendary Nasrullah, who came to America from England, won the Ohio Derby, the Sheridan Handicap and nearly $400,000. So the purchaser of On Dancer, inspecting that notable pedigree, could be forgiven for thinking he had a princely prize on his hands.

But the plans came to nothing. The horse became difficult to train, and although he had 24 starts in 2 years never finished higher than third. A later owner is of the opinion that he thought too much for his own good - that his active brain puzzled too much about the ways and wherefores of his profession, to ever come to terms with racing.

Perhaps he needed companionship - not from his stablemates in the yard, but from his human mentors, the people around him. He is a horse that needs to be reassured, to be consulted, to know exactly what he is being asked to do - and why. Above all, he needs to understand, and to knowingly share in a partnership.

David Broome says of him now: "He is tremendously intelligent, and has a lot of character. And he really needs to communicate. As a ride, he is a bit "dead" in the mouth, but I attribute that to a hangover from his racing days. What impresses me about him in his conscientiousness - you don't find that very often in a horse. Riding him is quite an experience, because he thinks quickly and can weigh up situations in a flash."

In early 1973 On Dancer, by this time a very novice showjumper, was sold by Mike Cohen of Spring Valley, N. Y. to Harry Gill, the Pennsylvania quarry and construction magnate. For a fortnight in Florida, Harry Gill's rider Rodney Jenkins rode On Dancer but although the horse scarcely made a single mistake in competition, he won no money. And in fact there is a curious story about his winnings that only came to light 20 months later.

David Broome and his patron, Phil Harris, thinking On Dancer had won at least $280 - $300 showjumping, put him in the Intermediate division when he started to compete in England. Those

Continued on page 19

MY SHORTLIVED EQUITATION CAREER ON NEW ETTA

New Etta and I competing in the Equitation

When I left home in New York City at fourteen years old to ride for Mike Cohen, he wanted me to start out correctly and do some equitation, along with riding every other horse on the place. Equitation is a division at the shows which judges the rider on their style and technique. The smoothest and most classical rider wins. It is a fabulous foundation for a young rider.

Mike had a small, bay, 15.3 hand Thoroughbred mare off the racetrack named "New Etta" - a lovely, sweet, wonderful mare who had a little experience in the three-foot hunters at a few shows. This was the most experienced horse that Mike owned, as all the other horses were right off the racetrack. Hence New Etta became my equitation partner. I started posting trot without stirrups for two hours per day on different horses, to make my leg especially strong and secure. New Etta and I showed in all of the equitation classes at the smaller shows and we won everything. I thought that I was the "Equitation Queen", UNTIL we showed up for the Maclay Finals at Madison Square Garden in New York City.

I knew we were in trouble as soon as I saw the course. I thought we were going to die for certain after I walked it. The first line was a long four strides away from the in gate - or a comfortable, flowing, continuing six strides for New Etta.

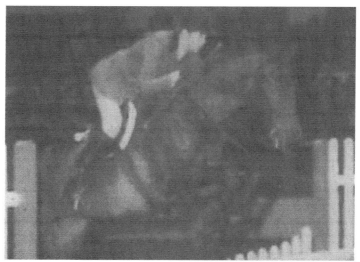

New Etta and Jessamy - An "Out of Body" Ride in the Maclay Finals, Madison Square Garden

The jumps looked huge and very serious – tons of flowers and all kinds of décor around them. New Etta and I had never seen so many flowers and different kinds of jumps - or such long distances. I was so terrified that I was probably what medical people would call "in a state of shock." I was sheet white and my heart was pounding so hard that I could hear it. I was trembling like a leaf.

When our turn came, New Etta and I walked in the gate to the majestic arena of the great Madison Square Garden. I honestly am not able to tell you what happened on course, because it was a total and complete out of body experience. All I know is that by some miracle, New Etta and I made it around the correct course alive and left it standing. The one thing I can guarantee for certain is that New Etta and I did many, many more strides around that course and took up much more time scratching, crawling and climbing our way around than anyone else in the class. The double and triple combinations were particularly tough for us, but we survived.

Upon completion of my one and only Maclay Final, the first thing I had to say was "Thank you New Etta and God Bless you". I threw my arms around her neck, kissed her endlessly and offered her all the carrots she could eat.

I think to this day of that courageous little mare tackling that course, which was way, way, way over her head. She certainly didn't have any help from her rider. Somehow New Etta's huge, generous and courageous heart got us around. I'll always love that mare for allowing me to be here today to tell this story. New Etta retired after this monumental event and went on to be a wonderful broodmare. I retired from the equitation division and came back to Madison Square Garden the next year on Dreamy Sam. Sam and I showed in the International Open Jumper Division. We had just won the Grand Prix of Harrisburg and we did extremely well at the Garden as well.

Of importance is the fact that I was completely relaxed and cool about everything, because no course looked too big after surviving the insurmountable Maclay Finals with the courageous New Etta.

Just another little story about how much we owe the wonderful horses who do these insane things for us every day. No foal ever born stood up and said, "I want to be in a horse show or run around a racetrack."

They do it for us, out of the generosity of their hearts. Please praise and love your horses every day for their valiant, generous efforts. We can only dream of having hearts as big and courageous as those of our horses.

DREAMY SAM

THE HORSE WHO MADE MY DREAMS COME TRUE

Dreamy Sam and Jessamy at Madison Square Garden

Ever since I was a little girl watching Bold Minstrel and the legendary William Steinkraus jump the 7'3" Puissance wall at Madison Square Garden in 1967, I had wanted to ride jumpers at the Garden. When asked who I credit with my early start in the World of Showjumping, I immediately reply: Mike Cohen and Dreamy Sam.

Those two wonderful souls gave me my start in the Big Time and extremely competitive horse show circuit. They have a place in my heart forever. As I've said, Mike had found Dreamy Sam at a small Ohio racetrack for $600 shortly before I went to ride for him.

When I first saw Dreamy Sam, I thought he was the most elegant, refined, beautiful horse I had ever seen. He had a beautiful head and neck and was built like an athlete. Mike and I started Dreamy Sam in the jumper divisions at the smaller shows with great success. It was time to address a bigger challenge.

Mike decided that we were ready for the big shows and we began our memorable venture to the Florida circuit in 1973. Mike took Dreamy Sam, On Dancer aka Philco, and the small gray Quarter Horse mare, Sanbar's Samantha. Our trademark was our three gray horses which drew much admiration from all.

Dreamy Sam started out in what was then called the Preliminary Jumper Division. There wasn't a low and a high preliminary – it was just preliminary. Schooling jumper was the only option for young horses which offered smaller jumps.

There were over a hundred horses in the preliminary classes, just about all carrying top riders. The jumps were quite big for young horses too. One had to make sure they had done their homework and were ready for this caliber of show and competition, before even entering. Fortunately, we had done our homework. Dreamy Sam won his very first preliminary class in Florida and stayed a consistent winner throughout the entire circuit. People took notice. On Dancer, (Philco), was the talk of the show with his extravagant jumping style. As I said earlier, Philco was sold early in the circuit to sponsor Harry Gill for the great rider Rodney Jenkins. They sold him almost immediately to Phil Harris, (hence On Dancer's new name), for Britain's legendary rider, David Broome.

Sanbar's Samantha was also fantastic and won up a storm in the junior jumper division. (The junior divisions were for children who were eighteen years and younger.) Samantha's owner Maria had bought her as a young horse out of an ad in the local paper for $900. Sanbar's Samantha turned out to be a little green for Maria, so I was given the ride. This pretty little mare was soon winning at the smaller shows, so she was able to accompany us to the Florida circuit as well. Samantha was fabulous in Florida, winning quite a bit in the junior jumpers. Maria was thrilled with her mare and never sold her, despite many generous offers.

So many juniors wanted Sanbar's Samantha, but Maria kept Samantha for her entire life and loved her to the very end. Maria cherished Samantha and Samantha led Maria into a wonderful lifetime with horses.

Dreamy Sam and Sanbar's Samantha continued their winning ways on the circuit following Florida. Dreamy Sam moved up to the Intermediate Jumper Division, which was a step before the Big Time Open Jumper Division. Dreamy Sam made the transition into the open division at a show in New Brunswick, New Jersey. We won the big class there against some excellent riders, including the wonderful USET rider Carol Hoffman, who was second in the class.

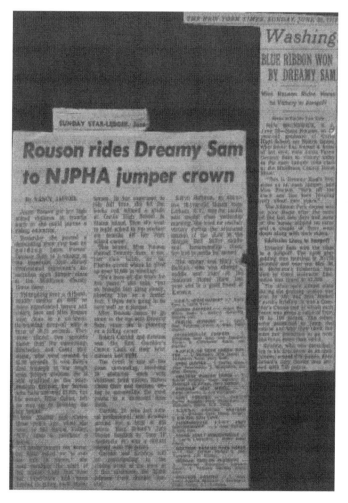

We then moved on to the Orange County Show in New York. The open classes during the week were held at night under the lights. We soon learned that Dreamy Sam did not like the lights at all.

We knew we had a problem in the schooling area when Sam was star gazing at the lights and not willing to go towards them. We did the best we could, catching some warm up jumps by allowing Sam to follow another horse, but we were feeling quite tenuous at best.

When Sam and I went into the ring alone, with no other horses to follow or give Sam moral support, I couldn't even get him into a canter. Sam was doing an extended trot with his head straight up in the air. His eyes were very wide and wild and he was staring at the lights. I realized that this was not going to happen under the lights.

I gently pulled Sam up, pet him and waved to the Judges Stand. That notorious wave to the Judges which all riders hate to do. The wave which says, "Never mind. We're leaving now. We obviously need to rethink this. Sorry to have taken up your time."

Now we knew that Dreamy Sam did not care to perform at night and under the lights. Good to know. We did not ask him to do any night classes after that ordeal. The good news was that the big class of the show, the East Coast Challenge Cup, was held on Sunday afternoon. We were back in the game. Dreamy Sam went around the East Coast Challenge Cup course beautifully and flawlessly. The course was tricky and there were only a few clear rounds. There were several exceptional horses and riders in that class as well.

Sam and I went in the jump off and flew around the course, cutting three seconds off of the previous best time held by the very talented "Night Murmur", ridden by the excellent horseman Gene Estep. Dreamy Sam was fabulous and we were the winners of the East Coast Challenge Cup. A joyful day and one heck of a comeback for us.

Dreamy Sam and I winning the East Coast Challenge Cup

Dreamy Sam looks for the champagne in the championship cooler as Miss Jessie Rouson looks on.
— Record photos by David Levine

SANBAR'S SAMANTHA

FROM A $900 AD IN THE NEWSPAPER TO A WINNING JUNIOR JUMPER

San Bar's Samantha and Jessamy - Junior Jumper Division

Sanbar's Samantha, the little gray Quarter Horse mare who could run and jump, quickly took the Junior Jumper Division by storm and became a Champion. As I've said, Samantha was purchased by her owner Maria Lull as a riding horse from an ad in the newspaper. She cost $900. Samantha proved to be too green for Maria in the beginning, so to my pleasure I got the ride on her. We taught her to jump and she became a Queen in the Junior Jumper Division.

Samantha also became a Queen as a trail horse for Maria, which is what helped to keep her fit for her jumping career. Maria and her husband Bob were tremendously supportive of Samantha's career. They attended every school at home, as well as every horse show. Bob, with his trademark "Black Label" beer in hand, was a particularly enthusiastic cheerleader for Samantha and was the one who convinced Maria to let her go on and be a star at the horse shows.

Samantha was a winning junior jumper everywhere we took her, including the big Florida circuit. Many a young rider wanted to own Samantha, but Maria turned down multiple very generous offers and kept Samantha through her old age and until Samantha's very last day.

After her show career, Samantha became a fabulous hunt horse for Maria. Samantha even inspired Bob to get a horse and start riding. Samantha also inspired Maria to make horses a big part of her life and Maria bred top thoroughbreds on her own farm for several years after.

One never knows how a horse could change your life and take you down an exciting and adventurous path.

JUNIOR OLYMPIC TOUR
PUERTO RICO & MEXICO CITY

There was a highly respected and well-known trainer in New York named Carl Knee. Carl had worked with Benny O'Meara and had known Mike going back to those days. Carl had a very successful show barn with some extremely wealthy clients. I liked Carl very much and had a great deal of respect for him as a horseman and a trainer. One day Carl called Mike. Carl said that he was the Chief de Equipe for the United States Junior Team and headed to International Junior Olympic competitions to be held in Puerto Rico and Mexico City.

Carl said that he was putting together a team of four horses and riders to compete against teams from Canada, Puerto Rico and Mexico. He had selected three of his own clients for the team, but told Mike that he wanted me to come with the team as the anchor rider. Carl explained that the riders would be riding their own horses in Puerto Rico, but in Mexico the riders would be riding Mexican horses provided by the Mexican government. Carl told Mike that of the four horses offered by Mexico for the competition, he would pick the easiest, steadiest and the most reliable ones for his clients. He wanted me there in case there was a difficult horse, as his clients had no experience whatsoever with riding difficult horses.

Carl's clients were very wealthy kids who had only ridden extremely well trained, expensive horses. Mike immediately said "Perfect!" A paid vacation with beaches, sunshine and plenty of marijuana available. Exactly what Mike dreamed of - a perfect escape. When the horses were flown to Puerto Rico, I flew with the horses to be certain that they were relaxed and comfortable about the experience. Dreamy Sam had never flown and was a tad nervous, but everything went smoothly.

We arrived safely and settled the horses into their stabling. After letting them relax for two days, we began our work. To our dismay, most of the classes in Puerto Rico were going to be held at night under the lights. We knew by now that Dreamy Sam was terrified of being under the lights, but we hoped daylight would hold out for the event. It was dark when we competed the first day and the lights were glaring. Sam was not happy. Once again, I had to do my "Dying Swan" wave to the Judges and leave the ring. Mike just shrugged and lit a joint.

Fortunately for all of us, the Nations Cup went on Sunday afternoon and Dreamy Sam was happy again. The band played The National Anthem and Sam immediately became patriotic and wanted to jump for his country. I was the anchor ride, which meant I had to go last and go clear on the course. Dreamy Sam was wonderful and we were clear both rounds. Our American Team had won the Nation's Cup against Canada, Puerto Rico and Mexico. Everyone was happy and the horses flew back to New York the next day. Mike flew home with Dreamy Sam.

Now came the Mexican part of the tour. It began in a Mexican government plane, which had to date back to WW I. It was an old battleship green war plane, which had seen a good bit of wear and tear over several decades. It looked like it had been shot out of the sky a few times as well. I have never seen or ridden in such a rickety, dilapidated, shaky plane in my entire life.

To make it worse, we hit severe turbulence and we honestly thought we heard bits and pieces of the plane falling off into the atmosphere. Everyone on the plane was completely mortified and ashen white.

Junior Olympic Tour

We were all certain that we were going to die, but by some miracle we made it to Mexico City alive. Upon arrival we were treated like Royalty. We went to a lovely Mexican restaurant and stayed in a beautiful hotel in Mexico City. The next day, we would be introduced to our yet unknown mounts.

The riders were all quite excited, but Carl was nervous. I realized why when we went to the stables the next day. Carl had been given a description of each horse's temperament by the Mexican trainer at the stable.

The first three horses to appear were steady and reliable, but Carl had told the stable owner to bring those out first as the trainer had told him that the last horse was "Special". The word "Special" does not always mean what one would assume when discussing horses. Sometimes it means that the horse has some personality and temperament quirks, making the horse quite tricky to manage or ride.

Each horse came out well-groomed with their own very tidy, attentive groom leading them. The first three horses went smoothly and Carl was beginning to relax. Carl designated one of his clients to each one, matching them as well as possible. So far, so good.

Everyone was happy and enjoying themselves, but I knew better. I had a good idea about what was coming and I was right. Out of the barn came a scruffy, disheveled old man leading a skinny grey horse. The horse's head was straight up in the air, with a wild, suspicious eye. His name was "Mecurio". It appeared that neither Mecurio, nor his old groom, had enjoyed a bath in quite a while.

Carl gave me a leg up and we began our walk to the ring. Rather than join the other grooms who stayed devotedly by their horses, my groom plopped down under a big shade tree. He then had a few healthy swigs of tequila from a flask which he had pulled from his pocket. My groom then proceeded to fall asleep instantly. It was siesta time for him. The Mexican trainer explained that the old groom had come with the stable and had been there for decades. He thought Mecurio had been under this groom's care for a long time as well.

When we got to the ring, Carl's worst fears about this adventure were realized. Mecurio reared straight up at the gate entering the ring and clearly was not interested in doing any work whatsoever – plus he wanted to fight about it. He was intent on not going into that ring. This act had made Mecurio quite infamous among all the horse people around Mexico City. They all knew Mecurio and what he had done to many a rider. I looked at Carl and he told me that it was okay to do whatever I had to do to fix the problem. Carl said, "This is your horse for the week, so get to work."

Therefore I was back to the old spin in tight circles and then kicking the horse forward and into the ring. Mecurio was shocked that anyone would challenge him and send him forward like that, but he came to respect me. With a bewildered expression, he went into the ring and jumped all of the obstacles which Carl had set up. Mecurio was actually a very adequate jumper and may have been a decent horse years before he had been ruined and become a rogue.

But Mecurio and I now had somewhat of an understanding. This was a good thing, because we were shipping to the big, fancy coliseum for the competition the next day.

The Junior Olympic Competition was held in a large indoor coliseum in Mexico City with big stands and a large crowd attending around the ring. Carl's riders were pretty good, but Carl needed clean rounds out of me in order to win the Nation's Cup.

I rode Mecurio down the alleyway to the in-gate of the ring and was completely ready for his act at the gate. Carl stood way back and told everyone to do the same. Before Mecurio could even raise his head to stand up, I had his head pinned to my knee, turned him in three tight circles and told the ring crew to open the gate. I kicked Mecurio forward and into the ring, sat up and gave him the very best ride I could.

We were clean both rounds and in good style I might add. America had won the Nation's Cup over Mexico, Canada and Puerto Rico and the crowd was very excited – one could even say wild.

It was announced that I was awarded the Most Outstanding Rider Award, the Leading Foreign Rider award, the Leading Woman Rider Award, and the Best Style and Technique award. I gave old Mecurio several carrots, many generous pats and sincerely thanked him. He was the horse who saved the night for our team and he seemed to know it. Mecurio looked very proud of himself when I handed him to his groom. Even his groom seemed elated and relatively sober.

I asked the groom to give Mecurio an extra good, warm soap bath and to please take good care of him forever after. The now happy and smiling old man assured me that he absolutely would take the very best care of Mecurio, because now he had the very best horse in the barn. He was really, really proud of his horse.

I thanked Mecurio and the groom again and left to get ready for the award ceremony. The ceremony was held in an exquisite hotel in Mexico City and was quite a fancy affair. Many of the important people and politicians in Mexico City were there, as well as the wealthy horse owners.

The awards were presented with great fanfare and I was given a standing ovation with each presentation. I owe that enthusiasm to Mecurio, who turned out to be much more infamous than I had realized. Everyone knew of Mecurio, as well as all of his tricks which had terrified so many of their riders. I received effusive praise and admiration for how I had ridden him with style and done a good job. I thanked everyone and told them that it was all Mecurio.

I said, "Mecurio is a wonderful horse. Please take good care of him. It's Mecurio who deserves the credit, with his courageous heart of gold – the heart of a true Champion, he won the night." Carl got a kick out of that.

After an evening of happy and joyous celebration, we all flew home the next morning as Champions.

THE HARRISBURG GRAND PRIX

Pennsylvania National

The 28th renewal of the Penn National was again held in the spacious Farm Show Arena in Harrisburg. This year over 1,000 horses were quartered for the eight-day event.

The Penn National is staged for a worthwhile cause - The Kiwanis Youth Fund, a project which has seen Kiwanis donate $201,339.00 to 26 different mid-state organizations in the last 15 years. The Fund receives 100 per cent of the show's profits for youth programs and other charitable groups.

The world famous Valley Forge Military Academy Band was on parade Friday and both the afternoon and evening performances Saturday. Friday night was Master of Fox Hounds Night with Dr. Rife Gingrich, a Penn National board member and MFH of the Beaufort Hunt as the honored guest.

The open jumping division belonged to 19-year-old Tony D'Ambrosio, who won the championship with Alligator Farms' Sympatico, with 19 points. Tony also won the leading rider title with 42 points.

A 17-year-old girl, Jessie Rousen, aboard Lotus Farm's Dreamy Sam, outrode the 18 starters in the Prix des Penn National open jumper stakes by turning in the only perfect tour around the pretzel-like seven fence jumpoff course.

In the amateur owner jumping division, it was Michelle McEvoy all the way. In addition to capturing the leading rider title, she won the division title on her horse, Vesuvius by winning two classes and by placing second in another class to collect 13 points.

In the amateur owner hunter division, again it was Michelle McEvoy aboard High Hope Farm's Computer who was champion with 13 points.

Sue Frischmann's Riot Free was the green working hunter and second year green working hunter champion by collecting 18 points, 16 over fences.

Winning the green conformation hunter title with 19 points was Nancy Easton's Bonnycastle, who had won three classes, including the stakes class and under saddle.

Fox Lake Farm's Automation, piloted by Rodney Jenkins was the regular conformation hunter champion with 20 points, collected by winning three classes, including the stakes. J.P.

Rodney Jenkins rode Morton B. Turbow's San Felipe to win the 1st year green working hunter championship at the Penna. National Show. (Budd)

Sue Frischmann's Riot Free was the grand green working hunter champion and the 2nd year green working hunter champion at the Penna. National Show. (Budd)

67

In those days the three big indoor shows started in Harrisburg, Pennsylvania. This was followed by The Washington International and then the ultimate of all shows - Madison Square Garden.

These were international divisions at the indoor shows, so they were not only filled with America's top horses and riders, they also had several of Europe's top entries. The courses were very big and quite technical. The competition was superb and extremely tough to beat.

Dreamy Sam and I competed in a couple of the classes during the week so he was comfortable in the Coliseum. Sam had never been in a coliseum before, so we gave him those early classes in order to acclimate. We received good placings, but the seasoned riders on the top horses were not expecting us to be a threat in the Grand Prix on Sunday. After all, I was a seventeen-year-old girl who was riding a relatively inexperienced $600 Thoroughbred horse.

Just before the Grand Prix began, the band played the National Anthem. Sam pricked his ears and looked as fresh and ready to jump as ever. Mike always made sure to have Sam hear the National Anthem before the big classes.

We went clear in the first round, along with some of the very top horses and riders. Everyone who had gone clear prepared for the jump off. When our turn came, Dreamy Sam walked in that coliseum like he owned it. He was clean and fast – absolutely fabulous – and the unbelievable happened. Dreamy Sam and I had just won the Grand Prix of Harrisburg against some of the top horses and riders in the world. The very talented Bernie Traurig was second on "The Cardinal", followed by the other outstanding and world class horse and rider partnerships.

When Dreamy Sam and I walked in the ring for the presentation, we received a standing ovation. Sam was extremely proud of himself and walked in that Coliseum like a World Champion. Mike Cohen was so excited, his Tareyton fell out of his mouth. It was an unbelievably thrilling moment for all of us. The gray thoroughbred who was purchased off a small racetrack for $600, had just beat several of the world's top horses and riders. We decided to skip the Washington International and save Sam for our dream, Madison Square Garden.

MY DREAM

SHOWING JUMPERS AT MADISON SQUARE GARDEN

Dreamy Sam and Jessamy at Madison Square Garden

Ever since I was a young child and had watched the great William Steinkraus and Bold Minstrel jump a huge Puissance wall at the National Horse Show, I had wanted to be a top jumper rider. Riding jumpers at Madison Square Garden was the pinnacle of my dreams. Now Dreamy Sam and I were going to show at the Garden.

The National Horse Show at Madison Square Garden is an entirely different experience than any other show. First of all, one is shipping horses into the middle of a hectic and electric Manhattan and unloading them onto a very busy city street. From there the horses are led up a very steep ramp and into Madison Square Garden's stabling area.

At the top of the ramp was the schooling area, which was a small dirt area with huge concrete support pillars straight down the middle. The entrance gate to the grand arena was to the left. Walking in the arena, one felt as though they had just left a tunnel and were now in the light. One could feel the aura of the many great athletes who had performed in that majestic arena. It radiated excellence. It made one proud to be there.

The small stabling area was set up with temporary stalls on the concrete floor, just beyond the schooling area. One needed to order a tremendous amount of bedding so the horses would be comfortable. The stabling area also had the huge concrete pillars and the stalls were set up around them. It was very tight quarters with just barely enough room to get a horse out of the stall and into the aisle. This is how the very best of the show horses lived after earning the honor of competing at Madison Square Garden. Being such generous creatures, they took it all in stride.

The schooling area was always crowded and hectic, filled with the horses competing in whatever class was going on. If one wanted to work their horse, they had to do so at a specified time in the very early morning – usually between three and five o'clock in the morning. There was no space to even hand walk a horse. Everything at Madison Square Garden was scheduled down to the very last minute and the rules were very strictly enforced. There was no walking your horse around at leisure or working the horse whenever you pleased. One had to adhere to the strict schedule. That includes when one could ship a horse into the Garden and when one must ship the horse out, after that horse's competitions were finished.

Grooms and riders worked with very little sleep, as they often had to ride their horses in the coliseum before dawn and then show late at night.

The show ran like clockwork and although everyone was exhausted during the day, they all came alive when the show started and the stands were packed with spectators.

The Open Jumper classes generally went during the evening performances when there were the biggest crowds of spectators. Of course the spectators had no idea of the incredible amount of work going on behind the scenes in order to produce the fabulous performances which they watched in the arena. In fact, for many of the spectators, the Horse Show was an extremely formal, yet festive affair. The VIPs and High Society patrons came out in droves for the show. The Madison Square Garden VIP spectators were often dressed in tuxedos and evening gowns, with a generous display of precious jewels.

The VIPs watched the show from extremely expensive and regal private boxes, while sipping Champagne and enjoying hors d'oeuvres of great delicacies. There was always an orchestra to entertain them between classes during the changing of courses. In those days, Doc Severinsen from the Johnny Carson show was the bandleader. It was an extremely enjoyable time for the audience – particularly the high rollers.

While the audience was having a grand time, the horsemen were working extremely hard to have their horses shine in the ring. After all the hard work involved in preparation, a horse and rider needed to walk into that World famous, majestic arena and perform at their highest level. They needed to be the epitome of class, style, beauty and athleticism, giving the audience their ultimate performance. The Regal and Grand Old Madison Square Garden demanded it.

Because this was an international show, I had the opportunity to meet some of the world's top riders. Having just come off a big win at Harrisburg, I was now well accepted and made to feel like a peer, despite being a teenager. It was an honor to meet these riders and fascinating to hear their view on the courses.

Dreamy Sam and Jessamy competing at Madison Square Garden

Dreamy Sam and I adapted to the insane schooling area, jumping a few jumps before going into the palatial arena for our turn against some of the world's greatest horse and rider partnerships. Unlike my tenuous experience during the Maclay Finals, I walked into that arena with confidence and pride. I fully believed in my horse and I believed in myself. I owe that confidence to Dreamy Sam and to Mike Cohen, as they both believed in me from the start.

Dreamy Sam jumped beautifully in his competitions and consistently won superb placings. We were very proud to be highly competitive among the best of the best.

I thank Dreamy Sam for being the horse who made my dreams come true. I think back on his great heart, his tremendous talent and his courage. I am forever grateful to him to this day. I loved that horse.

Dreamy Sam and Jessamy competing at Madison Square Garden

NORTHERN IRELAND & ENGLAND

Jessamy and Brass Tacks - a $300 Rescue to a Champion

Earlier in the year while in Florida, England's legendary David Broome and his good friend from Northern Ireland, Frank Kernan, told me that I had a standing invitation to come to Europe and ride for them. They knew that I was the rider who had started Philco's career and they had watched me show Dreamy Sam. Frank Kernan was a superb horseman and probably the biggest horse dealer in all of Europe at that time.

Frank was a short, stout, jovial, red faced Irishman - usually found holding his trademark rum and coke. Frank loved his rum and coke. Frank's place was in Crossmaglen, Northern Ireland – a notoriously rough part of the world during that decade, particularly in 1974.

Frank Kernan and David Broome came back into my life when they came to New York and bought another Thoroughbred horse I was showing named Brass Tacks. Brass Tacks was a horse which a friend of Mike's had sent for me to ride and for us to show and sell. Mike's friend had owned a big hack and boarding stable in New York City and had bought Brass Tacks at Bunchy Grant's Auction in Metuchen, New Jersey for $300 – a Killer's price.

So a piece of Bunchy's Auction came back into my life - this time in the form of a very green, but talented $300 Thoroughbred. Brass Tacks was a 16.1 hand chestnut gelding who had been mishandled and abused in his past. The very fact that he came from Bunchy Grant's auction spoke volumes to that history. Brass Tacks proved to be too much horse for the riders of Mike's friend, so the horse was sent to Mike explicitly for me to ride.

I worked with Brass Tacks and through proper training and the building of his trust and confidence, he became a big winner. Frank and David were looking for a horse for a top junior rider named Debbie Johnsey, who lived near David in Wales. They had heard about Brass Tacks and had come to buy him for Debbie. At that time, Frank had again asked me to come and ride for him in Northern Ireland. This time he stuffed several hundred-dollar bills in my pocket and told me to call him when I was going to arrive in Ireland.

Mike Cohen and I were having problems, so we parted ways at the end of 1973. It was heartbreaking for both of us. I was particularly heartbroken to see other riders on Dreamy Sam, as I had made Sam as much as he had made me.

Sam went from a horse off the racetrack to a winner in the international division at the big indoor shows with me – we were a team. That is as much to Sam's credit as to mine, but I felt he was my horse and it shattered my heart to watch someone else ride him.

It was a rough time and I needed an escape.

CROSSMAGLEN, NORTHERN IRELAND
"THE TROUBLES"
A COUNTRY AT WAR

Crossmaglen, Northern Ireland - British Soldiers in Town in the 1970's

- 16 March 1974 - Roy Bedford and Philip James both members of the British Army, were shot and killed by IRA snipers.
- 13 August 1974 - Dennis Leach and Michael Southern both members of the British Army, were killed in an IRA remote-controlled bomb attack
- 6 November 1974 - Stephen Windsor and Brian Allen were shot and killed by an IRA sniper while on foot patrol.

During the Troubles in Crossmaglen, at least fifty-eight police officers and one hundred and twenty-four soldiers were killed by the Provisional IRA in South Armagh - many in Crossmaglen itself. Incidents in Crossmaglen during the Troubles resulted in several fatalities.

"The Troubles" refers to the three-decade conflict between Nationalists, mainly self-identified as Irish or Roman Catholic, and Unionists, mainly self-identified as British or Protestant.

The term "Troubles" had previously been used in conjunction with the 17th century "Wars of the Three Kingdoms", as well as to describe the Irish Revolutionary period in the early twentieth century. It was subsequently adopted to refer to the escalating violence in Northern Ireland after 1969.

The violence was characterized by the armed campaigns of Irish Republican and Ulster paramilitary groups known as the IRA, and British state security forces, which included the British Army and the Royal Ulster Constabulary, RUC. It thus became the focus for the longest major campaign in the history of the British Army. The British government's position on this matter was that its forces were neutral in the conflict, trying to uphold law and order in Northern Ireland and the right of the people of Northern Ireland to democratic self-determination. The Nationalists regarded the state forces as forces of occupation or partisan combatants in the conflict.

The British security forces focused on republican paramilitaries and activists, and the "Ballast" investigation by the Police Ombudsman confirmed that British forces colluded on several occasions with loyalist paramilitaries. They were involved in murder and furthermore obstructed the course of justice, when claims of collusion and murder were investigated.

The Troubles were brought to an uneasy end by a peace process that included the declaration of ceasefires by most paramilitary organizations, the complete decommissioning of the IRA's weapons, the reform of the police, and the corresponding withdrawal of the British Army from the streets and sensitive Irish border areas such as Crossmaglen and County Fermanagh. This peace was agreed upon by the signatories to the Belfast Agreement - commonly known as the "Good Friday Agreement".

One part of the Agreement states that Northern Ireland will remain within the United Kingdom, unless a majority of the Northern Irish electorate vote otherwise. It also established the Northern Ireland executive, a devolved power-sharing government, must consist of both unionist and nationalist parties.

Although the number of active participants was relatively small, the Troubles affected many in Northern Ireland on a daily basis. The impact sometimes spread to England and the Republic of Ireland, and occasionally to parts of mainland Europe.

RIDING IN CROSSMAGLEN NORTHERN IRELAND

DURING "THE TROUBLES" IN 1974

When Mike Cohen and I had parted ways at the end of 1973, I decided to go to Northern Ireland in early 1974 to ride for Frank Kernan in Crossmaglen, Northern Ireland. This was the time of "The Troubles" in Crossmaglen and I unknowingly ended up in the middle of a war zone.

When I was packing to leave for Northern Ireland, I didn't just pack my clothes and my saddle. I had a sense that there would be many difficult horses at Frank's place as he had over a hundred horses on his yard. I sensed that he wanted me to ride for him because he knew that I had a successful history in riding and developing difficult horses. In addition, because showjumping was such a macho sport in Europe at that time and women riders were generally frowned upon, Frank felt that a girl riding his horses and showing them off well would be good for his sales business.

Knowing that I had a rough road ahead of me, I packed every conceivable bit for every type of difficult horse imaginable. I filled one suitcase with nothing but bits and had to pay exorbitant overweight fees on my luggage at the airports. However, it proved to be worth it. This was my first venture over to Europe and I wanted to be prepared for any type of horse I may encounter while riding there.

When I arrived in Northern Ireland, I was surprised that there was a bar in the airport lobby and pick up area. Almost everyone had a drink in their hands – holding true to the Irish stereotype of liquor being a mainstay amongst the Irish. I was met at the airport by a cheery old and shriveled Irishman, carrying a cardboard sign with my name on it. I was exhausted from the flight when I piled my suitcases into his old, beaten up car.

Crossmaglen, Northern Ireland

My fatigue didn't stop my chauffeur from stopping at a few local pubs on route to the stables. I learned quickly that I would be turning down drinks constantly during my tour in Northern Ireland. It seemed physically impossible to keep up with their drinking habits, so I didn't even try. Plus, they drank hardcore whiskey, scotch, bourbon or rum. While I was in Northern Ireland, I never saw any fun mixed drinks, such as pina-coladas or margaritas. Those were unheard of and simply did not exist in Northern Ireland, from everything that I could see.

It was clear from the antiquated airport, to the badly war-torn countryside that Northern Ireland was going to be a very rough place to work. The small towns we drove through were virtually devastated by the number of bombs which had been dropped on them. Many homes had been completely destroyed and the buildings ransacked. Poverty was rampant and people were suffering.

We had to stop at many road barricades guarded by heavily armed British soldiers. They would ask several questions and search the car each time. They were particularly curious as to what an American girl was doing in Northern Ireland during wartime. I was seriously beginning to wonder that myself.

Gun Post in Crossmaglen, Northern Ireland

(Photo credit: wikiwand.com)

During the drive to Frank's stable I heard endless gunfire all around. The sound of gunfire was something that I soon became accustomed to and took for granted. It was as much a part of Northern Ireland at that time as the rolling hills. I had expected Ireland to be very green, so it was a shock to see that the reality was gray and bleak. The hillsides and towns were bare, while the air was filled with smoke from the constant bombings and gunfire

Now I understood why Frank Kernan was willing to pay me to ride for him. It was because no one else was foolish enough to go to Northern Ireland. I had no idea that things were this bad in Northern Ireland, and 1974 was the absolute worst of times to go to Crossmaglen.

Another Gun Post in Crossmaglen, Ireland

Constant Road Stops by British Soldiers in Northern Ireland

It's true that I was so naïve at seventeen that I had no clue Northern Ireland was a war zone. I quickly learned that Northern Ireland was an extremely dangerous place to be. I also learned that Crossmaglen, where Frank's stable was located, was an especially hot spot for the fighting. They called the war in Crossmaglen "The Troubles".

I should have read the newspapers and watched the news. Good lesson to learn. Know something about the place you're going BEFORE you get there. I was thinking about what one soldier at a stop had said after reading my passport: "Why the hell is a seventeen-year-old American girl in Northern Ireland?" It was an excellent question. My answer to the soldiers was the truth – I was here to ride horses. Now I was beginning to wonder if this was the best career choice. I consoled myself with the fact that this would be the first time I had ever earned a real salary - $200 per week, which seemed like a fortune to me at that time.

It was dark when we pulled into Frank's place and we went straight to the house. The house was a large, old dwelling which looked as though it had survived both World Wars. My driver delivered me into a big, old kitchen and announced that he was leaving to the pub.

British Soldiers Guarding the Streets of Crossmaglen in the 1970's.

Bombed Building in the Background

(Photo credit flashback.com)

The kitchen had huge pots boiling away on a stove which was as old as the house. The pots were filled with potatoes and cabbage – mainstay meals in Northern Ireland. There I met Frank and his wife, as well as his daughter Shirley and his son James. James was fourteen years old and the riding talent in the family. He was a very handsome, friendly guy, and we got along instantly. I was only three years older than James, but I was also there to teach James the "American way of riding." In other words, riding in a smooth, classic style just as William Steinkraus had ridden. Shirley was James' groom and she was extremely loyal to him.

I could tell that she felt as though I was an intrusion into her close bond with James, so I sensed immediately that it was going to be a rocky relationship with Shirley.

They asked me about my trip and if I would like a drink, as well as something to eat. I passed on the drink, but said that I was hungry as I hadn't eaten since I left America - other than the peanuts on the flight. I was given a glass of water and a big steaming bowl of boiled potatoes and cabbage. I soon learned that boiled potatoes and cabbage were the constant daily meal at this Irish household. The women who worked in the kitchen also made the most wonderful bread and it was fresh every day. That was really a treat.

The Kernan's occasionally had meat, poultry, eggs or cheese, but they did not share those delicacies with the help. Such things were far too precious in this poor, war-torn country at that time.

After I had eaten, I was shown to my sleeping quarters. Shirley informed me that I would be sharing her small bedroom with her – something which she clearly was not happy about. We went up a rickety old staircase which creaked with each step. Shirley's room had two very narrow twin beds and I was shown mine. I was able to hang a few things in the small closet, but I mainly lived out of a suitcase. There was only one bathroom on that floor and it was down the hall. I went to the bathroom to take a shower, but realized that there was no shower. There was only a big old-fashioned bathtub with legs in the basement below. The entire Kernan family used this old bathtub for their bathing needs, but I learned from Frank's wife that this was generally a once per week event.

When I told her that I would be bathing every day after riding the horses, I was sternly admonished. This became a point of contention between Frank's wife and myself. I could tell that she did not like me from the moment we had met in the kitchen. Now she really didn't like me for using her bathtub and hot water. Her disapproval of me remained a constant factor during my tenure there, although occasionally she seemed to warm up to me. Shirley also resented me for intruding on her space. These two women wanted to make my stay at the farm quite a miserable one and they succeeded in their mission admirably.

In the very early morning, I would meet up with James and Shirley in the kitchen. We had some steamed coffee and milk which the ladies in the kitchen had prepared, as well as some of their wonderful bread and jam. Then James, Shirley and I headed to the stables. There were several rows of cement stalls, all filled with horses. Frank had over a hundred horses of varying ages and levels of training on his place. A few rough, hardy men were cleaning the stalls, including my driver from the evening before.

When I was shown the tack room, I was surprised to see that the old, thick bridles all had only a few types of bits – several big egg butt snaffles, a few Pelham bridles and a couple of hackamores. That apparently was the order of succession of bridles for any difficult horse which may arrive. Almost all of the horses had been ridden in fat egg butt snaffles and as I had anticipated, the horses were strong as hell. These were all big, tough Irish horses, with very little Thoroughbred blood mixed in their bloodlines. I was so glad that I had the foresight to bring my suitcase full of bits. Those bits began James' education into the "American Way" and he was very grateful for them as well. These Irish horses began my education into riding the heavier warmblood horses, as I had mainly ridden Thoroughbreds up until this point.

British Army Base in Northern Ireland

James informed me that all of our riding would take place in the indoor ring - or what they called the riding hall. He explained that this was necessary so that we did not get shot. While I was in Northern Ireland the gunfire remained a constant all day and often all night.

The ride from the stables to the riding hall was quite tenuous, as the riding hall sat on top of a hill. Gunfire was all around and we wanted to get up that hill and into the hall as quickly as possible.

Often my old driver from the airport would be in a corner of the riding hall wrestling with some big, strong, young horse, getting the horse broke to ride. He was a fearless, old Irish horseman and he did a hell of a good job with those youngsters. The Irish horses were generally big, tough, heavily muscled horses – particularly back then, before they had gotten more Thoroughbred blood into their bloodlines.

James and I rode all day long until it was dark. We did this every day, with only a break for lunch. In Ireland, as in most of Europe, the big meal of the day is served in the middle of the day. We would all pile into the kitchen and have a seat at the large table there.

A Fairly Common Scene in Crossmaglen, Northern Ireland in 1974

The ladies who worked in the kitchen would serve us each a big, steaming bowl of boiled potatoes and cabbage, along with their fabulous bread. Looking back, it's a good thing I rode all day long in order to work off the calories from this high starch diet.

The conversation would center on the horses we had worked so far and how they were progressing. I would explain the different training techniques that we were now using and how they helped a horse to ride significantly more smoothly and become "Americanized".

After our plates were cleared, the ladies served everyone a big mug of steaming coffee and milk. Sometimes one of the ladies would bake a cake, which was always a joy.

Niceties were very rare in Northern Ireland at that time – all the nice, little things that we take for granted in America simply did not exist there. Everything at the Kernan stables was based on being functional, not pleasurable. This experience made me realize how much I loved America.

After this meal, James and I would head back up to the stable and start riding again. Horse after horse after horse – what seemed like an endless string of big, strong, tough Irish horses - all needing to be "Americanized".

I helped James with his riding as well. James was only fourteen, but he was a very talented rider and went on to ride for the Irish team years later. My job was to "Americanize" James' style and to make him as smooth as possible. This was not difficult, as James was a superb talent. Working with James and improving his style and technique were the easy parts of my job. The exhausting part was "Americanizing" the horses.

Day of Bombing in Northern Ireland in the 1970's

When darkness came upon us, we headed back to the house and sat in the kitchen for "tea". "Tea" was generally another serving of bread and coffee with milk. If desired, boiled potatoes and cabbage were always available. We chatted about the horses and their training, even after the dishes had been cleared. We'd sip on our coffee and milk completely exhausted, until everyone finally headed up the stairs to bed. This was our routine, every single day.

Riding tough horses with a backdrop of gunfire and eating potatoes, cabbage and bread, along with our coffee. I'd turn in early, totally exhausted. I would have to ask permission from Frank's wife every night, in order to take a bath. As I've said, this was a huge point of contention between us, as they generally bathed once per week. Mrs. Kernan felt that I was wasting water. She gave me a bath towel to use that was no more than a small square of linen. Additionally, she would only allow me to fill the bathtub one-quarter of the way up, which she would check every single night. After bathing, I would crawl into my little, narrow bed and fall immediately asleep.

Some weekends we would take horses to a small show that was nearby. Frank would proudly introduce me as his "American rider" and the gentlemen would all offer to buy me drinks. If we was sitting at a table, I would have at least twenty untouched drinks sitting in front of me, which had been purchased in my honor.

On one of these occasions I met Eddie Macken. Eddie was starting a big young bay horse named Boomerang. It was clear to me that this pair were going to make history and that they did. Eddie and Boomerang were one of the winningest teams in the world on an International level for many years. A truly remarkable and legendary pair. I am proud to say that I saw them at their start.

Eddie used to ride Boomerang in a hackamore bridle – meaning no bit in the horse's mouth. After Boomerang became internationally famous, people around the world were buying hackamores like crazy and putting them on their horses. Surely, they reasoned, the hackamore had to be the key to success. Needless to say, the success came from Eddie and Boomerang's sensational talent.

Local Farmers in Crossmaglen, Northern Ireland tending their Herds in the Town Marketplace (Credit rte.ie)

My days were filled from morning to night with riding horses and helping James with his horses. Because I was so exhausted, I would generally turn in to bed once we were finished with Tea.

British Solder in Crossmaglen, Northern Ireland 1974

One night something harrowing and horrifying happened. In the middle of the night, while Shirley and I were fast asleep in our beds, the door of the room suddenly crashed open. We both sat up trembling in absolute fear, when we saw a huge British soldier standing in the doorway wearing full combat gear.

He was carrying a machine gun and had black charcoal marks on his face, as a soldier would have on a battlefield. The soldier ordered us to go to the kitchen. When we went to the kitchen, Frank and his wife were already there with James. They were visibly shaken and lined up against the kitchen wall.

The soldiers ordered Shirley and me to join them. The lieutenant in charge took Frank off to another room to question him and Frank appeared extremely frightened. It suddenly occurred to me that we could all die on this night and that we may be awaiting a brutal execution.

Another great big soldier in full combat attire and carrying a machine gun came over and asked me questions. The first question he asked was, "Are you American?" I said yes, I am an American. Then came the question that I had been asking myself ever since I had arrived in this war-torn, God forsaken country. The officer asked me, "Why are you here?" Excellent question. I explained that I was here to ride horses for Frank and to help the horses and James develop a quieter, softer, more American style of riding. I told him that I rode horses all day, every day and that was all I did. That was the truth. By some miracle, I stayed calm and somehow was able to convince this huge soldier that I was not there as some kind of American sympathizer to the opposing faction.

A Day of Bombing in Crossmaglen

The soldiers asked Mrs. Kernan, James and Shirley a few questions, but they answered that they didn't know anything about anything. The soldiers' main interest was focused on Frank and the "American", which they had heard was now here in Northern Ireland.

British Soldiers Guarding the Border at Crossmaglen

British Soldiers on the Streets of Crossmaglen, Ireland 1970's

Then an entire battalion of soldiers completely tore apart the house. They went through every drawer, closet and cabinet, tossing out the contents in order to look thoroughly for weapons. They even went through my suitcase, throwing clothes everywhere. Then incredibly, some of the soldiers started tearing up the floor boards of the house – all in search of weapons. They had demolished a good portion of the house before they went outside to tear up floor boards in the stables and search through everything there.

A huge soldier stood guard over those of us in the kitchen, while the staff from the house and the stables were questioned outside. It was very early in the morning before the soldiers finally left. They found no weapons and they were finally satisfied with our statements. They left Frank's place in shambles, but at least everyone was alive. Fortunately, they had not hurt the horses or other animals.

We all gathered around the kitchen table with our coffee. I was expecting some sort of an explanation from Frank or his wife regarding what had just happened. None was forthcoming.

Frank was still visibly shaken and sat at the table without saying a word. In fact, no one spoke a word. It was as though they completely understood what had happened and were not going to discuss it. That horrid evening was never discussed again. Someone grumbled something about putting things back in order, so we spent the day cleaning up the mess the soldiers had left behind.

The work men repaired the floor boards in the house and the stables. It took the entire day to put things back together, after which we ate some potatoes, cabbage and bread and went back to bed.

I wrote to my parents regarding this entire incident. My loving, kind, gentle, brilliant mother wanted me to come home immediately. My WWII veteran father thought that this was all "wonderful experience" and firmly stated that I should stay in Crossmaglen. This is a guy who thought WWII was the best time of his life.

As I've said before, my British father was not like an American parent at all. He was a very tough man and thought I should be tough too. He told me that he had wanted a son. Life can be so damn disappointing sometimes. My father divorced my mother a few years after I was born because she did not produce a son – among an array of other issues. I lived back and forth between the two of them. The horses became my rock of stability in the world.

But back to Crossmaglen, Northern Ireland.

IRA Soldiers in Crossmaglen, Northern Ireland in 1974

Northern Ireland wanted to be free from the British Empire 1970's

The next day everyone went back to their normal routine, but there was palpable fear and death in the air. Frank was extremely nervous all the time after that terrifying night. He was also gone a great deal and money became very tight for him. Frank began asking me to wait until the following week to be paid and he had less interest in the horses. To this day, I don't know why that invasion happened or what Frank knew about the situation, although I suspected that part of it was because I was an "American" in Northern Ireland and Frank and his family were Catholics. However I did know that it was time to leave Northern Ireland.

Sign Entering Crossmaglen, Northern Ireland

Horrible Violence with No End in Sight

Photo credit: belfasttelegraph.co.uk

The next day I called David Broome and flew to England shortly after. The feeling on that flight from Ireland to England was one of such tremendous relief and an overwhelming feeling of freedom. I felt that I was literally escaping certain death. That feeling of relief and freedom was so strong, that it has stuck with me to this day whenever I think back on those times.

I was overjoyed to be going back to a sane, safe world – no gunfire, no bombs, no constant feeling of fear or death in the air - no soldiers parading amongst civilians or into households. Plus, I could now have something to eat other than potatoes and cabbage. I was picked up at the airport by one of David's staff and we drove to David's place in Wales. I don't think that I have ever felt so relieved or so grateful to be alive.

RIDING IN WALES FOR THE LEGENDARY DAVID BROOME

David Broome on Philco

David's place was a lovely old English yard. One could feel the greatness of horseflesh that was there and had been there over the years. I saw my friend Philco again and he was already on his way to being a world-famous show jumper. I was surprised to see that there were only two jumps in David's riding area. One vertical and one oxer. Just rails. No fill for the jumps whatsoever. I realized that this was going to be an interesting experience.

The plan was that I would ride for David for a few weeks and then go to the Johnsey's place. Mr. Johnsey had bought Brass Tacks from Mike Cohen and me for his daughter Debbie. Mr. Johnsey wanted me to come to his place and train Debbie for a while. I was happy to be doing all of this – anything was better than Northern Ireland.

Windsor Castle and the Surrounding Grounds

I rode young horses for David and occasionally warmed Philco up for him. No one was allowed to ride Philco, so riding him drew great admiration. The crowds in Europe are extremely enthusiastic about showjumping. International Showjumping is the favorite sport in Britain, just behind soccer. It is constantly on the television and in the newspaper, unlike in America where it rarely received public attention at that time.

I rode some young horses for David at the Royal Windsor Show, which was quite a treat. Beautiful grounds on which to have a big show jumping event, with the majestic Windsor Castle as a backdrop for the show. David introduced me to several dignitaries there, as well as many of the other top riders.

David is a major Hero in Britain and deservedly so, as he had won most of the major international and Olympic events. The entire tour was a wonderful and memorable experience, but now I was wanted in Wales at the Johnsey's lovely yard.

MY TIME IN WALES WITH THE JOHNSEY FAMILY

BRASS TACKS – FROM A $300 KILLER AUCTION TO JUNIOR EUROPEAN CHAMPION

Brass Tacks and Jessamy winning the Championship at The Orange County Show New York

As I have previously stated, when I was riding for Mike Cohen one of the horses on which I had great success was a horse named Brass Tacks. Brass Tacks was a young, 16.1h chestnut Thoroughbred gelding who came out of Bunchy Grant's auction for $300. He was definitely headed to a Kill Buyer had a friend of Mike's not stepped in and purchased him. This friend sent Brass Tacks to Mike for us to ride, train and eventually sell, as he proved to be too much horse for the riders at his place.

I worked with Brass Tacks and found that all he needed was some tender loving care and proper training. He needed to be understood. Brass Tacks began as a very nervous horse, probably with PTSD from his racetrack days.

However, with constant daily love, care and proper training, Brass Tacks soon became a big winner in the show ring. David Broome and Frank Kernan had come to Mike's place and purchased Brass Tacks in 1973 – shortly after they had purchased Philco for David. They sold Brass Tacks to Mr. Johnsey for his daughter Debbie to ride.

Soon afterward Debbie Johnsey became Junior European Champion. As I was at David's place and close by, Mr. Johnsey asked me to come to his place and work with Debbie.

WALES AND PARIS

The White-domed Basilica, Champs-Elysees and Eiffel Tower

As was the case with James Kernan, Debbie was a superb talent and had already enjoyed great success with her pony "Champ". In later years she went on to ride on the British team. Training Debbie was an easy, enjoyable task.

All of the Johnsey family were wonderful and a joy to be with. While I was working with Debbie and showing her various American riding and training techniques, I became great friends with her brother Kevin. Kevin was not as involved with the horses as Debbie, but was a truly wonderful person. One day while we were chatting, I said that I would love to see Paris. Kevin immediately said, "Let's go!" So, Kevin and I found the least expensive way to go to Paris and off we went – Lowest Level Tourist Class all the way.

We checked into the cheapest hotel we could find, right near the center of Paris. I was shocked to find that the hotel rooms had no bathrooms - only a bidet. Different priorities, I guess. The bathroom was down the hall and the bathtub was in the basement of the hotel. Once again, the towels and the beds were tiny, but they did at least serve a continental breakfast.

Kevin and I had a fabulous time exploring all the sights of Paris, from the Eiffel Tower, to the Champs-Elysees, to Montmartre. As the tour books will tell you, The Champs-Elysees is known for its glory and grandeur. This is the most famous avenue in the world. If the monuments and symmetrical landscaping don't convince you, remember that Champs-Elysees means "Elysian Fields". This indicates that someone thought this street was heaven on earth.

Montmartre is primarily known for its artistic history, the white-domed Basilica of the Sacré-Cœur on its summit, and as a nightclub district. Kevin and I even went to the infamous club, the "Moulin Rouge". We were shocked to see virtually naked women on stage with lots of feathers – the famous Showgirls of the Moulin Rouge. We were both blushing terribly.

Kevin and I had a fabulous time in Paris enjoying the sights and the wonderful food. It was time to go back to Wales, as our terrific week in Paris had ended.

Kevin Johnsey, by the Eiffel Tower

Jessamy in Montmartre, Paris

BACK TO AMERICA
MY RIDE ON "THE SENATOR" AT MADISON SQUARE GARDEN

Once back in Wales, I realized that I was really homesick for America. Sometimes we don't realize how much we love and appreciate America until we actually leave. I said my goodbyes to the Johnsey family, as well as all of my friends in Britain. Then I flew back to New York.

Upon arrival in New York I immediately began looking for a riding job at a good show stable which focused on show jumpers. I discovered that the great rider Gay Wiles was leaving her riding position at a Long Island stable, because she was headed to Veterinary school. I called Jack Amon, the trainer at Gay Wiles' old stable, and I became the rider for Gay's horses. One of those horses was the fabulous jumper, "The Senator".

The Senator was a legendary jumper and had been PHA Open Jumper Champion, (Professional Horseman's Association), with his wonderful owner Frank Andrea. He was a big, sweet, extremely wise, ultra-talented and generous chestnut horse, who knew more about showjumping than most riders - including me. It was a true honor to ride him. The Senator was nineteen years old and I was eighteen. Frank Andrea and his trainer Jack Amon had told me that The Senator was a Standardbred. He did have a straight nose and a very unusual canter which took some real getting used to. It was a rock 'n roll gallop that you just had to go with. That was The Senator's way and it could not be questioned if one wished to do well with him. I quickly figured out that to win the most with The Senator you had to let him do things completely his way.

I had started out trying to give him a perfect ride - just as I had always tried to do with all the horses I had ridden and brought along. But The Senator said, "Thanks Sweetie - I've got this." After all, he had been winning in this sport while I was still back at the hack stable.

I discovered that the most successful ride on The Senator was to sit up and let him go free, doing his rock 'n roll gallop down to the jumps with a loose rein - no matter how big the course. He liked to ramble on down there and deal with the entire matter himself - no rider assistance needed or wanted. That's how Frank Andrea had ridden him and he had won a ton.

One could not doubt The Senator. This took a little adjustment on my part - particularly in the very small warm up area at the Garden. This schooling area was a tiny patch of dirt inside the Garden complex with what seemed like a hundred horses and riders at one time.

Everyone had to go in the same direction, because there were giant support posts for the building - all in a line down the middle of this tiny patch of dirt. There was a jump on either side of the posts. Everyone went around like a merry-go-round and jumped a couple of big jumps before going in the ring. That was the warm-up. So The Senator and I rambled around the schooling area and jumped a couple of huge jumps which Jack Amon had set.

Then we went in the ring. I threw the reins to that wise old horse, allowing him to ramble around the course as he pleased. Like magic, we did extremely well and made the front page of the NY Daily News. To this day I say thank you and God Bless to The Senator for his wisdom, generosity, amazing talent and giant heart. It was a true honor to know him and to ride him. I loved The Senator and miss him to this day.

PART TWO

THE START OF MY OWN BUSINESS
SHOWSTOCK STABLES LTD

The Beautiful Stable at Bridlespur Farm in Keswick, Virginia

Most of the horses I was riding in Long Island were older than I was, so I realized it may be time to move on as the horses were all retiring. I took a few odd riding jobs, but I was tired of working for people by this point. At eighteen years of age I wanted to set out and start my own business. I had saved up $1,000 from riding in Europe and was ready to be my own Boss.

While I was working a short-term riding engagement in Maryland, I met up with a friend named Robin Hughes. One day Robin asked me if I would like to accompany her to Keswick, Virginia as she had a horse there for sale. I went along for the ride and it changed my life. We happened to visit Keswick during dogwood season and the trees were in full bloom. Driving down the Keswick road felt like driving through heaven. Beautiful lush horse farms lined both sides of the road. The road itself had a glorious canopy of dogwood trees and was showered with blossoms.

I absolutely fell in love with Keswick and decided that this was the place that I wanted to start my business. Keswick would be a gorgeous place to live. When Robin took me for a tour of the beautiful Bridlespur Farm in Keswick, I fell in love with the stable and decided that was exactly where I wanted to begin my new business - Showstock Stables, Ltd. I made securing this stable my next mission.

I rented a room for $50 per month in a very small, cheap motel in Gordonsville called the Inwood Motel. The Inwood is quite close to Keswick and has been around for decades upon decades. I rented room number 3. I gathered all of my showjumping photos and news articles which I had collected up to that point in my career. I placed them neatly in a scrapbook and decided it was time to meet the owners of Bridlespur Farm.

I had learned that Bridlespur was owned by Mr. and Mrs. Buddy McIntyre. The McIntyre's had owned top Saddlebreds at least twenty years before and had housed them in the magnificent stable on Bridlespur. The stable had twenty four stalls - all a good size at twelve foot by twelve foot. It had a wash stall, a feed room and a little office. It also had a twelve foot by twelve-foot lounge for entertaining, with a small cabinet bar and sink in the corner. I thought it was the most perfect stable that I had ever seen.

Due to neglect and lack of use, the majestic stable had lost its glamour. The beautiful wood on the fronts of the varnished stalls was dull and scratched. The stalls and rooms were dusty and filled with cobwebs. It looked as though no one had tended to the barn in many years. But I saw the beauty and majesty in that stable and I wanted it badly.

I scratched together my best outfit and with my scrapbook in hand, I bravely drove to Bridlespur and knocked on the front door of the elegant house. Mr. McIntyre opened the door and I introduced myself. I explained that I had ridden professionally for years with great success. I was now going to start my own business and would like very much to rent his stable.

Mr. McIntyre politely stated that he was not interested in renting the stable and slowly began to close the door. I gently pushed back on the door and kept talking. I showed him all of my photos and newspaper clippings, describing each one and telling him the related story. Mr. McIntyre seemed to be enjoying all of this attention.

It was probably the most exciting thing to happen on Bridlespur for many years. Mr. McIntyre was a very kind man and he became somewhat intrigued and amused by my insistent tenacity and determination, as well as my stories.

He continued to listen intently and I could tell that I was breaking through the initial ice. This entire conversation took place in the doorway of Mr. McIntyre's beautiful home. Finally Mr. McIntyre gave in and agreed to rent me the stable. He said the rent would be $1,500 per month. This was a major problem as I only had $1,000 to my name and no family or any other help offered whatsoever. This situation required more talking in the doorway.

I said that I would scrub the stable until it was immaculate and re-varnish the entire inside, bringing it back to its glory. I said that I would clean and paint the rooms so that they looked fresh and new, and I would paint the huge white doors at all four entrances to the stable. I promised Mr. McIntyre that when I was finished, the stable would once again be magnificent - just as it had been when he was showing his great Saddlebreds.

Mr. McIntyre seemed very interested in all of this free labor offered from an energetic teenager. I believe my story and background impressed him. It seemed as though he now believed in me, despite the fact that we had just met. From his kind and generous heart, Mr. McIntyre told me that I could rent the stable for $500 per month and that he would never raise the rent while I was there. He said that if I left the stable, he would never rent it to anyone else. Mr. McIntyre even said that he would buy all the paint, varnish and supplies for me to do this job up to both of our high expectations. Still in the doorway, we shook hands. That handshake proved to be my very secure lease for the next ten years - until Mr. McIntyre passed away. I shall forever be grateful to Mr. McIntyre for his kindness, generosity and for his belief in me.

PREPARING THE STABLE FOR MY NEW BUSINESS

The Inside of the Stable on Bridlespur Farm after I had varnished it

Now came the hard work. Mr. McIntyre brought many cans of paint and varnish down to the barn and seemed very excited to have this new project in the works. I believe my stable renovation was a breath of fresh air for Mr. McIntyre. It gave him something to do each day which he really enjoyed. My renovation project brought Mr. McIntyre back to life, as he remembered the glory of his past with the horses in this stable. Mr. McIntyre was having one heck of a good time.

Meanwhile, I was totally alone as I did not know a soul in Keswick. I would drive from my room at the Inwood Motel, to Bridlespur Farm very early in the morning. Then I would start scrubbing that entire barn, wearing old shorts and a tank top. I believe Mr. McIntyre got a kick out of that too.

There was a good twenty years' worth of bird droppings on the stalls. It took several weeks of scrubbing with pine sol disinfectant, hot water and brushes to get everything spotless, but it was finally clean and smelled fresh.

Now it was time to begin varnishing. I started at one end of that long barn aisle, painstaking varnishing each stall front until it was perfect. Then I'd move on to the next stall front and then the next, leaving each one sparkling with fresh vanish. As you can see, it was a long barn and it looked longer and longer every day. It seemed like a task with no end in sight. Mr. McIntyre came to the barn every day and was thrilled with my progress and the difference in the appearance of the barn. He was very encouraging. Mr. McIntyre was the only person I saw all day long.

I would varnish from very early in the morning, to well after dark. The barn had lights in the aisle, so working late was not a problem. Sometimes Mr. McIntyre would bring me a sandwich or a piece of cake and bottled water. I was thrilled, because all I ate every single day was hard boiled eggs. Eggs were all I could afford. I had a small hot plate in my little motel room at the Inwood and boiled a few eggs every night. Thinking back, at $50 per month I probably should have stayed there. I'd have a lot of money by now.

It took endless weeks to finally have varnished the entire inside of the stable. However the wood was so old and dry that it soaked up a good part of the varnish. Mr. McIntyre and I examined it and he was ecstatic, but I told him that I felt I needed to put on another coat of varnish. Then Mr. McIntyre was really excited and said that he would go to the hardware store and buy more varnish immediately.

So it was back to the end of the barn, beginning all over. I'd varnish from very early in the morning until well after dark – every single day. I never took a day off. I didn't know anyone and it didn't make sense to sit in my little motel room and do nothing when I had a business to get started.

Every night I would come back to my room covered in varnish and absolutely filthy. I'd throw the shorts and top into a laundry basket and take a long hot shower to scrub off the dirt and varnish.

Then I'd eat a couple of hard-boiled eggs, brush my teeth, get in the bed and fall straight into a coma like sleep, totally exhausted. That was my life for the entire spring, summer and into the fall – varnish and paint, shower, eat a couple of boiled eggs and then crash to bed - every single day.

Finally the second coat of varnish was finished. Then I started painting the four rooms. The small lounge type room was wood paneled, so I varnished that too. Mr. McIntyre brought me great big buckets of white paint, new paint brushes and a very tall ladder, because these were big, tall doors on the stable's entrances. I also painted the fancy little white wrought iron benches which were a part of the beautiful entrance to the barn. Of course the doors, benches and rooms also got two coats.

Finally, I moved in one Thoroughbred jumper named "HUD", which Maria and Bob Lull had been kind enough to buy for me to ride and train. I charged them $8 per day for full board, care, riding and training. That gave me a little monthly income, which is a good thing because I had just about depleted my $1,000. At this point in my life, I had never owned a horse of my own. Eventually I sold HUD to a junior rider in Puerto Rico.

I gave Mr. McIntyre a check for $500 for the first month and I had to pay the Inwood Motel $50 each month as well. Plus I needed to buy hay, feed and bedding for HUD and eggs for myself. I had a phone hooked up as well, for all the business that I anticipated I would be generating.

I also needed jumps. I had heard that Rodney Jenkins was selling his old set of jumps for $500, so I told him that I would take all of them. I gathered my board checks for a couple of months and bought the jumps from Rodney. There was a fellow who did some work on the farm and he had a truck. I talked him into helping me pick up all of Rodney's jumps and proudly set them in the beautiful field behind the barn at Bridlespur. Then I painted those jumps for weeks on end until I had a beautiful course. Of course the jumps got two coats of paint too.

I may not have had much, but I felt happy and free. I now had my very own business and would never have to work for anyone again. I was ready to tell anyone who would listen that I was open for business.

HUD - Owned by Mr. and Mrs. Robert Lull

THE EARLY DAYS OF SHOWSTOCK STABLES

THE INFAMOUS LARRY STORY

The Entrance to the Stable at Bridlespur - Scene of the Larry Incident

Although I really didn't know anyone in Virginia, (aside from Rodney Jenkins), I went about calling every single horse person in the area to let them know that I was now open for business. The only person who showed up to welcome me to town was the great Enis Jenkins - Rodney Jenkins' father. It was a huge honor and it revealed the true class and kindness of the gentleman. If Rodney had to name one person to thank and credit for his tremendous success, I'm sure that he would say that person would be his father - the great horseman Enis.

To my dismay, most of the high society people who I contacted really shunned me. There was apparently an extremely wary attitude which was, "Who is this young Yankee girl who is now renting the beautiful stable at Bridlespur? What nerve that girl has to come down here from up North and infiltrate our tightknit group of horse people! Who the hell does she think she is????" These people would not even acknowledge my presence in the post office. I would say hello and there would be absolutely no response. They would not even look in my direction.

They definitely shut me out and shunned me at every opportunity. I soon discovered that it was extremely difficult to break into the old money Virginia society – especially if you were a teenage girl from New York City with no money.

However Mark Perry, a great horseman from Florida, said that he would send me a horse to sell. I was thrilled. My very first sale horse. Mark was a short, stocky little man with very small round eyeglasses and a trademark cigar stub in his mouth. Mark was the trainer of such great show horses as "Touch the Sun" and "Mr. Demeanor", as well as several top winning racehorses. He was also married to Rodney Jenkin's sister.

Mark Perry wanted $2,500 for the horse and was sending him "on the cuff", which meant that I paid all expenses on the horse and kept any sale profits over $2,500. The horse arrived – a big 16.2 hand, ten-year-old attractive chestnut with four white stockings and a big white blaze. I named him "Mark". Mark had a good bit of experience in the three foot and three foot six divisions, so I thought he would be easy to sell for a profit - plus he was a nice mover and jumped in good form for a junior or amateur show hunter.

Mark had one little snag to him. He would go around like a Champion for me or for any decent rider, but he would stop at the jumps with an inexperienced or bad rider. Mark wasn't mean when he stopped with these people. He would just slow down and fade to a stop right in front of the jump. Mark would go from cantering around the course like a Champion, to wilting like a dying flower. He didn't hurt or throw anyone off, but he obviously had to be matched with the right rider in order for his sale to be a successful one. Mark wanted to choose his riders carefully.

Some local people named Bill and Poo Johnson came with their daughter Kathy to try Mark. They had a small horse farm in Keswick. Kathy was an excellent junior rider, so she was a wonderful match for Mark. I sold him for $5,000, sent Mark Perry his $2,500 and felt very rich. This is more money than I had ever seen in my entire life.

Then I received a call from a fellow named Larry. He was riding for a big show hunter stable in the area and was apparently hustling some sales horses on the side, unbeknownst to his Boss.

Larry wanted to move half a dozen sale horses into my stable and I was thrilled. I would be getting eight dollars per day per horse for total care. This included feeding, cleaning the stalls, turning out and riding these horses daily, as well as for potential customers. I did all of the work at that time, so my overhead was under control. I thought I was really rolling.

As I had a little bit of money now, I purchased two bridles for Showstock Stables at $50 each. I immediately realized that I had overextended myself, but fortunately Larry said that he would buy one of the bridles and give me a check later.

Things went smoothly for a month or so. I rode Larry's horses every day and whenever he brought customers to preview the horses. Larry's horses always looked fabulous and went around the course perfectly, as I worked with them every day for hours on end.

Larry sold several horses and things were going along fine, although Larry never seemed to have a check with him. Getting paid for my work was becoming extremely difficult. One very early morning I arrived as usual to feed the horses, turn them out into their paddocks and clean the stalls - all before I began riding.

To my shock, Larry's car was already there parked at the entrance to the stable and in the courtyard. He was loading his horses onto a van. It was blatantly obvious that Larry was trying to skip out on paying the board, so I went right up to him and asked him what he thought he was doing. I told him to come back to my office so I could give him the bill and he could pay me what he owed me on the spot.

I sat behind my desk, wrote out Larry's bill and he begrudgingly gave me a check for the board which he owed. It suddenly hit me that I had forgotten about the bridle which Larry had committed to buy for $50. I told Larry that he needed to give me a check for the $50 bridle as well.

At my desk, preparing Larry's bill

This is when the problem started. Larry was leaning against the doorway of my office, just as smug as he could be. He smirked and in the cockiest possible way said, "Sorry Hon. I lost it."

With that he turned on his heel and strutted away, headed to his car. The blood immediately began to boil in my head and while jumping up to go after Larry, I turned over my desk. I didn't have a husband, or boyfriend, or father or even an employee to help me, so I knew that I needed to handle this myself. This was not right and could not stand. I believe in justice.

Larry had just gotten into his car and the car door was still open. Without saying a word, I ran to the side of the car, grabbed Larry by his fancy shirt, pulled him up and punched him right in the face as hard as I could. Larry immediately fell over into the next seat, just like a carnival dummy falls when struck with a ball. Larry was cursing wildly and calling me unprintable names.

When Larry finally got himself upright in his seat, his shirt was torn and his nose was bleeding pretty badly - but he was still cursing up a storm. I never said a word. I just grabbed him by the shirt again and punched him in the face with as much power as I could possibly muster.

Larry again fell straight down onto the other seat. Still cursing like a wild man, he eventually straightened himself up again – now with even more blood on his face and shirt from a cut over his eye. Never speaking a word, I grabbed him again and punched him so hard that I thought I'd knocked him out. Larry was a mess by now and a sight to be seen.

Larry stayed down for a bit and I thought that I may have really hurt him, but then he started cursing like a crazy person again and wobbled his way back to the driver's seat. This time, as he was getting up, Larry threw the car into reverse and tore out of the courtyard backwards before I could hit him again. He took off out the driveway with the door of his car still open, burning rubber the entire way in a cloud of dust and smoke. Although I didn't get my $50 or my bridle, I'll admit that I felt pretty good. I had just dealt with my very first business altercation and decided that I had handled it well.

Then the most amazing thing of all happened. The phone in the stable rang. This was a big deal onto itself, as no one ever called me. I answered the phone and it was Larry.

He said, "Hi Hon, I found your bridle." I said, "Great Larry! Bring it over." Larry stated that he'd be sending it with a girl instead. I guess Larry had seen enough of me for one day.

Then a young, trembling girl drove into the courtyard in her fancy BMW. The girl got out of the car with the bridle in her hand and was shaking all over. I guess this girl had just seen Larry's bloody face and shirt. This girl quickly reached over and stretched to hand me the bridle, keeping as much distance between us as physically possible. The poor girl then ran to her car, jumped in and took off almost as fast as Larry had escaped. Now I really felt great. My very first altercation ended in Total Victory.

My wonderful farrier Eddie Watson arrived shortly after this event to shoe the couple of remaining horses in the stable. We were chatting and I told him that he wouldn't believe what had just happened.

I told Eddie the entire story about Larry, the bridle and our altercation. Eddie was laughing so hard that he had to put the horse's foot down.

Apparently Larry had taken a lot of people in this area for money and it was clear that Larry did not have many friends. He had burned many bridges in the Keswick area and elsewhere across the country.

After Eddie had finished his shoeing, I went back to my work and riding without another thought about the Larry incident. However the most amazing thing of all happened over the next couple of weeks.

Apparently Eddie had spread the story of the Larry incident, as only a blacksmith can. It had traveled far and wide. The television and radio could not have informed more people than Eddie had apparently reached.

All kinds of people were showing up to congratulate me and tell me they thought that I was terrific. These were the same high society folks who had shunned me so badly ever since my arrival in Keswick. I had suddenly become extremely popular overnight. I was finally welcomed into this tightknit group of wealthy Virginia horse people - heartily and enthusiastically. I was invited to all kinds of social events after that.

I suddenly became the Darling of these Keswick people, because as one of them said, "It's about time someone straightened out that little punk!!" Had I known that all I had to do to be accepted was knock out Larry, I would have done it weeks before. It no longer mattered that I was a teenager with no money from New York City. I was the gal who knocked Larry out and that made me quite popular. This was probably the most exciting thing that had happened in Keswick for decades.

About a week later, two police officers showed up at Bridlespur Farm and drove up to the stable. I came out to greet them and they informed me that an assault claim had been filed by Larry. The officers said that they were here to investigate. So I told them the entire story, from start to finish.

I told them that I was eighteen years old, had started my business with $1,000 and had overextended myself with the $50 purchase of the extra bridle. I told them how Larry had said he'd buy the bridle and then had smirked so condescendingly at me when I had asked for a check. I told the officers that it was clear Larry had no intention of paying for the bridle. I told them how smug and cocky Larry had behaved.

I also pointed out that Larry was taller and weighed more than I did, as well as the fact that he was a grown man and I was a teenage girl.

I told the officers exactly how I had handled the situation, blow by blow. By the time I had gotten to this part of the story, the officers were laughing so hard that I had to run into the office to get them some tissues. Tears of laughter were rolling down their faces as they asked me if I wished to file any charges against Larry. I told them that I felt I had resolved the situation with an excellent result. The officers started laughing uproariously again and I had to run and get them more tissues.

When the officers were getting back in their car, they said that this had been the best call of the day. They told me that if I ever needed anything at all, to call them immediately. They made sure they gave me their cards and numbers. Then still laughing, they asked me to try not to knock out any more men. I promised them that I would try my very best, but the horse business was a tough business and some situations must be addressed immediately. No time to call the police and no need, if I had the situation under control.

While still laughing their heads off the officers finally left, waving to me all the way down the driveway. I could tell this story would spread around the police department and the Virginia police would now be my friends too.

THE FABULOUS GUCCI

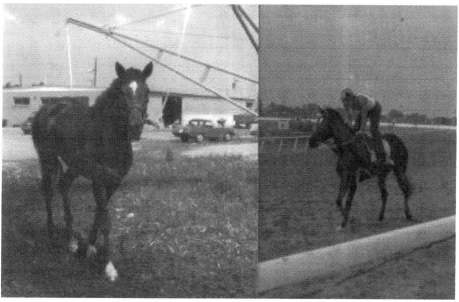

Loppy, (Gucci), .at the Charlestown Racetrack

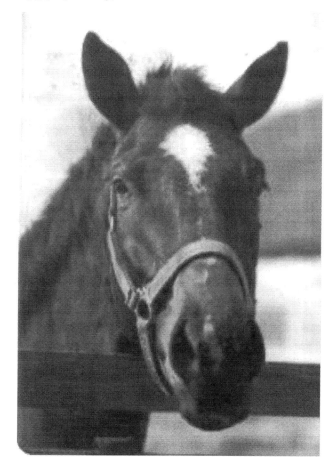

I kept in touch with my friend Robin Hughes and she told me about a four year old dark brown Thoroughbred gelding at Charlestown racetrack. Robin said that the horse was about 16 hands and had lop ears - meaning his ears tipped to each side of his head. Robin said that she had a good feeling about this horse and believed he could jump. He was priced at $2,500. Robin had an excellent eye for a horse and had been a top rider herself in years past. I trusted her judgement and when I saw the horse, I fell in love. I called him Loppy and proudly brought him back to my stable at Bridlespur Farm.

I worked on Loppy every day and felt that he would be my special horse. He arrived quite thin, with a very poor coat. I groomed and rubbed on Loppy for hours until his coat was shiny and beautiful. Loppy gained the weight he needed in the next few months and turned into a very handsome guy. I rode and trained Loppy, teaching him the ropes on the flat and over fences. He showed a great deal of ability. Despite Loppy's relatively small size, he had a huge stride and a lofty jump. Loppy felt like a great big horse when I rode him.

I began Loppy at the smaller shows in the hunter divisions and built him up over a few months until he was ready to compete in the young jumper classes. I named Loppy "Little Sport" for his horse show name - named after one of my father's comic strips. I showed Loppy around Virginia and as far away as Memphis, Tennessee. Loppy was becoming my young Star.

While I was training Loppy, I also had a wonderful 17 hand, 12 year old bay Thoroughbred gelding named "Toss the Coin". I will discuss Toss the Coin in the next chapter, as he deserves a chapter of his own. I was competing Toss the Coin at the Washington International Horse Show that year and he was very competitive, winning an excellent placing and check in every single class, despite the fact that he was extremely new to the jumper world.

Loppy, (Gucci), schooling with Jessamy at Bridlespur Farm

Toss the Coin had been a junior hunter all of his life, but after I purchased him, I started him on his jumper career. Washington was only his sixth jumper horse show, but he was wonderful in the International Open Division. We drew quite a bit of attention.

Bernie Traurig, an extremely talented rider with a very impressive record of winning on a national and international level, expressed interest regarding Toss the Coin. Bernie was one of the very best riders in the country, so this was quite a compliment.

Bernie and I planned for him to drive down to Keswick after the Washington Show so he may have a ride on Toss the Coin. Bernie came and rode Toss the Coin in the field at Bridlespur Farm. Toss the Coin was wonderful, but Bernie felt that at 17 hands he was too big a horse for him to feel really comfortable. Bernie asked me what other horses I may have and I told him about my good, young Preliminary Jumper Loppy.

Bernie asked me to ride Loppy so that he could watch him jump. I tacked up Loppy and rode to the jump course. After I had ridden Loppy around and jumped a medium size course, Bernie started putting up a really big oxer. When Loppy jumped that with ease, Bernie began putting up a vertical. I jumped back and forth over the vertical easily, so Bernie put the jump to the very top of the six foot standards. A big jump for a young horse, or any horse for that matter, but I believed in my horse. I cantered down to the vertical and Loppy jumped it with room to spare. I then spun him right back around like a western horse and jumped it again, with only a couple of strides on the approach. Loppy jumped it confidently and with loft and style. Bernie said, "That's it. We need to talk." and he quickly turned and began walking to the stable. I followed Bernie back to the stable, praising my wonderful young horse the entire way.

After I made sure that Loppy was tended to, I went in the lounge to chat with Bernie. I told Bernie the price I wanted, which I felt was quite steep for a young horse. Bernie agreed to buy him on the spot and we shook hands. He had Loppy vetted and paid for within seventy-two hours. Bernie wanted Loppy shipped to his farm in Ohio immediately and paid me $350 to drive him there myself. I drove Loppy to Bernie's place, which was gorgeous. Bernie was very excited about his new prospect and pampered him from the start. He named Loppy "Gucci" and went on to do great things with him.

By the time the Washington International Horse Show came around the following year, Bernie had Gucci there to compete, along with his other fabulous horses.

Gucci and Bernie won every single Intermediate Jumper Class at Washington that year and it was clear they were headed towards real greatness. The next year, Bernie began Gucci in the Grand Prix classes and Gucci was sensational.

Bernie also came and purchased a wonderful 16 hand, 5 year old steel gray Thoroughbred gelding who I had just bought off of Beulah Park racetrack. His name was "London Fog". London Fog went on to be a winner in the Midwest Grand Prixs with my friend Will Simpson riding.

I'll admit that it hurts to sell a horse which you love as much as I loved Loppy, but if you're in the horse business and not a wealthy person, selling horses is the only way to survive. I learned this from my early days while riding for Mike Cohen. I loved Philco too, but I always understood that at some point he would be sold. Most of the horses I rode were sold.

The only reason that Mike decided to keep Dreamy Sam was that Sam was nerved and not a sound horse. This is a surgery which severs the nerves just above the heel of the hoof, so that the horse cannot feel any pain in his foot. Sam would never pass a veterinary exam. Nerving was a common procedure back then, but is almost never performed nowadays.

So the fact that Dreamy Sam could never be sold turned out to be my good fortune, as well as Sam's. Mike gave him a wonderful retirement until his last days.

THE WONDERFUL TOSS THE COIN

Toss the Coin and Jessamy competing at the Palm Beach Show

During my very first year of business I had a wonderful horse sent to me to sell. The horse's name was "Toss the Coin". He was a big 17 hand, 12 year old handsome bay Thoroughbred gelding. Toss the Coin was an extremely kind horse who moved and jumped very well. He had been an excellent junior hunter in Buffalo, New York. His rider was now going to college and Toss the Coin was sent to me to be sold. I quickly discovered that Toss the Coin was not sound. I informed his owners and the decision was made to have him thoroughly gone over by Dr. Daniel Flynn, a top veterinarian in the area. Dr. Flynn felt that the lameness was from chronic navicular disease, so the decision was made to "nerve" Toss the Coin – the same surgery which Dreamy Sam had undergone. The owners were in agreement with Dr. Flynn and Toss the Coin was nerved. I cared for Toss the Coin throughout his recovery from surgery, which took several months. Indeed, Toss the Coin was now sound, but I soon realized that it is extremely difficult to sell a horse which has been nerved.

Toss the Coin and Jessamy - Washington International Show

I decided to show him in the jumpers and purchased him from his owners for $5,000. I competed Toss the Coin at the Virginia shows and took him to the show in Memphis as well, where he was Champion in the Preliminary Jumper Division. Toss the Coin won everywhere he went, even when I moved him up to the Intermediate Jumper Division at some very competitive shows.

My old friend Mark Perry showed up at the stable one day. I schooled Toss the Coin for him and Mark was impressed. Mark said that if I got some weight off of Toss the Coin and made him fitter, he believed that Washington would be an ideal place to show the horse in the big Open and International division. I told Mark that Toss the Coin had only been to five shows as a jumper, although he did win at all of them. Mark really believed in the horse and he really believed in my ability to ride him around the big division at Washington. He told me to gallop him daily like a racehorse in order to get him fit. Mark promised that he would be at Washington to help me in the schooling area.

With that commitment, I entered Toss the Coin in the International Open Division at the Washington International Horse Show and began galloping him like a racehorse in training.

When Toss the Coin and I showed up in Washington, we went to our two stalls – one for Toss the Coin and one for my feed and equipment. All of the big barns and top riders in the country were there with many horses each. I was probably the only person at the show competing in the Open and International division with only one horse.

Toss the Coin and Jessamy - Washington International Show

I proudly led Toss the Coin down the ramp and hacked him in the coliseum the day before the show began. Toss the Coin was as cool about this as he was about everything else. I presume that when he was a junior hunter he had shown just about everywhere, including Washington. Mark was there and we decided which classes would suit us the best. We entered the big evening classes and avoided the speed classes, as Toss the Coin was not a speed horse.

The next evening Toss the Coin and I went in our first class at the Washington International Horse Show. Mark set the jumps in the tiny schooling area and we did just enough to make him comfortable.

Toss the Coin walked in that coliseum like he owned it and jumped around the big course without a fault. He was wonderful in the jump off as well and we won an excellent placing and a decent size check. I was back in the big division, thanks to this generous horse.

This same thing happened each night. Toss the Coin would jump around the big course clear and finish up with an excellent ribbon and a good check after the jump off. Mark was so thrilled that he lost his cigar stub a few times. When Toss the Coin was a junior hunter, no one had believed that he would even make a four foot working hunter. Toss the Coin had proven all of those professionals to be wrong. I was so very proud of him.

I gave Toss the Coin a little time off and then prepared to go to the Florida circuit. Bernie Traurig had just purchased Gucci and London Fog, so Toss the Coin was my main jumper for Florida.

I also had a 17.3 hand, four year old Thoroughbred who I had bought in Ohio from River Downs racetrack. He would be showing in the First Year Green Hunters. In honor of my beloved Toss the Coin, I named my new prospect "Flip the Coin". I'll talk about him in a few chapters.

We arrived in Florida and I showed Toss the Coin lightly in the open jumper division with hopes of having him ready for the big American Invitational at the end of the circuit. Toss the Coin was wonderfully consistent throughout the Florida circuit and won some excellent classes and placings. He always won enough prize money to easily pay our way. At the end of the circuit, we had to ship to Tampa Stadium for the American Invitational. The class was held at night under the lights in the huge stadium. All of the very best were there, so I was extremely proud that Toss the Coin had won enough throughout the Florida circuit to qualify for the Invitational.

Toss the Coin and Jessamy
The American Invitational in Florida

Toss the Coin had never experienced anything like this. He had never shown in a big class in a stadium under the lights. Despite his lack of experience, Toss the Coin schooled well and bravely walked into that stadium. He jumped the course beautifully and courageously. We had one unlucky rail down which put us out of the ribbons, but I was so immensely proud of my horse. Many of the top people came up and complimented me on our performance and said the horse had jumped around like a lovely hunter. That was my boy - he always tried and he courageously tackled any challenge I presented to him. Toss the Coin always went around as smoothly as a top hunter and he jumped in beautiful style. We shipped back to Virginia to give Toss the Coin a well-deserved rest.

One day when I was bringing him in from the paddock, I noticed that Toss the Coin was not sound. I called Dr. Flynn who came out immediately and examined him. The news was heartbreaking. Toss the Coin had ruptured the flexor tendon within his hoof, where it ties into the coffin joint right behind the navicular bone.

This is something that can happen with horses which have been nerved, which is why people are wary of buying a horse who has undergone this procedure. Dr. Flynn had told me that this was a risk at the time he nerved Toss the Coin, but I was willing to take the chance. Dr. Flynn told me that Toss the Coin's jumping and showing career was now over. I was totally devastated. Eddie Watson constructed a special shoe, hoping to ease Toss the Coin's pain so that he could retire in comfort.

I kept Toss the Coin for many months after this, hoping that he would become more comfortable in his retirement. As the months wore on, Toss the Coin began losing weight and condition due to his discomfort. When Toss the Coin did not want to eat his grain and hay, I knew it was time.

I believe that is how animals tell us when they are ready to go – they stop eating and drinking. It broke my heart, but Dr. Flynn said that it was now time to put him to sleep. Toss the Coin is buried at Bridlespur just overlooking the jump course where he had made the transition from a hunter to a competitive Open Jumper.

I loved that horse. To this day, I thank Toss the Coin for his tremendously generous heart. Toss the Coin gave me some wonderful experiences and he always made me very proud. There are not too many horses which one can say that about. Toss the Coin was always a perfect gentleman and he always gave me his very best. I think of him often and love him to this very day.

My father did a beautiful oil painting of Toss the Coin and I over a big oxer in Palm Beach. I treasure that painting.

John Henry Rouson's Oil Painting of Toss the Coin and Jessamy[2]

---

[2] John Henry Rouson's work can be found on equineartofdistinction.com

THE LOVELY COOL FELLOW
FROM CHARLESTOWN RACETRACK TO MADISON SQUARE GARDEN

Cool Fellow and Jessamy -- Champion at Memphis

Shortly after I began Showstock Stables, a horse was sent to be sold from some wonderful people in Richmond, Virginia named King. Mr. Robert King came to Bridlespur with his daughter Roxanne, right after their horse had been shipped to me. I had evaluated the horse and told Mr. King that I felt I could sell him fairly quickly, after we established a price for the horse.

I offered Mr. King my thoughts and he agreed completely. Both Mr. King and Roxanne seemed to like me and were impressed with the stable at Bridlespur. Mr. King asked if Roxanne could come and visit the horse, to which I answered "Absolutely. In fact, Roxanne is welcome to stay up here, as I could use the help." Mr. King was thrilled because he felt that this adventure would be a positive influence for Roxanne. Roxanne was just out of school and like so many kids, she was feeling a little lost as to what direction to turn at that point in her life. Roxanne thereafter became my right-hand person and my great friend. She was by my side helping me from that day on. It was wonderful to finally have such a great support system.

Mr. King was a big man and an extremely friendly, kind, jovial and generous person. He owned a huge Ford dealership in Richmond, Virginia and was a very successful businessman. When I sold his horse, Mr. King came up to visit and I handed him a check for the horse. Mr. King waved it away and said that he wanted me to invest the money in another prospect which Roxanne and I could work with together. After that, I sold Mr. King an interest in just about every good horse I came upon in those days. This was also a huge help with the showing expenses involved in developing these horses.

Loppy was his first investment. When Loppy was sold, Mr. King asked me to re-invest in another horse. Our next venture was a young, gray Thoroughbred gelding, about 16 hands. He was by "Young Emperor", out of a "Princequillo" mare. This horse was from Charlestown Racetrack and his papered Jockey Club name was "Cool Fellow". "Young Emperor" was an extremely popular and successful bloodline in those days. There were the sensational hunters "Market Rise" and "Market Street", both by Young Emperor, among several others. Rodney Jenkins had many of these winning horses by Young Emperor. Additionally, "Princequillo" was a classic bloodline which showed up in some of the best horses in the world – hunters, jumpers and racehorses.

My friend Robin had told me about this horse from Charlestown racetrack and I fell in love with him as soon as I saw him. I bought him for $3,000 and sold an interest in him to Mr. King. Roxanne and I called him "Gray Baby" for his barn name.

When I picked up Cool Fellow, he was a thin, young horse who needed a little time to gain weight and relax after the track. We gave him some time off, and then began slowly teaching him how to jump. Just like his relatives before, Cool Fellow was a lovely mover and a wonderful jumper. He was only 16 hands, but he had a big stride.

We brought him along through the pre-green division and once I felt that he was ready, we began showing him in the Green Conformation Division. Cool Fellow had blossomed into a beautiful horse and the judges loved him

The first show we went to outside of Virginia was the beautiful Memphis show. Cool Fellow won every class in the Green Conformation Division and was Champion. Roxanne and Mr. King were ecstatic. By the end of the year, Cool Fellow had qualified for the prestigious show at Madison Square Garden.

Cool Fellow had never been in a coliseum environment such as the Garden, but he was brave and performed admirably. He won an excellent placing in every class and he made all of us extremely proud. Cool Fellow also developed some real admirers. He had caught the eye of a gal from Florida named Kim, who had fallen in love with his beautiful, elegant way of going. Kim came down to the schooling area to ask me about him. We made arrangements for her to sit on Cool Fellow very early the next morning, during the Garden's schooling hours. The next morning at 5:00, I rode Cool Fellow a bit in the ring before Kim hopped on. It seemed as though a hundred horses were in the ring. There were only two jumps – one oxer and one vertical. Kim and her trainer did the best they could in that hectic environment, but it was probably the most difficult and inappropriate place imaginable to try a horse. They didn't care. They told me they loved him and wanted to buy him.

Cool Fellow and Jessamy
Green Conformation Division at Madison Square Garden

As I was shipping Cool Fellow home in the next couple of hours, I asked them to contact me in Virginia and gave them my number.

I think it bears mentioning here exactly how I shipped the horses around in those days. In the early days, I used to borrow a four horse Imperatore van from a wonderful friend - Jake Carle, the local Huntsman. Jake was a very good looking, friendly, generous guy, who had money and just enjoyed life. I think he got a kick out of how hard I worked and didn't mind that I borrowed his van whenever I needed to ship horses. I always returned the van to Jake in immaculate condition, with a full tank of gas and a thank you note. This went on for a few years.

Cool Fellow and Jessamy at Madison Square Garden

Cool Fellow and Jessamy at Madison Square Garden

However this shipping arrangement was not acceptable to Mr. King. He didn't want "His Girls" borrowing equipment from anyone, least of all this handsome, debonair, young Huntsman. Mr. King, as the owner of a huge Ford Dealership, immediately ordered a six horse Imperatore van with a Ford truck. He had it custom painted in my stable colors of blue and gray, as well as having my name and Showstock Stables, Ltd beautifully detailed on each side. The next thing I know, Mr. King came to Bridlespur as his driver drove the truck in and parked it. Mr. King handed me the keys and said "Have fun Girls!"

Cool Fellow and Jessamy at Madison Square Garden

Mr. King also took offense to my old, beat up car, which happened to be an unfortunate bright, tacky lemon-yellow Capri. He felt it was an eyesore and immediately ordered a brand-new Eldorado – silver with blue leather interior. Mr. King gave me a deal on the Eldorado way below cost which I could not refuse. I had a payment each month, but I now had a respectable car. Mr. King had the fancy new Eldorado driven to Bridlespur by one of his salesmen. He then had the same driver remove my old, tacky yellow car. Now Mr. King was happy. Both of "His Girls" had brand new, fancy Fords.

Mr. King wanted me to come up with another prospect to become a Champion, as Cool Fellow was sold to the lovely gal in Florida. We did see Cool Fellow again the next year in Florida.

Cool Fellow was winning with his new owner in the Amateur Owner Hunter Division and she absolutely loved him. She had won the High Point Amateur Hunter Award for all of Florida State.

This is yet another story of a horse purchased very affordably and saved from a very difficult background. These horses, when given a second chance, proper care and training, as well as lots of love and attention, often become Champions.

I encourage everyone who is able, to find and rescue a potential Champion for themselves. As I have said, these horses can be found at the smaller racetracks across the country – both Thoroughbred and Quarter Horse tracks. They can be found in cheap auctions, where Killer buyers are often lurking and waiting to buy them. They can even be found in Kill Pens, awaiting a certain and horrible death. These horses are begging to be discovered and rescued. I can tell you from my personal experience of buying hundreds and hundreds of these horses, that they will reward you tenfold. They will also help one become a better rider. However, a buyer of such a horse should work with a knowledgeable and experienced trainer – someone who knows how to condition and bring such a horse along. For the good horseperson, there is a wealth of very affordable talent across the entire country, just waiting to be discovered, rescued and developed.

Now I had a brand-new van with which to go find my next Champion. I would drive this van to a racetrack at night and settle into a cheap, nearby motel. I'd get up at 4:00 in the morning so that I could be on the track looking for horses before 5:00 am. I'd walk every single shed row, asking about horses for sale and looking at hundreds of horses at each track. Then at 11:00 am, I would go to the track kitchen and speak with the trainers and grooms who were taking their coffee break. I'd ask about young horses for sale and often got several great tips. I'd even leave to look at horses on farms by the racetrack. I hit all the tracks out west, from Charlestown and Penn National, to Beulah Park, Waterford Park, Thistledown, Latonia and River Downs. Every day was an adventure and an opportunity to discover a Champion. I even bought some nice horses off a racetrack in Spokane, Washington.

FLIP THE COIN

RIVER DOWNS RACETRACK TO CHAMPION OF OKLAHOMA

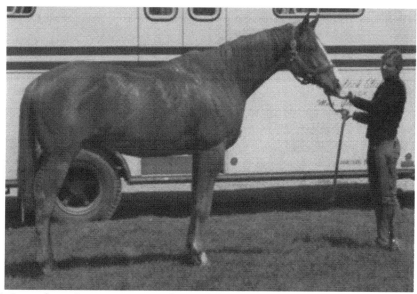

Flip the Coin, when Jessamy purchased him at River Downs Standing by the Showstock van.

Flip the Coin and his Owner and Breeder, Kitty Holding him as Jessamy gives him a bath

I have bought hundreds and hundreds of Thoroughbred horses over the years - too many to write about, but a few stand out. There was a 17.3 hand, four year old Thoroughbred at River Downs racetrack which I wanted in the worst way. I followed this horse's career for a year before I could finally purchase him.

Flip the Coin's first cross rail on the Ohio farm

This 17.3 hand wonder was owned by an older couple who had bred him themselves on their farm in Ohio. Their names were John and Kitty Barnesfather and they soon became my dear friends. This couple loved their big chestnut baby, despite the fact that he was not very impressive as a racehorse. I had constantly called the horse's trainer, Jim Saylor, to ask about the horse. Jim said I should speak with the owner and told me when John Barnesfather would be at the racetrack. I drove all night and made sure that I was there to meet him in the morning. John Barnesfather was truly a classy, old fashioned gentleman in his eighties and an excellent horseman. His wife Kitty was a British woman, also in her eighties and a wonderful horsewoman as well. They had met during WWII while John was in England with the US Army.

John and I got along instantly. John insisted that I come to his farm and meet Kitty, as well as view his other horses. So I followed John to the big old farm, which had many horses everywhere. I met Kitty and we got along wonderfully. John and Kitty insisted that I stay for dinner and spend the night in their wonderful old farmhouse. John grumbled, "There's no damn sense in staying in a shabby motel, when we have a perfectly good room upstairs. Now that's settled! You're staying with us whenever you're in Ohio."

Kitty chimed in immediately in her British accent, "John is right. It makes no bloody sense for you to stay anywhere but here. A young girl must not be staying in that fleabag motel by the racetrack. God only knows who's been in those rooms." I came to dearly love John and Kitty. They were my Ohio Mom and Dad and they treated me as though I was their daughter. I am grateful to them to this very day and miss them terribly.

John and Kitty showed me all of their horses, including their beloved stallion. I was amazed that Kitty handled all the horses entirely by herself. I was also astonished that Kitty did all the work by herself - from feeding, to turning the horses out, to cleaning stalls. She handled the stallion, the mares and the foals – never a problem. These horses loved her and behaved remarkably well. Kitty may have been an elderly woman, but she was one hell of a horsewoman. Kitty had handled these horses from the minute they were born and taught them how to behave from the very beginning. When the horses were ready to be prepared for the track, they were sent to their trainer Jim Saylor. Jim Saylor is a truly great horseman himself, plus he could really ride and break horses beautifully – all in a western saddle. Jim and I became good friends and I ended up buying several horses from him over the years while he was training at the Latonia track in Kentucky and the River Downs track in Ohio.

I loved to buy horses from Jim because they were wonderfully broke and soft to ride, plus they were ready to go on and learn how to jump. Jim's horses already had such a superb foundation. They knew all the aids and how to walk, trot, canter, turn and back up. Not one other horse that I had ever purchased from the racetrack knew all of these aids. Usually the horses off the racetrack needed to learn everything right from the start.

Jim was a great cowboy and in his younger years had ridden saddle broncs successfully on the professional rodeo circuit. The man really knew how to train and ride a horse. He'd lope his Thoroughbred horses in a slow, soft Tea Cup canter, yet have them ready to win on the track. A horse from Jim Saylor was a pleasure to ride and I bought several of them.

Back at the farm, I told John and Kitty that I needed to get up at 4:00 in the morning so that I could be at the racetrack by 5:00 to look at horses. John and Kitty insisted that they would get me up. Sure enough, Kitty woke me at 4:00 and already had coffee ready and breakfast cooking. John was sitting at the kitchen table drinking his coffee and waiting for me.

John was dressed like the perfect British country gentleman, ready to go horse shopping. A tweed jacket and vest, with nice slacks. After saying "Good Morning", I stated that I would have a quick cup of coffee and head to the track as it took a little longer in the horse van.

John immediately barked. "You have to eat some damn breakfast and get something in your stomach. You can't be walking around that damn racetrack on an empty stomach. Not having it! Now sit down and eat." The Boss had spoken, so I took a seat at the table immediately. Then John added, "I'm driving you to the track and the van can stay here. You don't want to be driving that damn thing around unless you need to."

It was very clear that I had been adopted and now had two people in my life who were going to make sure I was safe and cared for while I was in Ohio or Kentucky. The Barnesfather's house became my second home whenever I was in Ohio, or headed to Kentucky. It never mattered how late I would show up – they were always waiting for me, yet still the first ones up in the morning. John and Kitty were truly remarkable people. I loved them dearly.

I said, "Okay. You're the Boss." I had a plate of Kitty's fabulous breakfast, thanked her again and then John and I headed to his car. John insisted on driving, so at a maddeningly slow 40 to 50 miles per hour we headed to the track. John had both hands securely on the wheel and was focused intently on the road ahead. He had on his little round eyeglasses, along with a British cap. To my utter amazement, John had us at River Downs at exactly 5:00 am. This stately gentleman knew what he was doing.

On the way to the track, as well as during the time we were enjoying Kitty's meals at home, John would tell me endless stories about how he had met Kitty during WWII and fallen in love. John said that he was a young officer in the army and had wanted to go riding one day. He'd heard about a place in England where he would be able to rent a horse to ride for the day. With great pride, he would speak of the lovely young woman who worked with the horses at that place and rode all day long.

Glowingly he would recount how this remarkable woman could get on any horse and ride it – "There was nothing that beautiful damn English woman could not do with a horse." That beautiful young woman was Kitty. John, a very handsome young officer at the time, courted Kitty relentlessly until she finally said the magic word – Yes. And so, this incredible couple had now been married for over sixty years and were as in love on this day as they were the first day they had met. Maybe even more so.

I realized that their dedication to each other and to their horses was why they produced such fabulous, gentle, kind horses. I consider it one of my greatest honors to have been close friends with this loving, wise couple. They became my Ohio/Kentucky parents whenever I was there, regardless of what time I arrived.

When John and I arrived at the track, I got out at the first shed row and began walking past the stalls and asking about horses. John would wait in his car and follow me from shed row to shed row.

If I liked a horse and it was brought out of the stall for me to examine, John immediately jumped out of the car and inspected the horse alongside me.

John was a truly wonderful horse shopping partner, because he had a good eye for a horse as well and knew many of the trainers. Between John, Kitty and Jim, there wasn't anything I couldn't find out about a trainer or a horse. I had a terrific team of solid friends to help me while I was touring the Ohio and Kentucky racetracks.

As John, Kitty and I had become such great friends, they decided to sell me their 17.3 hand baby. John said that he would like $5,000 for his giant horse. Although $5,000 was an extremely fair price for a horse of that quality, it was more than I had ever spent for a horse straight off the racetrack. I told John that his horse was certainly well worth every bit of $5,000, but that I was a tad nervous buying a horse for that much money when I didn't know if he could jump or how he would be to ride. John immediately said, "Well let's bring him to the damn farm so that you can ride him and let's see if the Big Bugger can jump! I'd like to know what the hell he can do too." So, I drove my van to the track the next morning, picked up this giant baby and brought him to the farm.

John and Kitty were very excited to see me ride him and Jim was thrilled that the horse was going to have a career other than racing. Jim wanted winners and horses who could and would really run. That was not this horse.

When we got to the farm, we let the big horse settle in his stall while we had the terrific lunch Kitty had prepared. I was very impressed with how well behaved this big, young horse was to handle and ship. He was a real gentleman, just like his owner. First, I set up some old standards and rails that were on the farm in a flat field that would be good for riding. I left the rails on the ground to start, as this horse had never jumped before.

When I got on him, I was amazed at how calm, quiet, soft and gentle he was to ride. I rode him around on the flat and the horse was incredibly well trained already – thanks to Jim Saylor. This horse knew his leads, had a long stride and a fabulous slow, floaty canter. He was an absolute saint to ride and a real pleasure. I have never purchased a horse off the racetrack which was as quiet, well trained and ready to move on to the jumps as this horse. Again, the great cowboy Jim Saylor deserves the credit for this, as well as Kitty and John for their loving care of their horses from foals on up.

I walked and trotted the big horse over the rails on the ground and he was very willing to please. I asked John and Kitty to set up a tiny cross rail for us to try.

This horse hopped over it in stride and showed many appealing qualities. He seemed to have a very nice jump in him. Everything was so easy for this horse. It seemed clear that bigger jumps in the future would not be a problem for him. He jumped in good style and was also a truly beautiful mover. I realized right then that this was going to be a fancy hunter. I gave John a check right after I had bathed and taken care of the horse. We all hugged our goodbyes and I happily loaded my new prospect onto my new Imperatore van and headed home. I had worked for a year to buy this horse and now he was mine. I felt like a kid with a new toy – a toy which had been wanted all year.

I decided to name my new giant four year old baby "Flip the Coin" - in honor of my beloved "Toss the Coin". Flip the Coin was as easy to ride at home as he had been at John and Kitty's farm, He was ready to begin to learn to jump. I started with the basics, building him up to trotting a gymnastic. When his style had solidified through the gymnastics, I began trotting small jumps. Flip the Coin was so willing and capable, that he was a joy to ride and train. Soon Flip the Coin was cantering jumps beautifully and ready for his first horse show. Needless to say, he was perfect. I showed Flip the Coin in the three foot divisions at some Virginia shows. Flip the Coin was very brave and not the least bit spooky. He adapted to the show environment immediately and went around his courses with a lovely cadence.

Flip the Coin and Jessamy at the Palm Beach Shows

Flip the Coin consistently won top ribbons. He was gaining weight and condition as well. He was beginning to look like a real show horse. However it soon became apparent that the three foot divisions were way too easy for him. Flip the Coin was ready to step up to the First Year Green Division and jump 3'6" jumps. As it was the end of the year, I waited until the Florida circuit to break Flip the Coin's first year green status. I showed Flip the Coin all through the Florida circuit. He was absolutely wonderful and earned some top prizes over fences, as well as in the hacks.

After Florida, I showed him at few more Virginia shows. Flip the Coin was fabulous. Everyone adored him and they loved standing next to him to see exactly how big he actually was. Although Flip the Coin was a big horse, he was so handsome and elegant that his size was not an issue. Plus he was a truly beautiful mover and very light on his feet. He floated when he moved.

I decided to take Flip the Coin to the big horse show in Oklahoma City. This show was held in a beautiful big coliseum – something Flip the Coin had never seen before. However he was as cool as ever. Flip the Coin performed beautifully and ended up being Champion in the First Green Division at the Oklahoma show.

A lovely young girl approached me, along with her parents, to ask about Flip the Coin and if he was for sale. I priced Flip the Coin with a good healthy profit in mind, as he was a very special, wonderful horse. These people were completely unfazed and bought him on the spot. Their daughter was clearly in love with him. I later heard that Flip the Coin was the Zone Champion Large Junior Hunter of Oklahoma. What a wonderful horse he was indeed. John and Kitty's big baby was now a true Champion. He made all of us extremely proud.

WHISPER WHY

FROM LATONIA RACETRACK
TO CHAMPION OF THE ARIZONA CIRCUIT

Whisper Why and Jessamy in the Pre-green Division in Arizona

One day I received a phone call from Jim Saylor. He told me about a chestnut four year old at Latonia racetrack which he felt I would like. So I headed to the Latonia racetrack in Kentucky the next day.

I drove my horse van there, as Jim had been quite convincing. I stayed at John and Kitty's home upon arrival, and got up early the next morning to see this young horse. John and Kitty always made me feel welcome in their home – even if I arrived in the middle of the night. It was wonderful to have such a warm, comfortable place to rest after a long day of driving. The next morning, John again insisted on driving me to the racetrack. We went straight to Jim Saylor's barn and had our warm greetings.

Then Jim brought a lovely four year old chestnut gelding out of a stall. Jim said that his Jockey Club name was "Bravo Bret" and that he was a very kind, quiet horse to ride and handle. I liked the horse immediately. He was about 16.1 hands and had a dished face with a blaze. Plus he had three white stockings. I looked him over and he was very clean legged. The horse needed weight, as most of the horses at the racetrack do, but he had a wonderfully correct frame. I really don't mind looking at horses which are in racing weight, because it's actually easier to observe the horse's frame and bone structure. Weight often covers many faults.

I asked Jim if I may see the horse walk and trot. Jim walked the horse out of the barn to the pavement outside. He walked the horse down the pavement and I liked everything I saw – he was very fluid and looked like he was going to move well. Then Jim trotted the horse back and I fell totally in love. This was one of the very best movers I had ever seen. He would be a hack winner for sure. I asked Jim how much he wanted for the horse and he said $2,000. I wrote him a check right there and then.

The next day I walked the entire track at Latonia, looking to see if there were any other horses which should come home with me. I didn't find anything else I wanted which was for sale, but "Bravo Bret" made the entire trip worthwhile. After another wonderful night at John and Kitty's farm, I drove my horse van to Latonia to pick up my new prospect. Jim was at the barn and I thanked him again for thinking of me when he got this horse into his stable. Jim promised that he would call me about any interesting horses the minute he saw them. I considered myself very lucky to have such a good horseman on the lookout for quality horses at the tracks. It makes all the difference in the world.

Jim helped me load my new horse and after thanking Jim and John again, I was back on the highway towards Virginia. I decided to name my new prospect "Whisper Why", because he was such a soft, quiet, easy going horse. I'd call him Whisper for his barn name. Whisper settled in beautifully. As with all my new horses, regardless of where they are from, I wormed him and had his teeth floated by the veterinarian. It is so important that a horse's teeth are floated every year so that they are able to chew and digest their food properly. It also makes a huge difference in how the horses ride – they are much more accepting of the bit and rider contact. This is so important, yet so many people overlook this significant step.

Floating of the teeth involves filing down any sharp edges, as well as checking the teeth for anything which would cause discomfort, such as a broken or infected tooth. This can be done by a veterinarian or a professional equine dentist.

Once he had settled in, I began riding Whisper Why. Just as Jim Saylor had said, he was a very quiet horse. Thanks to Jim's training, he was already lovely to ride and knew the basic aids. It wasn't long until Whisper was jumping beautifully around my course and had learned his lead changes. My new Baby was now ready for a horse show.

It was autumn by now, so I began Whisper in the young hunter divisions at the Virginia shows. He was wonderful from the very first show on. Whisper accepted the noise and activity of the shows extremely well. He always jumped around beautifully and he always won the hack classes. I decided to take my horses to the Arizona circuit in the New Year. It was a long drive, but it proved to be well worth the journey.

The Arizona shows were beautifully done and thoroughly enjoyable. Plus the weather was fabulous most of the time. I showed Whisper in the Pre-Green Hunter Division and he was a superstar. He was Champion every single week. Whisper Why ended up Circuit Champion of the entire series of Arizona shows.

While Whisper was showing, he had many admirers. One very nice girl from California had really fallen in love with him and bought him right at the show. She said that she had to have him and she was right. Whisper Why ended up being a winning Amateur Hunter in California and he was greatly loved by his young new owner.

My jumper Sportif, (who has his own chapter), had a very successful circuit as well, plus I had sold another lovely Thoroughbred horse quite well to California. I definitely planned on coming back to Arizona the following year. I absolutely loved it.

MY COWBOY DAYS

My Roping Horse - The Great Caesar

There was another reason that I wanted to go to the Arizona show circuit, which I feel I should tell you. I believe the saying goes, "Behind every great woman, there's a good man."

Although it is true that I worked ninety-nine percent of the time, there is that one percent which I believe needs to be discussed in the interest of full disclosure. I am going to tell you the story of my Cowboy and Roping days, which I have kept very secretive until now. This is a story about a special man and a special horse – both which touched my heart and my life. I have only the very fondest and most loving of memories left from those times.

The winter before I went to the Arizona show circuit, I was on the Florida circuit. My groom and I had done all of our work and went to pick up a few supplies at the local tack shop.

We had a little time to kill before it was feeding time for the horses, so we were browsing through the magazines on display. There was a magazine called PRCA World Championship Edition. PRCA stands for the Professional Rodeo Cowboy Association. This caught my attention as it was chock full of rugged, fit, good looking young men in cowboy hats.

My groom and I were flipping through the pages saying things like, "He's good looking. Wait – look at this one! Oh My God – look at him." We were carrying on like a couple of silly, giggly teenage girls until my groom flipped over one more page. That's when it happened. I saw what I honestly believed was the best-looking man I had ever seen in my entire life. It was in his brown eyes and his somewhat unruly brown hair, highlighted by a black cowboy hat. I felt as though I knew him – as crazy as that sounds. I just froze in place and stared at the photo. All I could say was, "Wow!"

My groom piped up and said, "I saw him first. I saw him first." Then I said as definitively as possible, "You may have seen him first, but he will be mine – and he will be mine within the next thirty days!" As I've mentioned before, I know what I want when I see it.

I purchased the magazine and lived with it non-stop. I read it from cover to cover and it had become quite dog eared, but I kept it by my side. I needed to finish out the last couple of weeks of the circuit, but I had made up my mind that I would meet this man, one way or another, once I arrived back in Virginia to rest the horses. There would be a tiny window where I could take a little personal time for myself – something I almost never did.

I studied the magazine and figured out where the next big rodeo was going to take place. The choice was clear. The next really big rodeo was in Las Vegas, Nevada. This man was a world class cowboy and this was a huge rodeo, so there was no doubt in my mind that he would be there. I made the decision right then that I would be at that rodeo in Las Vegas as well.

I bought a ticket to Las Vegas and reserved a room at the Landmark Hotel, which was within walking distance to the coliseum where the rodeo would take place. I took a taxi to the hotel, checked in and waited until evening when the rodeo was going to begin.

When evening came, I walked to the coliseum and walked right in the "Contestant's Entrance", just like I owned it – the same way I always had walked onto racetracks. The Contestant's Entrance is where all the cowboys entered the coliseum. It was clearly the place to be. When not competing or working with the horses or livestock, the cowboys generally hung around in the lower rotunda of the coliseum near the entrance.

This area was open to the public and the cowboys would often mingle with the crowd. There was a bar and it was a smoky, noisy area, but I knew it was the place I needed to be. I waited by the bar that night, right near the gate to the coliseum's contestant's entrance, but I never saw him.

Several really attractive cowboys tried to speak to me, but my mind was laser focused – just like my mind would be focused on a horse that I truly wanted. This went on for three days. During the day I would lie by the hotel pool and get a suntan. At night I tidied up and walked over to the rodeo.

On the third night, I was at the rodeo and my man sauntered into the lower part of the rotunda. I knew it was him. His eyes caught mine and we were staring at each other with such a strong, magnetic energy that it is impossible to properly describe in words. As hectic, loud and electric as the rodeo atmosphere was, particularly a rodeo of this size, it was suddenly as though there was nothing else going on – only silence and the fixed stare between us. He slowly and tentatively walked over to me and said in a very soft spoken, articulate and polite voice, "Do I know you?" I said, "No. I'm from Virginia. I ride Grand Prix horses." We were both breathless. Never taking his eyes off of mine he said that he had to compete very soon, but in the softest and most gentle voice, he asked if he may have my phone number.

He wrote it down on his contestant entry number and said that he would call. Then he was gone. The entire meeting took less than three minutes. That was it. Gone.

I watched him compete that night from the stands. He missed the steer and received a score of zero. Something on his mind perhaps? I thought so and it made me smile a little. I thought that he was the most perfect man I had ever met.

I never saw him again that night, but I flew home the next morning feeling as though my mission had been accomplished. I knew it was love at first sight. This had never happened to me before, nor since. I knew I loved him, just from his picture. As absolutely insane as that sounds, I was actually right. I had known exactly what he would be like and I was spot on. Past lives perhaps? I don't have the answers, but all I can say is that this is exactly how it happened.

The next morning, I took the first flight back to Virginia and went back to working non-stop with the horses. At that time, I was renting a tiny, tiny one-bedroom cabin which was close to my rented stable at Bridlespur Farm. I worked with the horses all day, came home to the tiny cabin each evening, showered and ate a little something. I would then fall soundly asleep, totally exhausted.

That was my life, until the third night after my return from Las Vegas. The phone rang. It was very late at night and I was sound asleep. But it was him. In a very soft voice he said, "Hello. It's me." I asked him, "Where are you?" We were both totally breathless. He said, "Rock Springs, Wyoming." I said, "I will be at the Rock Springs Airport, by 11:00 am tomorrow" and he said, "I will be there." Then we hung up.

I figured that I could surely buy a ticket to get into Rock Springs by 11:00 am and I did. I bought a ticket that night, packed a few things and left in the middle of the night for my flight to Rock Springs, Wyoming. When I got off the plane at the tiny Rock Springs Airport, he was waiting there. It was as though we had known each other for our entire lives. We immediately hugged tightly like long lost friends.

We were so comfortable together and we instantly became best friends. It turned out to be an extremely sensual and exciting romance which lasted eight years. It was the greatest relationship of my life – no question. It was also a wonderful friendship because we innately understood each other from the start.

He took me to a restaurant so that we could get to know each other. We had strawberry daiquiris and that became our staple drink for the next eight years of our relationship. I still have the key from the small hotel room we checked into.

From the very first minute I saw him, I knew that we understood each other and were meant to be together – at least for the eight years during which we were a couple. He felt the same way.

He was from the West coast and I was from Virginia, so we would meet in places like Lincoln, Nebraska; Billings, Montana; Sioux Falls, South Dakota; Little Rock, Arkansas; Salt Lake City, Utah; Great Falls, Montana; Denver and Boulder Colorado; Houston and Dallas Texas; and our original meeting place; Las Vegas, Nevada. I visited every single state on the West Coast. He also came to my place in Virginia several times, as well as my condo in California when I had the horses there for a year. As my mother said, it was a truly beautiful, intense, sensual romance.

I would often meet him at roping schools or clinics, where he made a living teaching people how to rope steers as supplemental income to his rodeo winnings. One such school was at his friend's place in Boulder, Colorado. It was suggested that I attempt to rope.

My man said, "I know that you can really ride a horse and you have been watching me teach roping techniques for months. Why not try to rope?"

I was curious, yet skeptical as to if I could actually rope, but I said that I would try.

Then his friend led out a very small, 16 year old, scruffy chestnut Quarter Horse gelding with a big western saddle on him. This horse was barely bigger than a large pony at 14.3 hands, but he was very stocky and compact. I could tell that this horse was a wise old soul and I was right. He had a very wise, knowing eye. I asked what his name was and our friend said, "Caesar." I got on Caesar and realized right away that Caesar knew exactly what he was doing.

Although I was a successful Grand Prix rider, I did not have a clue of what the hell I was doing on a roping horse or in the roping world. But my ignorance didn't matter, because Caesar knew exactly what to do. I'm sure that I was not the first idiot which Caesar had tolerated.

My man's friend put the slowest steer he owned in the chute - possibly the slowest steer in the entire country. Both men gave me last minute instructions.

They told me exactly how I had to swing the rope and exactly how to position my horse next to the steer, which were both extremely complex feats. Then they told me exactly what spot to focus on the steer's back leg as he bolted out of the chute. They had me practice swinging the rope several times until they were satisfied that I wouldn't hang myself. Caesar just stood there, completely bored and totally cool – his eyes were half closed and he was soaking in the Colorado sun. He was probably wondering why he always got stuck with the idiots who didn't know what the hell they were doing.

They told me to back Caesar in the chute. They said to break out of the chute when the steer breaks and start swinging the rope. I was wary, but I was willing to try. They said to remember how to position your horse for the catch, and went through all of the tedious and intricate details of that entire procedure again.

It was a lot to digest, but I felt as ready as I was ever going to be at that point in time. I nudged Caesar awake from his nap and backed him into the chute. All of a sudden, I was no longer on a sleepy pony. Caesar had his ears pricked forward and his eyes attentively on the steer's every move in the box. He never took his eyes off of that steer. Caesar was like an alley cat ready to spring and he suddenly felt like a big, powerful horse underneath me.

When the steer broke from the gate, Caesar bolted out of the box and was right by his side in exactly the perfect position where we were supposed to be. My man roped the horns and turned the steer. I thought thank God I don't have to worry about the horse, because I have all this rope in my hands which I need to swing and I'm overwhelmed. I just dropped the reins. Caesar positioned himself perfectly and patiently loped beside the old steer waiting for me to throw the rope. If Caesar could have thrown the rope, he would have done that too.

Then I saw the spot on the steer's leg that they had been telling me about and I threw the rope – not having a clue what I was doing. It appeared that the throw was going to be a little too high, but Caesar lowered his body towards the ground and by some miracle, I actually caught the steer by both hind legs. I pulled the rope tight and then I immediately dallied, which is when you wrap the rope around the saddle horn in order to secure the catch.

Caesar pulled himself up and backed up enough to make the rope tight and secure. Caesar had just caught the steer.

The men were elated. Caesar seemed pleased that he hadn't lost his rider and that this complete novice had actually caught the steer – with his help of course. All of this took a few minutes. To put things in proper perspective, the winning times for professional team ropers are only a few seconds – often around four to five seconds for the entire process from the chute to the catch and dally.

The first thing I said after we'd let the steer go was, "How much for the horse?" My new friend, believing that he was going to get rich off of this fancy East Coast gal, said $2,500, which I know he believed was an outrageous price for such an old horse. I immediately said, "Sold".

I got off of Caesar, patted him effusively and loosened the cinch. Then I left Caesar waiting patiently for me as I wrote the man a check for $2,500. I told him that I wanted Caesar delivered to Virginia as soon as possible. That was it. The beginning of my roping career and my partnership with the Great Caesar.

I now owned a roping horse and in my personal and bias opinion, the best one ever created. I loved Caesar's intelligence, his understanding and forgiving soul, plus his extensive knowledge about the sport of roping steers. I knew that if I was going to try to rope, I needed Caesar – no question. Caesar did absolutely everything but throw the rope. That was my job, but he made it as easy as possible for me.

Caesar arrived the next week. He seemed bewildered when I put him in a big twelve by twelve stall in my fancy show barn. He had a foot of shavings as bedding and all the hay he could eat. I gave him a bag of carrots and fussed over him for well over an hour. Caesar was looking with wonder at all of the big Thoroughbred horses in the barn. He had a confused stare. I don't believe Caesar had ever seen a horse more than 15.0 hands in his entire life - until now.

My Thoroughbred horses were generally between 16 hands and 17.3 hands. Caesar had no idea what all of this was about, as he had never experienced this kind of treatment before, but he knew he liked it. I bathed him the next day and groomed him until his coat shined.

My Roping Steers and Roping Arena, up on the Hill at my farm

Caesar and I became the closest of buddies and I trusted him to no end. In my mind, Caesar was a truly great horse. To paraphrase Shakespeare, "Though he be but small, he is mighty".

I built a roping arena on my place with lights, in order to rope at night after work. With the help of a local farmer, I went to the Orange Livestock Market and bought some steers with horns. It wasn't long before word got out and the local cowboys began hanging around. Before long we had a roping practice at my place at least two or three nights a week.

Of course this was a major shock to the wealthy local Keswick horse society, but they took it in stride – perhaps even found it entertaining. After all, they believed that you never know what to expect out of a damn Yankee from New York City. First, she knocks out the horrid Larry. Then she becomes a super horse salesperson, rider and trainer. Now she's roping steers with a bunch of cowboys at night. Let's just have another mint julep and watch.

Given all of this history, you can see why the Arizona circuit was looking a lot better to me than the Florida circuit. I went to Arizona and then continued on to Southern California. I set up shop in Southern California for the entire year of 1980. I was horse showing and my cowboy was at the rodeos, but we were together a great deal and he called every single night without fail. So, to those who ask, "Is there love at first sight?" My answer is, "Yes. I believe in love at first sight."

Caesar passed away some years later when he was well over twenty years old. I never roped again. It was something special that I had with Caesar and I could not do it without him. He is buried in an honorary place on my farm. I love Caesar to this very day with all my heart. I thank him for his wisdom and for putting up with me. Caesar was a saint on earth and is now a saint in Heaven. I miss him terribly.

Once Caesar died, I let the romance with the cowboy die too. It was time for the cowboy to settle down and raise a family. I had no interest in that as I was so wrapped up in my business.

It was time to let the cowboy go on with his life on the West Coast, but I have the most wonderful, fond memories of him to this very day. He was a very positive influence for me and the love of my life – no question.

However my love for the western horses never died. I wanted to have a very kind, gentle, quiet horse to enjoy on the trail and around my farm. I called Grady Duncan, a top cutting horse trainer. I told him that I didn't need a fancy cutting or roping horse. I just wanted a really quiet, unflappable horse to enjoy.

Grady said that he thought his friend owned a horse which would be perfect for me. He told me to come up to his farm in Millwood, Virginia and he would have the horse there so that I may take a look.

I drove up to Grady's farm in Millwood and it was a buzz of activity. Grady was working with a number of horses and riders – a pandemonium of horses, cattle and people everywhere. I saw a little red and white Paint horse tied to the fence and looking very forlorn. He was wearing a big western saddle. Grady waved to the horse and said, "That's him. Hop on and ride him all over the farm. Do anything you want with him. See what you think."

So I went over to this sweet horse and the first thing I noticed was his intelligent eye and how kind he was. He had one blue eye and one brown eye, which made him that much more adorable. He was only seven years old, but he had the manners and temperament of a much older horse. I untied him, slipped on a hackamore, adjusted the cinch and hopped on. I noticed straight away that he felt like a much bigger horse to ride than he appeared standing. Although he was not very tall at barely fifteen hands, he was stocky and well-built with a long neck.

There was plenty of neck in front of me and plenty of body to fill out his girth. We headed off on Grady's enormous farm so that we could get to know each other. We walked through a huge field and picked up a little jog by the second field – all with a very loose rein. The horse was very comfortable to sit on and I decided to nudge him into a canter. He had a nice lope, but was uneducated about picking up his leads. I played with him for about ten minutes, teaching him how to pick up his leads and praising him the entire time. This was a very intelligent horse and after our ten minute school, he never picked up the wrong lead again – never, ever. His ears were up the entire ride. This was just a super cool horse.

I rode him back to the barn, untacked him and sponged him off. He stood like a statue and a perfect gentleman. I gave him a few carrots and went to talk to Grady. I asked Grady what the horse's name was, as he was a papered Paint horse. Grady handed me his papers. This horse's name was, "Cody Can Glide", by "Philly Show Boy", out of "Miss Tardy Tuffy". He was born April 20, 1994.

This was not breeding that I had ever heard of before, but the horse was perfect. I asked Grady what he wanted for the horse. He told me $6,500, obviously trying to make himself a little extra money on a riding horse. I told Grady that I would write a check for $5,000 right now, if he wanted it, and that I would pick up the horse the next day. Grady took my check for $5,000 and I now owned a seven year old, barely 15 hand Paint gelding. I called him "Cody" and he is still with me today. Cody is now well into his twenties and I love him to no end.

After Cody came home and settled in, I decided to ride him up the mountain trail. I had never done this before. It was late afternoon when I had finished my other work and put Cody's hackamore and western saddle on him. I brought a wine cooler in my saddle bag, so I could really relax with my new horse and unwind from the day's work.

Cody and I meandered up the winding trail towards the mountain top, crossing beautiful, clear streams and having a fabulous time. I never had to touch the reins. Cody was so calm, cool and sure footed, that I simply enjoyed the scenery, the spring blossoms, the wildlife and the ride.

Even deer leaping out of the woods did not bother Cody. He just looked at them as if to say, "Hi. Nice day, isn't it?" Cody and I had been riding up this unknown trail to the mountaintop for quite a while. Only then did I realize that it was starting to get dark.

I had tried to pick out landmarks along the way up the mountain, so that we could find our path back home. However it suddenly dawned on me that I had no idea where the hell I was. All of my landmarks were hidden with forest growth and all the trees and shrubs I had counted on looked exactly the same – particularly with the sun setting. I didn't know what to do.

So I dropped my reins on Cody's neck, gave him a big pat, and softly asked him to please take us home. I told Cody that this is why I bought him. Someone had to be thinking and paying attention on these rides, and it clearly was not going to be me. Cody understood that I was an idiot and that he would need to handle this entire situation.

Cody gently turned himself around and very slowly and carefully began the walk down the mountain. Cody's eyes and ears were on full alert for mountain lions, snakes or any other legitimate danger, but he remained as calm and cool as ever.

I had no clue where we were and it was getting darker by the minute. But Cody knew exactly what he was doing. He surefootedly put one foot in front of the other and safely walked us down the mountain. I never questioned Cody's wise judgement and I never touched the reins. With no reins and certainly no help from me, Cody delivered us back to the farm to the exact spot that I had gotten on him. He turned around and looked at me as if to say, "Ride's over Honey. We're home now."

Needless to say, Cody was given every possible treat available in the barn, as well as a nice warm Vetrolin bath. I knew right then that this was the best horse I had ever bought in so many different ways, along with Caesar of course. Cody's intelligence and calm, cool demeanor alone was priceless. In return, Cody received more loving than he had ever known in his entire life.

During one of our many card games at Cismont Manor Farm, I told my dear friend Sallie Wheeler about my new western horse. I told her that I was thinking of getting a companion for Cody, in case any friend ever wanted to trail ride with me. The next day, the Cismont Manor van drove in and unloaded a black and white Paint horse.

This was a horse which Sallie had purchased for her son Douglas to ride, but the horse had apparently bucked Douglas off. That was the end of his stay at Cismont Manor Farm. This horse did have a buck for sure, but with some work I was able to get him to come around and behave like a good trail horse. He had two blue eyes and I named him Morocco. Morocco was never going to be a Cody, but at least I had a guest horse and a companion for Cody. Those two were immediately joined at the hip and the best of friends. But Cody is the King.

Cody and Morocco

I have another little Cody story, in the event that I have not yet convinced you that Cody is the best horse in the world. This incident took place not too long ago. I decided I wanted to go for a nice relaxing ride and asked my groom Rogelio to tack up both Cody and Morocco.

Neither horse had been ridden in quite a while. I told Rogelio that he'd be riding Morocco to keep us company. Rogelio can ride and he actually helped break many of the two year olds from my breeding operation. He used to be an exercise boy at the racetracks in Mexico and is very competent around a horse. Therefore he could ride the bucker.

I stepped onto Cody from the fence, just because I was lazy. Rogelio hopped on Morocco and we went for a nice walk around the farm.

When we returned, Rogelio hopped off of Morocco and I swung my leg over Cody to step off too. Apparently Rogelio had not tightened the cinch on Cody's saddle sufficiently. When I went to step off, the entire saddle with me in it, saddlebags and all rolled underneath Cody's belly in one giant pile.

Anyone who has ever had this happen knows exactly how dangerous this can be. The normal horse is usually completely freaked out and flies backwards, trampling the rider and saddle beneath. Then the horse tries to take off and get away from this trauma, dragging the rider and saddle with them. Several riders have been badly injured or killed this way, which is why it is essential to always check your girth or cinch on a horse before getting on. This is a deadly serious and dangerous predicament to find oneself in and most horses will not tolerate it.

However my Perfect Cody never twitched, flicked an ear or blinked an eye. Here I was underneath him with the entire saddle in a huge pile. My head was between Cody's hind hooves. Cody never moved a hair. He let me sort myself out, get back on my feet and undo the saddle – all of which took several minutes. Cody stood stone still the entire time.

Right then I turned to Rogelio and said this is the best damn horse I have ever bought in my entire life. I have owned thousands of horses – many of which were Champions and became quite famous. But with the exception of Caesar, I have never, ever owned a horse who would react to this particular situation in this calm, cool manner and above all, be so careful to keep me safe and unharmed in any way.

Needless to say, there is no amount of money which could buy Cody. Cody does not have a price tag. I love him and trust him to no end. Cody is the Coolest of the Cool and he shall stay with me until his very last day. Perhaps he is Caesar reincarnated?

Cody and Jessamy in the Indoor Ring

THE SENSATIONAL SPORTIF
FOUR YEAR OLD BRONC TO WINNING GRAND PRIX HORSE

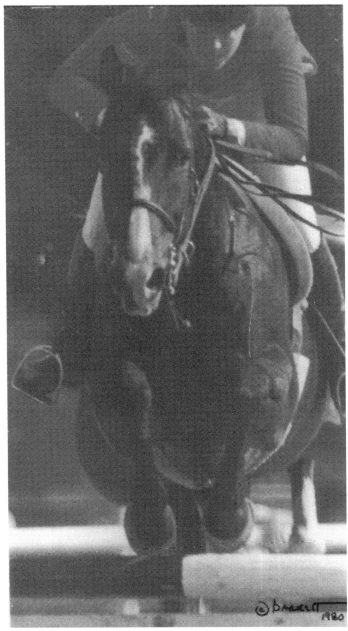

The Wonderful Sportif and Jessamy Winning a California Grand Prix

Sportif and Jessamy at Flintridge, California

I had been quite successful selling horses and I really wanted to buy a jumper prospect. I wanted to get back to the Grand Prix arena. There was an older woman with a riding and lesson stable nearby. I heard that this woman had a stocky 16 hand, four year old gelding by "New Twist", out of a Quarter Horse mare. "New Twist" was by "Bonne Nuit", who has produced a countless number of legendary international horses. New Twist also sired Frank Chapot's great stallion, "Good Twist", who I had watched win every single open jumper class he went in at Madison Square Garden.

This woman was having much difficulty with her four year old horse, because he consistently bucked everyone off - including the instructors and professionals. This horse also flipped over whenever the saddle was placed on his back. Due to his excessive personality, this four year old was priced quite affordably.

I thought that if this horse had such a wonderful bloodline and could buck that well, maybe he could jump. So I went to see this infamous young horse. True to form, he flipped over when the saddle went on. I asked the woman if he always did that and she said YES!

Then I asked if I may see him ridden and she adamantly said NO! She said that she did not have anyone who would ride him. However she did say that I was welcome to ride him. So I hopped on - after he had gotten himself up off the ground and I had dusted him off.

I rode through the initial bucking phase which was a little rough, but after I kicked him forward this young horse felt really good. At 16 hands he was not a tall horse in height, but he rode like a great big horse. He was a very wide chested, powerfully built, stocky horse, with a great big stride and a very powerful hind end. I jumped a little jump and he ballooned over it - just like one giant buck.

I bought the horse right there, gave the woman a check and picked him up that day. This woman was very happy to see him go. She was smiling and waving non-stop as I drove out of her driveway with my new prospect.

Sportif and Jessamy winning at A to Z show in Phoenix, Arizona

I named my new champion "Sportif", which is French for athletic. What no one seemed to understand about Sportif was that he was extremely sensitive about his girth. I believe this comes from people adjusting the girth too tightly during the breaking process, as well as when one first gets on the horse. So I left Sportif in the stall and paddock with an old saddle and a loose girth, with a soft, fuzzy girth cover.

Sportif and Jessamy winning in California

Sportif wore the saddle all day for the first week. Each day I'd tighten the girth a little tiny bit and give him lots of carrots. I'd walk Sportif around and let him get used to the girth and the saddle every day. Basically I broke him all over again - but the correct way. After a week of this, I began riding him. I'd get on with a looser girth and tighten the girth after we had walked around - little by little.

I trained Sportif at home and he became a winner straight away at the shows in the preliminary and later, the intermediate jumper divisions. Our next step into the open jumper division began on the Arizona Circuit. Sportif won every single open jumper class at Scottsdale, the very first show of the circuit.

He then won at the A to Z show in Phoenix and was spectacular in the Grand Prix there. Sportif and I finished an extremely close second place by 100th of a second, to the great talent and my wonderful friend, Gary Ryman.

I had put down a super trip and everyone was already congratulating me. Gary was the last to go, but he had been drinking scotch at the bar before the class and was carrying on in his usual jovial way. Gary did not seem that serious about the competition and did not appear to be a threat, as he stumbled over to his horse. He climbed on his mount for the class - an incredibly hot Thoroughbred horse, already in a lather. They looked like a totally disheveled and unimpressive pair.

When Gary entered the Coliseum, his hunt cap went flying off wildly on course early on. As he continued on course, his jacket buttons popped off and his jacket and tie were now flapping around as well.

But mega talent that he was, Gary somehow snaked the ultra-hot, difficult horse around the jump off - hitting and rattling every single jump. Gary beat me by a 100th of a second with a death-defying ride. That's showjumping folks. It's not over until it's over.

The same goes for life. I learned an important lesson here. That night I thought that Gary Ryman was the luckiest man alive. No one could have gotten away with his performance. Surely Gary was blessed with unbelievably good luck - something that I felt I had seldom experienced and therefore sometimes resented a little. Much later that year, we went on to the Cow Palace in California – the Madison Square Garden of the West Coast. There were rumors that Gary had not shown up. As always, Gary had many horses to ride and many owners and trainers counted on him.

People were concerned about why he was not at the show. There were many theories, but when the truth came out it was beyond horrifying. Gary had been killed by a gang of thugs the night before. They had robbed him of a big sales commission he had just earned and had in his pocket. Gary was found brutally murdered in a dumpster in the city.

This was an overwhelmingly heartbreaking event, which froze everyone in fear, horror and grief. No one knew what to do, so everyone tried to go through the motions of showing horses. But the sadness, despair and sheer grief was so palpable in the air, that one could cut it with a knife. Everyone kept saying, "Why Gary, who everyone loved? Why? Why?"

I guess if there is a lesson to be learned out of this horrific tragedy, it is that luck is not lasting – just as life is not lasting. We need to take things day by day, try to use our best judgment on how to handle ourselves and make an effort to enjoy every good day we have, because one never knows how quickly things can change. Don't take anything or anyone for granted. Try to live every day as a loving, positive day for yourself and for everyone around you. That is what Gary would have wanted.

RIDING ROGUES IN TEXAS

Sportif and Jessamy winning the Grand Prix at the Cow Palace

TRAINING ACTRESS LINDA BLAIR

After the Phoenix shows we went to Tucson and won the Grand Pix there in great style as well. I was having thoughts about California, as I had never been there and had always wanted to see it.

After the Arizona Circuit, I went to Magnolia, Texas on a job to ride, train and turn around some extremely difficult horses. These were horses from four to six years of age, which had barely been handled. One of the toughest horses was a chestnut Appendix Quarter Horse gelding, who actually turned out to be a very fancy horse. When I first got on this Appendix horse, I made the terrible mistake of not having someone there to hold his head. I got a leg up, but the horse bucked off before I even got in the saddle. I had a bad fall and had done serious damage to my back. I had to crawl to the car in order to go to the hospital, because I was unable to stand or walk due to excessive pain.

The doctors at the hospital gave me pain meds, which I then supplemented with pain relieving Butazolidine tablets for horses. This is not a healthy thing to do, as Butazolidine is damaging to the stomach. But it does work like magic. I was riding again the next day.

I got through a successful ride on the Appendix horse and was washing off another horse I had just ridden. It was hot, so I went to spray the horse off with the hose. As soon as I began to spray this horse, she reared up and slapped my hand with her newly shod hoof. It was a huge gaping wound, so I was once again back at the hospital. After more than thirty stitches and a big bandage, I was back at the farm and continuing my work.

All of the Texas horses ended up going really well and I sold them to various people around Texas and the surrounding states. I sold the fancy chestnut Appendix Quarter horse to Butch and Lou Thomas of California, and he became a top winning hunter for them.
Both Butch and Lou are superb horse people, so they were the perfect people for this talented young horse.

I had finished my work in Texas and was planning to head back to Virginia. Out of the blue, I received a phone call from a trainer named Eddie Connor. Eddie asked me to ride some investment horses that he had just bought in California for actress Linda Blair. So the horses and I were off to California and a whole new world. I rented a condo there at Cota de Caza and spent the whole year of 1980 in California.

Sportif and I showed and won all over the California Circuit. I was also training Linda Blair during this time, helping her with her new investment horses and her main horses, "Mink 'n Pearls" and "God Bless". This began a wonderful long-term friendship. I loved California, with the exception of the wild brush fires which forced me to evacuate Cota de Caza with the horses on two very stressful occasions. As much as I loved California, these fires confirmed my decision to come back to Virginia.

Linda was very successful on the California show circuit with her horses and won more than she had ever enjoyed before. Everything came together and she was riding beautifully. I kept the horses well trained for her and she did a wonderful job riding them. The big show at the end of the year was the Cow Palace in San Francisco. The Cow Palace was the Madison Square Garden of the West Coast.

The Cow Palace had a rodeo and a horse show going on in the coliseum at the same time, so it was always an electric and exciting time, as well as a lot of fun. I was still dating my PRCA World Champion cowboy at the time, so it worked out perfectly.

Linda won a great deal on her hunters and Sportif was wonderful all week. Sportif and I ended up winning the Grand Prix at the Cow Palace. I sold him to Linda Blair shortly after and she was very successful with him in the Amateur Jumpers. Linda then came back to Virginia with me at the end of 1980 and won on the East Coast as well.

**Linda Blair and Sportif at my
Bridlespur Farm in Virginia**

Linda Blair – Star Actress, Excellent Rider, Wonderful Friend

Linda Blair riding her jumper Floyd at Palm Beach

We also showed Linda's investment horses, which she had bought from Eddie Conner. Eddie Connor and I sold one named EF Hutton to Mike McCormick from Texas. Linda showed the other horse which was named Floyd. She was quite successful with Floyd, until he was sold as well.

To this day, I think of how many doors Sportif opened for me. His transformation into being a top winning Grand Prix horse, from a small, stocky, misunderstood four year old, who could buck like a bull and throw everyone in the dirt. What a great heart he had. Sportif was another fabulous lesson in my belief and favorite saying that I taught Linda all the time: It's not the horse's responsibility to understand us. It is our responsibility to understand the horse.

Horses communicate and speak all the time, in their own way. The most important and necessary part of being a good rider and trainer is to listen to the horse. They are telling you everything that you need to know, if you listen to them.

Listen and remember - constant praise and positive reinforcement for their efforts, so they know that you are listening and that you appreciate their cooperation. Skill and proper training techniques aside, I believe positive reinforcement towards the subject is the most important part of training any animal.

When one is able to understand and then transform horses happily and willingly all the time - resolving the problems of all kinds of different horses - one becomes a Horse Whisperer.

Jessamy and Sportif winning the Grand Prix at the Cow Palace

Linda Blair on her jumper Floyd, with Pamela Curruthers The Great British Course Designer, watching.

MERRY CHRISTMAS
from
Linda Blair
and
God Bless

PACIFIC HORSE CENTER
Champion Amateur Owner Hunter
GRAND NATIONAL
Reserve Champion Amateur Owner Hunter

Linda Blair, owner
Alias: Michael McNeill

Miss Jessamy Rouson, trainer
Showstock Stables, Ltd.

BUYING MY OWN FARM

UPON MY RETURN FROM CALIFORNIA

Showstock Stables, Ltd, Keswick, Virginia

After I had purchased more land, built the twenty-stall barn,

Indoor and outdoor rings, fencing and paddocks

While I was in California the end of 1980, I received a phone call from a friend who told me about a farm for sale in Keswick, Virginia. It was twelve acres with an eight-stall barn, board fenced paddocks and a house. It sounded promising so I wanted to follow up and see it. Incredibly this small farm was owned by my old friend Larry. I called Larry to speak to him about the farm. He had wanted to leave Keswick and move to Chicago where he had gotten into the racehorse business with his father in law.

Larry sounded like a motivated seller, so I said that I would fly from California to Virginia and see the place. I caught a flight into Virginia and met Larry at the farm the next day. Larry was extremely stressed, frazzled and disheveled. He really wanted to sell this farm and move on to Chicago. I did a quick walk through of the property and liked it.

There was an older ranch house, an old eight stall barn and a separate pretty good sized three car garage. There were a few paddocks with old three board fencing. I told Larry I would buy the place for the right price. Larry said he wanted $200,000 for the property and wouldn't take one dime less. I told him that I would not give him $200,000, but I would give him $125,000. That was all I would pay.

Sold! Larry wanted out and begrudging accepted the offer. We both had to fly back to Virginia the following week to sign the papers at the attorney's office. I put down $50,000 cash and financed the rest with my bank. It was a done deal, or so I thought.

The next week Larry called and said he wanted more money. I told him it was a done deal and that he did not have a leg to stand on. Larry said, "I know, but I'll hold this up in court for years and you'll never move in." I told him that he was a snake years ago and he was still a despicable snake. Larry said, "A leopard doesn't change its spots." What a piece of trash this guy was. He couldn't even be shamed. A call to my attorney took care of Larry's greedy meltdown and the farm was mine.

In early 1981 I spent several days moving my belongings into the house and settling in. I remember the first night I was lying in bed, looking out the window at the moon and the trees. I couldn't believe that I now owned my very own farm. I felt so happy and proud that I could barely sleep that night.

I had a pretty big operation with a lot of horses at that time, so I left the horses at Bridlespur while I renovated the farm. I bought five acres of land behind me and cleared it. By borrowing money from the bank against my farm, I built a twenty-stall barn and a big outdoor ring. The ring was 300 feet long and 150 feet wide. I put lights around it on telephone poles so that I could ride at night. It was a fortune in footing to get the surface just right, but it was all coming together.

Then I had all the fencing redone with four board white fence and built some lovely paddocks. My next project was a big indoor ring on top of the hill. I had it built 200 feet long by 80 feet wide, with sixteen stalls on one side and a lovely client's lounge with a bar on the other. Above the lounge, I built three small utility apartments for help.

I also had the garage on the property made into a two-bedroom apartment with a kitchen, where the help could eat their meals. A few years later my next-door neighbor passed away. I purchased her farm next door which had about seventeen acres, a house, a beautiful lake, and a small garage and apartment. It was fenced with old fencing. I had new four board white fencing put in and renovated the house and garage apartment. This gave me extra land on which to turn out horses. I rented the house and the apartment for some extra income.

In 1985, after shopping in Europe, I also rented a big farm in Keswick for my breeding program. It had huge fields with turn out sheds and was ideal for a breeding operation. The mares in foal and the mares with foals by their side lived there, as well as the yearlings and the two years olds.

I bred the two-year-old fillies, just as they do in Europe. I then bred them back again as three-year olds. They came into training as four-year olds after producing and weaning two foals each. I would bring the two-year-old colts over to Showstock, which was my training farm. We would break them and get them going lightly under saddle. Then they would be turned out until they were three years old. Once they became three-year olds, they lived at Showstock and began light training to become show horses.

My breeding operation grew to the point that I owned over two hundred horses. In 1997 I heard about another Keswick farm for sale which was one hundred and twenty-seven acres. The people who owned this farm really wanted out, so it was priced quite affordably. It was called Stonebridge because it had stone bridges built across all of the streams on the property. The farm had a charming stone house, an eight-stall stable, a lovely pond and a very large equipment shed with an apartment on both ends.

It had several large fields with turn out sheds, which were all fenced with black board fencing. I was on the property for maybe fifteen minutes and bought it that night. It was a steal and exactly what I needed for my large breeding operation. I decided to live in the stone house on the farm as it was so lovely and peaceful there.

Now I had Showstock Stables for my training and sales operation, and Stonebridge for my breeding operation and private residence.

I thank all of the horses in my life who made that possible.

BUYING HORSES AT THE RACETRACKS ACROSS THE COUNTRY

A Fancy Hunter – Deerhunter, from Penn National Racetrack

Once I had gotten on my feet in the business after 1975, the racetrack was my main source of horses for the next ten years. I was always looking for that really special horse - one which could become famous in the show ring and be a big winner as a hunter or a jumper.

I would drive my Imperatore horse van to small racetracks all across America and spend the night in whatever little seedy motel was closest to the track. If I went to the racetracks in Kentucky or Ohio, I would usually stay at John and Kitty Barnesfather's farm – a home away from home.

Starting at 5:00 am in the morning, I would walk every single shed row barn at each racetrack. I would ask all of the trainers, grooms and exercise riders if they had or knew of any young horses for sale. Then I would examine the horses which were available for purchase.

I would evaluate them extensively while they were standing and when they jogged down the lane. Then I would either buy the horse or I wouldn't, depending on how I felt about each horse. If I decided to buy a horse, I wrote the trainer a check right there on the spot. No vetting.

Things move very quickly on the racetrack. Horses change hands every day. As is the case with a horse auction, the racetrack is a place where one needs to be confident enough in their ability to recognize a good horse and to pay for that horse right there and then. The same horse may not be there tomorrow, or even that afternoon. The racetrack is not a place to doddle. I knew what I wanted as soon as I saw it and I'd buy the horse straight away. Sometimes I would get cash advances from my credit card so that I had the cash to buy horses for an even better price. Buying horses from the racetrack was sometimes like buying from street vendors – some haggling and back and forth until a price was determined and agreed upon by both parties.

Around eleven in the morning at the racetrack, I would always go to the track kitchen to speak with trainers, exercise riders and grooms on their coffee break. The search for good horses which I could train and resell never stopped once I arrived at a racetrack. In the afternoons, I would check back at the barns around feeding time just in case I had missed anyone with a good horse. Over time I managed to build up a number of contacts on the tracks. These were trainers who had dealt with me and trusted me. They would often call me about horses for sale and I would always come to look at them immediately.

I generally went to Penn National, which was near Harrisburg, and Waterford Park, which was in West Virginia. I also went to Thistledown, Beulah Park and River Downs in Ohio. I bought some nice horses at Latonia racetrack in Kentucky as well. If there was a small racetrack around, no matter where I was, I would be on it looking for horses. I even bought a couple of nice horses from the track in Spokane, Washington. Often I would look at horses on farms surrounding the racetracks as well, if I heard about some nice horses for sale.

Fancy hunter, "As You Like It" - from Waterford Park Racetrack

I would train these horses so that they could become hunters or jumpers. I also sold several as dressage prospects, as I always bought big moving horses. I purchased hundreds and hundreds of horses from the tracks. That is how I made a living and survived. Many of these horses went on to become quite famous.

Displayed are a few photos of some fancy hunters who came from the tracks. "Deerhunter" and "Speak the Truth" from Penn National Racetrack, as well as "As You Like It" from Waterford Park Racetrack.

Speak the Truth was an interesting purchase because when I looked at him on Penn National Racetrack, I noticed that he had a significant bump on one knee. He was sound and he flexed well. However I had his knees radiographed by the track veterinarian so that I would know exactly what was going on with him.

Speak the Truth, a Fancy Hunter From Penn National Racetrack

I really loved his type and believed that he would make a very fancy show hunter. The radiographs of his knee revealed a small carpal fracture known as a bone chip. I overnighted the radiographs to Dr. Flynn in Virginia in order to get his opinion. Dr. Flynn felt that the chip could be surgically removed nicely and that the horse should be able to be a sound show horse. So, I wrote the trainer a check for $2,500 and loaded him on my van.

Once back in Virginia, I had the knee surgery performed by Dr. Flynn and gave the horse the necessary time off to recover. As I knew very well that the carpal surgery would need to be discussed with any potential buyers, I named my beautiful new gray horse "Speak the Truth".

After several months of recovery, I began training Speak the Truth. He was everything that I thought he would be – a beautiful mover and he had a wonderful instinct to jump in good style. In addition, Speak the Truth had an outstanding disposition and temperament. I brought Speak the Truth along and began showing him in the pre-green hunter division. This is division for young horses over three-foot jumps and judged on their style and technique, as well as the overall smoothness of the ride.

Speak the Truth won a great deal in the pre-green division and drew the attention of an excellent horseman named Murray Kessler. Murray is now president of the United States Equestrian Federation. After trying Speak the Truth at my stable, Murray and his wife Teri fell in love with him and bought him. Speak the Truth went on to be a big winner in the Amateur Owner Hunter Division and made Murray, Teri and I extremely proud.

I had believed in the four-year-old horse who had suffered a carpal fracture at such a young age, while training at the racetrack. I bought him, did what was necessary to make him a truly sound horse, trained him and now had sold him to one of the top couples in the show horse world. I was extremely proud of Speak the Truth.

A few years later, I sold Murry and Teri another wonderful thoroughbred horse which I had developed from the racetrack. He was a handsome dark brown horse, a lovely mover and a fabulous jumper. His name was "Count the Ways". This horse went on to win a tremendous amount for Murray and Teri as well.

As I have preached before, I believe there is a tremendous wealth of talent and quality at the smaller racetracks, cheap auctions and even in Kill Pens all across America. Some horses may have small physical issues which can be overcome, as was the case with Speak the Truth. Some may be extremely thin and in horrible condition, as was the case with many of the horses I purchased off of the track. But for the good horse person with an eye for a horse, there is a wealth of talent and opportunity which can be purchased very affordably.

One must have the judgement to not only know what they are looking at, but what these horses could potentially be by just watching them stand and jog down the aisle. Truly good horsemen can do extremely well by buying and training horses off of the racetrack.

I would often drive my Imperatore van all night long in order to get to a racetrack and walk it first thing in the morning. If I only had a couple of horses on the van, I would divide the horse van into two large stalls with hay, a water bucket and a lot of bedding. This way I could stop and sleep on the way home if necessary, because I knew the horses would be comfortable.

There are so many potential Champions just waiting to be discovered, rescued and developed. My hope is that those who are able shall be inspired to rescue these horses which have so much to offer. I always lecture that there is a tremendous amount of raw talent at the racetracks, auctions and even the Kill Pens. These horses can be purchased very affordably. A person could buy a potentially top horse for very little money, as I did over and over. A world of talented Thoroughbreds, Quarter Horses and Warmbloods are out there just waiting to be discovered by those seeking a Champion. Go find them.

I'M AN EAGLE

I'm An Eagle and Jessamy competing on the Arizona Circuit

Around this time, I was sent a lovely five-year-old Thoroughbred horse by some wonderful people in Oregon who had bred him. His name was "I'm An Eagle". He was a very pretty dark gray gelding, about 16.1 hands. His wonderful owners, Greg and Leslie Lynch, had bred him to be a show horse at their fabulous farm called Willamette Thoroughbreds in Bend, Oregon.

I had met Greg and Leslie due to the fact that I had sold several nice horses to clients in California and Oregon. I also judged a horse show in Oregon and had spent all of 1980 in California. Greg and Leslie were wonderful, super cool people and we instantly became friends. They told me that they had bred a lovely dark gray thoroughbred horse, but had not had the time to work with him. Leslie was an obstetrician and was constantly delivering babies at the hospital. Greg was an attorney and always working at his firm. Although they both did a beautiful job caring for their horses, they had very little time to work with them.

Hence they decided to send me their beloved gelding, I'm An Eagle. I was to train, show and promote him, preparing him for a nice sale to worthy owners. I'm An Eagle arrived after the long trip from Oregon.

I let him settle in for a week so that he may be acclimated with the farm, his stall, paddock and the other horses. After I'm An Eagle was settled, I began riding him and teaching him the basics on the flat and over fences. I'm An Eagle was naturally a very good jumper and he was brave and careful. I believed that with some work he could become a winner. I brought I'm An Eagle along carefully and began showing him in the small jumper classes.

I'm an Eagle was fabulous from the beginning and it was not too long before he was winning in the Preliminary Jumper division. He was a very consistent horse and Greg and Leslie were extremely pleased with him. Once he was ready, I took I'm An Eagle to the Arizona Winter Circuit so that Greg and Leslie could watch him on the West Coast. He was very competitive in the Preliminary division and won quite a bit. He was careful and fast in the jump offs. Many people were interested in I'm An Eagle, but Greg and Leslie decided that he was ready to come back to them for Leslie to ride, as she had retired from medical practice. Leslie went on and rode I'm An Eagle successfully and kept him for his entire life.

This is one more example of a wonderful diplomat for Thoroughbred horses everywhere.

BEING SELECTED TO TRAIN AT THE USET HEADQUARTERS

WITH THE GREAT

BERT DE NEMETHY

**Training at the USET Headquarters in Bedminster, New Jersey
Riding "Take Notice"**

During the latter part of the 1970's, I had the great honor of being invited to train at the United States Equestrian Team (USET) Headquarters in Bedminster, New Jersey under the Legendary Bert de Némethy. Bert was the Coach of the USET and a historic figure in the tremendous progress of American showjumping over the decades.

Bert de Némethy is credited with the development and instillation of the smooth riding style and technique which American riders are now known for around the world. Bert de Némethy, (February 24, 1911 – January 16, 2002), began his career as a cavalry officer in Hungary. After much success, he later became the show jumping Coach for the United States Equestrian Team. While Bert was the coach, the US Show Jumping Team won the team silver at the 1960 and 1972 Olympics, the 1968 individual gold, and the 1972 individual bronze. Additionally, all four riders on the 1984 gold medal-winning team had been trained by Bert de Némethy. Bert de Nemethy's teams won the team gold medal at the Pan American Games in 1959, 1963, 1975, and 1979. His teams won 71 out of the 144 Nations Cups in which they had competed, as well as the FEI President's Trophy in 1966 and 1968. His riders individually won 72 International Grand Prixs and more than 400 international classes. After coaching the US Team, de Némethy was much sought-after as a course designer. Bert de Némethy was inducted into the Show Jumping Hall of Fame in 1987.

And so, it was a great honor when Bert selected me, along with a very small group of young riders which he wished to work with up at the Team Headquarters in New Jersey.

I believe I was extremely fortunate to be one of the selected riders, because I certainly had no wealth to donate or great, established horses to bring there. Bert also invited the young, but very talented Will Simpson, who also came with no money or great horses, but Will did become a top-notch rider in the years to follow as well. Some of the kids there were from wealthy families who had donated significant funds to the team and they were extremely well mounted on well trained, expensive horses – saintly horses really.

We were allowed to bring two horses each. I brought Sportif and a gray Thoroughbred mare named "Take Notice", who belonged to a racehorse trainer. I had a standby too, which was named "Highlander", a 12-year-old, 17 hand foxhunter owned by a local fireman in Virginia.

Bertalan de Némethy

Although these were relatively green horses at the time, they were the most experienced horses that I had available to me. Sportif was still four years old and a bronc. Take Notice was a six-year-old mare off the racetrack and it was quite early in her new jumping career. Highlander was a big, kind horse, but not really a show horse at all. However Highlander would jump anything and I showed him with some success at a couple of shows in Virginia.

The mornings were filled with long and intensive flat work sessions under the skilled eye and wise tutelage of Bert de Némethy. It was summer and it was extremely hot. Bert would be sitting up in a judge's stand with an umbrella, a loud speaker and a cold, icy drink of questionable contents. The rest of us were literally sweating it out in the sand ring. Take Notice and Highlander tolerated this reasonably well. However Sportif, being part bronc, was not happy with these tedious, highly disciplined and seemingly endless exercises on the flat. Sportif occasionally took off into a big-time bucking fit. I'd work that out with him outside of the ring and then return to the ring to finish the session.

The same thing happened to Will Simpson who had brought two hot Thoroughbred horses to the USET. One of them was "The Roofer", who had just jumped well over seven foot at a horse show in Chicago with Will. "The Roofer" was a small, plain, skinny dark brown Thoroughbred horse, with a tremendous heart and a rambunctious personality. Will was still a teenager, but he dealt with these traits extremely well, as Will is such a sensational natural talent.

Will's other horse was a tall, skinny, excessively hot chestnut Thoroughbred with white stockings and a big white blaze. This horse did not take well to the intensive degree of discipline expected at the Team at all. Will would often be seen off in a corner somewhere, turning this extremely lathered and frothy chestnut Thoroughbred horse in circles. They were not big participants in the flat sessions. At one-point Bert got on Will's hot chestnut thoroughbred, but that didn't last long. Bert handed the horse back to Will covered in foam. Bert told Will that he was doing one hell of a good job and should carry on with whatever it was that he was doing.

On these grueling flat days, the rich kids with the expensive and well-trained horses did exceptionally well and garnered much praise from Bert. Will and I - not so much. On our greener and more temperamental horses, Will and I rarely heard any of Bert's praise during the flat sessions, but we did hear some sharp reprimands. The other kids giggled.

In the afternoons, Bert would have us all do various gymnastic jumping exercises with our horses. Will and I fared a little better here, but it was still difficult to be smoother than the made, well trained, equitation type horses. However the end of the training period at the USET was highlighted with a jumping competition out on the huge grass Grand Prix field at the Team. The jumps were actually quite big and there were several natural obstacles, such as water, ditches and banks. The course was extremely technical, spooky and quite tricky – plus it went up and down hills. All of this is what really separated the true, natural riders from the rest.

The Equitation kids and their horses were overwhelmed with the size of the course, the natural obstacles, the technicality of the course and the huge rolling grass Grand Prix field itself. They were having a difficult time and the majority were not able to finish the course at all. Bert called them out of the field and they were often in tears. Will and I offered our condolences, because we knew that this was not going to be easy.

That said, Will and I proceeded to ride and jump our squirrely horses around that course with ease and style. Plus, we were the only ones clean and we both became Bert's new Heroes. Will and I were smothered with praise, which was a nice change from the preceding weeks. This new found respect for us from all of the contestants was truly evident when we had lunch at the Team clubhouse after the Competition.

Will and I proved that when things got tough, we got tougher. Our temperamental and inexperienced horses jumped around that big course like deer out in a field. Plus Will and I accomplished this in superb style, if I may say so myself. We proved that we were the natural riders in the bunch and it was a very happy ending for us.

Bert was talking to someone about me and said, "She's half wild and half tame." I'm not sure exactly what that meant, but I took it as a complement.

Training at the beautiful, majestic and historic USET headquarters with Bert Némethy was a truly fabulous experience and a tremendous honor. Although the highly disciplined early days were rough for Will and me, in the end we proved to be the ones who would and could ride under pressure and in a winning fashion. No one doubted that they would be hearing our names in the future. We were destined to be riders and are grateful for the horses who taught us all we know, regardless of how tough they were.

KEEP THE CHANGE

FROM AN UNKNOWN TO WINNING THE MACLAY FINALS MADISON SQUARE GARDEN

In the 1980's and 1990's, I was selling about a hundred horses per year from coast to coast. As well as developing my own horses, I was always checking in with other professionals to learn what horses they may have for sale. I wanted to see if any of those horses would fit into the various daily horse orders I had from clients at that time.

I had just gotten a new client in the barn from Richmond, Virginia. He was looking for a horse for his daughter, who was named Melanie. This man was a powerful CEO of a Fortune Five Hundred company. He frequented the cover of Forbes, the Wall Street Journal and multiple other top business magazines and papers. His name was Alex. He was a class act and a nice guy.

His daughter Melanie was a timid and somewhat limited rider, so I knew that I needed an especially kind, honest horse for this job. I called my friend and neighbor in Keswick, Jimmy Lee, to see what he may have in the way of horses which would carry a less experienced rider. I had sold many horses for Jimmy over the years and even rode for him for a while at his Belcort Farm in Keswick, which was great fun. Jimmy said he had a big seven-year-old bay horse who had been bred by Nina Bonnie. The horse was half warmblood and half thoroughbred, with an excellent disposition. Jimmy said that the horse may not be the very fanciest or prettiest of movers or jumpers, but that he did everything well enough and was a complete packer.

I picked up Jimmy's horse and brought him to my farm. The horse was as represented and a perfect saint, so I sold him to my new client. We named him "Keep the Change".

With the kindness and generosity of this horse and under my watchful, critical, yet supportive eye, Melanie eventually began to ride quite well and become very competitive at the shows – a totally new experience for her.In the beginning this took a great deal of firm guidance as Melanie was a somewhat wild teenager who was going through a punk rock phase at the time. Before they purchased the horse, Melanie would show up at my place in wild outfits, with her hair dyed green, purple, bright red or orange - or sometimes all the colors at one time.

Her parents were not happy about it, but they were unable to change her ways and felt helpless to do so. However this child's ways changed immediately and radically once she became a part of my stable.

This appearance and behavior could not and would not stand at Showstock. No way possible. Everyone needs to set standards as to what is acceptable and what is not. This is very important - particularly in the horse business. I'm sure Bert de Nemethy, George Morris and numerous other top trainers would agree with me.

Melanie showed up the very first day to ride her new horse in really tight pants with huge, psychedelic colored flowers plastered on them. Her black shredded tee shirt had skulls all over it. Her hair was green, bright red, orange and purple. She looked like a carnival act. This was not going to be happening at my place and had to be stopped immediately.

I saw Melanie drive in and stopped her just as she was getting out of her brand-new BMW, which she had completely trashed with fast food wrappers and cups. I walked right over to the driver's side of the new BMW and told Melanie to stop right there and not to even think about walking another step towards the stable. We needed to talk and straighten some things out immediately. Melanie was stunned and slightly intimidated, but she listened closely. And so began the "Big Talk" which her parents had tried and failed with so miserably. This was a child headed out of control, and not towards positive influences. Melanie's parents had just given up on trying to change her and felt completely helpless, as I'm sure so many parents do in this situation with a rebellious child.

I explained to Melanie in no uncertain terms that when she was on my place, she was a representation of me and the way I run my business. I explained that riding horses is a sport which requires tremendous discipline - not only from the horse, but from the rider and trainer as well. There were rules, standards and proper etiquette which had been established for decades and needed to be followed. Anyone who wanted to truly be successful with horses needed to follow the strict rules of good horsemanship.

Number one rule - The horse always, always comes first and is always treated with respect.

I told Melanie that I was very serious about good horsemanship and that if she wanted to see her horse, or even come to my place, she needed to be equally serious and have some pride in how she was turned out.

I guaranteed that her horse would always be beautifully turned out, because he was my responsibility. I told Melanie that she needed to show her horse the respect of arriving properly attired and that she definitely needed to show me that respect, or none of this was going to happen. With that said, I laid down the rules which would not be questioned going forward.

First, the outfit had to go. Melanie was only allowed to show up and ride in riding boots and breeches, or clean, trim jeans, with an appropriate belt, paddock boots and chaps. Her boots must be polished daily. I told Melanie that she would be wearing a long sleeve, button down shirt from now on, and could only roll up the sleeves if it was extremely hot outside. There would be no jewelry, no body piercings and no outlandish make-up. Simple, minimal, tasteful make up and sunscreen were allowed – nothing more.

Second, the hair had to go. Melanie was naturally blonde and was actually an attractive young lady under all of this horrific façade she put forth. I told her that she needed to go home to Richmond and dye her hair back to blonde. I didn't care what kind of blonde, as long as it looked like her natural hair.

Third, the fast food had to go. Why should your kind, generous horse carry around an overweight rider, when you are perfectly capable of eating healthy food and getting in shape at an acceptable weight?

I told Melanie that she would lose weight through the daily exercise of riding and eating properly, but that she needed to get back in her car, go back to Richmond and fix the hair and clothes right now. She could clean out and wash her car while she was at it. I then sent Melanie home, never allowing her to visit her horse that day.

Melanie got in her car and headed back to Richmond.

I then went back to my work when some hours later, I got a phone call from Melanie's father Alex. He was ecstatic. Alex said that Melanie had rushed home and told both of her parents about our "Talk". He said that Melanie and her mother Nancy had been busily sorting out appropriate clothes and the proper hair dye. He said that Nancy was busy dying

Melanie's hair blonde for an hour, and that Melanie looked great. She was now outside cleaning and washing her car.

Alex was thrilled. He said that he and his wife felt that they had their daughter back and could not possibly thank me enough. I thanked them for their kind words and told them to keep giving Melanie positive support for her positive changes.

I also suggested that they come up and watch Melanie ride and show sometimes. Melanie's mother and father came up often after this and supportively attended almost every horse show. It made for a happy family.

The greatest result of all was that Melanie really blossomed - not only as a rider, but as a person. She became a very attractive, happy, polite, respectful young lady and seemed to be glad to be rid of whatever rebellious demons had bothered her in the past. Everyone was happy – Alex, Nancy, Melanie, the horse and myself.

Melanie had a very successful show season and was now headed to college. Alex called and asked me if I could sell Keep the Change, as college would prevent Melanie from riding for now. I said that I could absolutely sell him because he was a wonderful horse. I began riding Keep the Change every day after that and prepared him for sale. I believed that he could be a superb equitation horse.

My next horse show was in Southampton, New York, so I took Keep the Change with me as New York and Connecticut are states where equitation rules. Equitation is a very prominent, serious and significant division there and the Maclay finals were held at the majestic Madison Square Garden.

Aside from the legendary George Morris, the top equitation trainers on the East Coast at that time were Bill Cooney and Frank Madden – both who had worked for George.

The name of their stable was "Beacon Hill" and it was a dominant and well-respected force within the equitation world. Marion Hulick, an excellent horsewoman herself, was also helping Bill and Frank at the time.

It was a lovely day in Southampton when we arrived and had settled in. I cleaned up Keep the Change and took him for a walk so he could graze around the showgrounds.

I led Keep the Change to Beacon Hill's stalls and found Bill and Frank right away. I said, "Hi Guys. I believe I have an outstanding equitation horse here, if you happen to be looking for one." They told me that they needed a horse for the equitation finals for Scott Hofstetter, who was a superb rider, and said that they would love to try my horse. The next morning, we tacked up Keep the Change at Beacon Hill and Scott gave him a ride around. Everyone loved him.

Bill and Frank asked if Scott may show Keep the Change in a couple of equitation classes at Southampton and I agreed. Scott won both equitation classes on Keep the Change.

Southampton is an extremely difficult place to win because the jumps are very spooky for a horse, the distances are long and the grass terrain is uneven. As Southampton is an extremely prestigious place to show and win, only the very best show up to compete at the highest level.

After Keep the Change had won those classes with Scott, there was no way that Bill, Frank and Marion were going to part with the horse. I couldn't have gotten him out of there with a tractor. Paul Greenwood, who owned Old Salem Farm where Bill, Frank and Marion all trained students, immediately wrote me a check. No way were they letting that horse out of their stable.

A couple of months later while the National Horse Show at Madison Square Garden was going on, I received a phone call from Bill Cooney. This took me somewhat by surprise as Bill was quite a reserved fellow – a man of few words. Bill told me that Scott had just won the Maclay Finals on Keep the Change and had been second in the Medal Finals and fourth in the USET finals. Bill wanted to thank me for selling them Keep the Change.

Bill's call was followed by one from Frank and then Marion. They were all absolutely thrilled with the horse and could not thank me enough. I thought it was very kind and touching that they took the time to call me. Most people don't bother to call when everything is a great success. I was really moved, particularly because it was clear how much they loved Keep the Change. It's always nice to be appreciated, but all the credit belonged with the horse.

All I did was recognize how good he was when no one had ever heard of him and Jimmy Lee was making a little fun of his plain jumping style. No one ever made fun of Keep the Change after those finals.

Keep the Change even started winning hacks and over fences classes in the large junior hunter division. It's amazing the changes that can happen when one believes in a horse, and then that horse, rider and trainer get the judges to believe in them. I believed in this horse from the beginning and am grateful that he had such a wonderful life from then on.

It's all in the history books now. Keep the Change became the most wanted equitation horse in the country for years. He was leased by Paul Greenwood for a fortune each year until he retired. No amount of money could ever have bought him. That is how it should have been and that is how it was. Keep the Change was a great horse because he had an incredible mind, courage, scope and class. Keep the Change was already a wise old soul at the young age of seven years. It was his intelligence and his cool attitude towards everything which made him shine above the rest.

The next year in Florida, Scott Hofstetter was no longer a junior rider and was looking for rides. Scott is an exceptionally gifted talent and the nicest guy in the world, so it was my pleasure to put him on such lovely horses as "In the Cards", "Something Special" and "All the Gold", as well as some super young jumper prospects. Scott never let me down and the horses loved Scott too. He always gave the horses a truly beautiful, professional ride and he was always very kind to them. Scott really appreciated the horses and the opportunity to ride them, which is very important to me. We would all be nothing in the business if not for the horses. Scott and I always had a wonderful time working together. I am extremely thankful to Keep the Change for making all of that happen.

THE OFFICER

BEGINNING OF MY SYNDICATES

An Article I wrote for Barron's in 1982, regarding the Investment Future of Grand Prix Horses

In September of 1982, I wrote an article for Barron's which appeared on the front page. Barron's was an extremely well-respected financial paper.

The article discussed the great investment opportunity in Grand Prix horses. I was proven to be correct not too long after this article appeared and for all of the years to follow.

The Officer and Jessamy competing in the Grand Prix at Cismont Manor Farm, in Keswick, Virginia

It had become very clear to me that the path of showjumping in America was beginning to model itself after the Europeans. Showjumping is one of the most popular sports in Europe, as it is readily available to be seen on European television by the public. It is second only to soccer.

The top European riders are viewed as Superstars and their horse shows draw enormous and very enthusiastic crowds. European riders often have big sponsors, as our American athletes do in football, basketball, tennis, as well as an array of other well televised, popular American sports. However at this time, American showjumping was behind Europe in regard to its interrelation with the media and the public. I believed that this was going to change during the coming decade. Hence I wrote the Barron's article.

I realized that unless one is independently wealthy and able to buy a string of talented horses themselves, it is extremely difficult to remain at the highest level of the sport. Wealthy owners and backers were needed in order to make a top rider's dreams come true. Although I had sold many horses to wealthy people which had gone on and done extremely well for them, I did not have a truly wealthy backer for my own career goals within the sport at that time.

This is when I came up with the concept of forming a syndicate of investors to buy and support a string of Grand Prix prospects. At the time, all I had was one good 17 hand, five-year-old Thoroughbred gelding by "Clavier", who I had purchased locally from a woman named Phyllis Jones. Phyllis had bred the horse on her farm and had started him at the smaller Virginia shows.

Phyllis called me one day and asked me to come and ride her horse. The horse was a tall, handsome chestnut with a blaze and white stockings. He was quite striking looking and was a big, powerfully built Thoroughbred horse. The horse had never raced, which was a positive thing.

The Officer and Jessamy competing in the Keswick Grand Prix

However this horse was still a very powerful, strong and complex horse to ride. He was not a ride for just anyone. As do many Thoroughbreds, this horse required an extremely quiet and sensitive ride. I felt the horse had a great deal of scope and that he was very brave. I got along with him extremely well so I bought the horse from Phyllis. I named him "The Officer", as the movie "Officer and a Gentleman" had just come out.

I began The Officer in the lower Preliminary Jumper Division, but he was soon ready to jump the High Preliminary courses, as he was so brave and jumped the Preliminary fences with ease. After The Officer quickly became comfortable in the High Preliminary Division, I stepped him up to the Intermediate Jumper Division.

Once again, The Officer became comfortable with the Intermediate courses after a few months and jumped them with confidence and scope. I stepped him into the Open Division and eventually the Grand Prix classes. The Officer was a very brave horse, but always needed that confident, yet very sensitive, empathetic, quiet ride. He was similar to Philco in regard to the type of ride he desired for the ultimate results.

The Officer was consistently jumping double clear rounds in the Grand Prixes and placing very well in these classes, from Virginia all the way to Arizona.

So I had one good horse, but I needed more horses in order to form a viable group which I thought could be sold as a syndicate to interested investors. Around this time a woman named Sarah had contacted me regarding jumper prospects for sale in New Zealand and had sent me some photos. The horses were not only appealing, but they were priced where I could afford to purchase them. I decided to go to New Zealand to take a look.

She's Riding High

By DANNY FINNEGAN
of The Progress Staff

To anyone who has ever dreamed the impossible dream, Jessamy Rouson should be an inspiration.

At 28, Rouson is a self-made millionaire. She also is one of the top riders on the U.S. Grand Prix horse jumping circuit and the mastermind of a horse syndicate worth more than $1.8 million.

The surprising thing is that she knew all along she could do it.

At 10, she decided she wanted to ride horses for a living. At 14, she started doing just that, and after three years of success as a rider, she broadened her goals. "When I was 17, I made up my mind I would have my own business and not work for anyone anymore."

Today, she will compete against many of the country's other top riders at the $25,000 Keswick Prand Prix Event at Cismont Manor Farm on Virginia 22 (3 p.m., $5 per car).

But Jessamy Rouson's talents extend far outside the ring.

She owns a 20-acre horse farm, Showstock Stables in Cismont, and is putting together a syndicate of show jumping horses worth slightly more than $1.8 million. This is the same girl who came to Virginia in 1975 with $1,000 in her pocket.

She isn't ready to slow down, either. The syndicate is still in the developmental stages, and she has big plans for it. Rouson, who has written a book and has a real estate license, also hopes to ride in the 1988 Olympics. And what Jessamy Rouson wants, she usually gets.

"I believe if you have the drive, you can get anything you want and I certainly have the drive," Rouson said, sitting in the comfortable den of her 11-room, ranch-style house on the

Jessamy Rouson With The Officer
'I Have A Lot Farther I Want To Go'

"I just fell in love with the area."

So, with $1,000 in her pocket, she rented a $50-a-month room at a small hotel in Gordonsville. She worked out a deal to lease a barn on the Bridlespur Farm from the McIntire family. Rouson paid $500 a month for the barn, with the agreement that she would fix it up and varnish it. She had one horse, which she rode in shows but did not own.

A few months later she saw something special in a skinny, floppy-eared horse and bought it. "I borrowed $4,500 and bought it. Then I sold it for $35,000 six months later. That was the first time I could breathe financially. I just went on buying and selling horses from there."

Two themes have been prevalent throughout Rouson's life — her love of animals in general and horses specifically, and her drive to excel.

"I always made sure I was around horses," said Rouson, who also owns six Great Danes and an Irish wolfhound. "I used to work in the hack stables around New York City just to be around horses.

"I love animals. There are a lot of times when they are a lot easier to deal with than people."

When Rouson was 14, she started working at Lotus Farm

ficer, have fared well on the Grand Prix circuit the past two years despite the fact that The Officer, a 7-year-old she bought in Crozet, is a relatively young horse in this style of competition. They placed in the $50,000 class at Culpeper last year as well as the $25,000 class at Oklahoma City and were in the Governor's Cup earlier this year in Richmond, and placed in the Virginia Jumper Classic.

Rouson has big plans for the syndicate, which currently consists of six performance horses, one a stallion, and 10 brood mares. Her goal is to produce horses that can compete for the World Cup with the Europeans.

She started looking towards syndication as soon as she saw how much the sport of horse jumping has grown in the United States in the last few years.

"The prize money has shot up 100% and the value of these horses has shot up 100%. Once you start getting corporate sponsorship and TV coverage, which is happening now, the horses will become even more valuable."

Rouson, one of the few riders who also manages her own farm, acts as a selling agent and oversees the training of all her

THE WONDERFUL WORLD OF NEW ZEALAND

Van Ark - a 10-year-old Thoroughbred Jumper I purchased in New Zealand during 1984

I finally arrived in Auckland, New Zealand after a grueling and exhausting twenty-four-hour flight. New Zealand is not only in a different time zone, the country is a day ahead of us in the USA. So, if it's a Monday here, it's a Tuesday in New Zealand. The seasons are also reversed, so that winter in America is actually summer in New Zealand. I knew right away that New Zealand was going to be a fascinating adventure. Sarah, the nice lady who had contacted me, picked me up from the airport and took me to a charming little Inn on the beautiful New Zealand hillside.

I was able to rest for the night before our first day of horse shopping. I slept like a rock for probably twelve straight hours. The Inn had a lovely breakfast prepared and I was ready for my new adventure.

The one thing I noticed straight away about New Zealand, aside from its beauty, was how wonderful and incredibly friendly the people are in this country. New Zealand is a truly fabulous place.

**Sarah, my New Zealand friend, holding Van Ark
Before I rode him at Hastings.**

My New Zealand friend Sarah picked me up at the Inn and we began our first day of horse shopping. I looked at many nice horses and met some fabulous people, but I had not as yet seen a horse with the scope and quality which I was seeking. We traveled all over the North Island of New Zealand, as the North Island has significantly more horses than New Zealand's South Island. I stayed in various lovely and charming country Inns along the way. Towards the end of my New Zealand trip, we went to a horse show in Hastings.

I watched horses in the schooling area and then sat in the stands watching all of the jumpers. I was hoping that one of these horses would catch my eye. There was a big, high jump class towards the end of the show and I thought this may be the opportunity to find a good horse.

Finally a wiry chestnut Thoroughbred horse named "Van Ark" came in the ring and jumped quite well. Van Ark came back to jump six foot, nine inches to win the class. This was an interesting horse, albeit a sensitive and tricky ride.

I approached Van Ark's rider in the schooling area and asked about the horse. The very friendly rider turned out to be Van Ark's owner and we had a delightful chat. He told me that Van Ark was ten years old, 16.1 hands and that he had owned Van Ark for most of his life.

He told me that Van Ark was extremely difficult to get on and that mounting him required three people – one to hold his head, one to give the rider a leg up and then of course, the rider. The owner said the horse was very brave and had a big jump, but was a very squirrely ride. All of this was said with the wonderful and charming New Zealand accent.

I realized that this gentleman was actually quite an excellent rider. I asked him a price to buy Van Ark and it was extremely reasonable. I said that I would like to ride him in the morning, just to get a feel of him.

The next morning, I got up and met Van Ark's wonderful owner at the barn. He showed me what was involved with getting on the horse and said that if this was not done properly, Van Ark would buck like a bull. Van Ark was extremely sensitive about his girth, reminding me of Sportif in the very beginning.

After we pulled the girth up just a bit and walked him around, then a little tighter girth and another walk, he held Van Ark's head as I got a leg up on his back. The horse was very sensitive and on the "hot" side, but he did jump very well for me. This drew an interested crowd of horse people, as they all knew of the very difficult Van Ark. My ride on Van Ark drew many compliments, as they never thought that "a girl" would be able to ride this difficult horse.

I felt confident that I could manage Van Ark's various quirks. This was not a horse for everyone, but I agreed to buy him. Van Ark's owner was thrilled. All in good humor he said, "I never thought that I'd ever get rid of this Miserable Old Bloke!"

After a satisfactory vetting at New Zealand's Veterinary School, Van Ark had a twenty-four-hour flight to America to begin a new career here.

While I was looking at horses, I also took a little time to see the wonderful and intriguing sights which New Zealand has to offer

The North Island is very volcanic and indeed there were active volcanos in Rotorua, along with boiling, bubbling mud bathes in Te Puia – some right in the middle of the road. The New Zealanders just drove around them and went on with their day.

I saw beaches with black sand from the volcanic dust, as well as gorgeous lakes, all surrounded by the beautiful New Zealand hills. I even saw a lake with black swans. There were many sheep farms in New Zealand with more sheep than I have ever seen in my life. I was fortunate to attend a sheep shearing contest and it was incredible how quickly these sheep shearers worked. They could shear an entire sheep in a minute or less.

Consequently New Zealand produces many beautiful wool products. Of course I had to buy a bunch of wonderful sweaters to ship home.

A baby lamb at a New Zealand sheep farm

New Zealand Cattle Farm in the Hills

Beautiful lake, surrounded by the hills of New Zealand

New Zealand was a wonderfully rustic, charming place. The cars seemed to be quite older models and no one seemed to drive recklessly or too fast.

The homes, cottage and country stores nestled in the hills were delightful to see as well. Auckland is a beautiful city with phenomenal views. Boat rides around the island and to the small surrounding islands are wonderful and relaxing excursions. Anyone who is able, should certainly visit the amazing country of New Zealand.

A New Zealand Country Store

PART THREE

MY NEW INVESTOR

BUYING HORSES IN EUROPE FOR MY SYNDICATE

Paul Schockemohle and Deister at Aachen

Now I had two horses for my syndicate, but I needed several more in order to make an attractive and viable offering for business people. Shortly after expressing these thoughts, I received a phone call from Mike Cohen which would change my life from that point on. Mike said that he had an investor to buy horses for my syndicate. I asked Mike the obvious question, "Why aren't you using his investment money for yourself?" Mike said, "Because I'm afraid of him." I said, "OK. When can I meet him?" Mike responded, "In Philadelphia at midnight tomorrow night - in his warehouse."

So, I drove to Philadelphia the next day. Mike, my new investor and I met at the allocated warehouse and I described my plan for the syndicate. I actually liked this man and got along with him very well. He was from New York City, just as I had been, so we had that instant comradery. Two days later, Mike, my New Investor and I were on a red eye flight to Amsterdam.

This is a good time to mention that the winter of 1985 was so bad, that it made front page news on all American and European newspapers. It was bitterly cold with an incredible amount of snow. Perfect time to go to horse shopping, as the sellers are a little less optimistic than they are in the spring. Even when I was buying horses off the racetracks, I mainly shopped in the winter when the weather was terrible. In my opinion, it's the best time for buyers.

Once we arrived in Amsterdam, Mike, Mr. Investor and I checked into our rooms at a small hotel. We met up again in the bar and bistro area. Given the free, anything goes atmosphere of Amsterdam, it was not long before my two comrades were out of control. Endless heavy drinking and a lot of talk about the fact that prostitution was legal in Amsterdam, as well as the fact that marijuana and recreational drugs were rampant and readily available.

Without going into excessively sordid detail, let's just say that my traveling partners were behaving like very wild teenage boys – which is to say, out of control. This behavior was totally unacceptable on my watch. After I put my foot down and ended all of this free-for-all activity, I can tell you the evening did not end well. It involved a lot of broken glass, including the drink I threw in Mr. Investor's face.

This particular evening also involved a short, chubby sixteen-year-old prostitute who miraculously showed up in the bar looking for my friends – just as she had been summoned to do. This poor young girl was wrapped up in a down vest and coat, a big wool hat and multiple scarfs – plus she was wearing snow boots. How sexy is that? She was half frozen from the weather, with most of her makeup running and washed off. She did not look like the sexy prostitute which my friends had probably imagined. However by that point, they were so plastered they didn't care.

They just giggled like idiots and laughed at her. It took me a couple of minutes to realize exactly what was going on, but once I did all hell broke loose. I put a stop to this nonsense immediately. I asked this young girl how much she was supposed to be paid for her time this evening. She told me a hundred dollars, so I gave her a hundred dollars.

I told this young teenager to go home to her parents and go back to school and get an education – in her case, I recommended both day school and night school to keep her out of trouble. I may just have saved that girl's life in the long run.

Well this did not go over well at all with my traveling partners. I told them that we were here to buy horses – not to drink until falling down drunk, or chase hookers, or search for drugs, or destroy the damn hotel. That's when I threw a drink in Mr. Investor's face, which turned out to be a really, really, really bad idea. He went absolutely, stark raving crazy and became violent.

I ran to my room and locked the door, while they destroyed their hotel room next door - yelling and cursing wildly the entire time. It didn't get quiet until about four o'clock in the morning. Around eight in the morning I got up and knocked on my traveling partners' hotel room door. All was quiet and I was afraid that they had abandoned me in Amsterdam. I knocked again and finally heard a little noise.

Then my new investor opened the door in his underwear, looking pretty rough from the night before. I could see Mike passed out on his bed in his underwear. There was broken glass and destroyed furniture everywhere.

So I said, "Are you guys going to breakfast or what?" My investor grumbled that they'd be right down and that was it. After the unfortunate incident the night before, these two guys became perfect gentlemen and extremely respectful.

I think they were actually grateful that I had saved them from themselves. They carried my bags, opened doors and behaved like ideal traveling partners. I was now the Boss. We were ready to go horse shopping.

LOOKING FOR TALENTED PROSPECTS IN AMSTERDAM

Our first stop was at the stables of the biggest horse dealer in Holland. The winter was brutal that year, so we watched all the horses in an indoor arena. There was a big sliding door that closed the arena off from the stabling area. The owner proceeded to show us a wide display of horses, all of which were extremely over prepared – meaning that the horses were made to be wary and suspicious of the jumps, so that they over jumped way up in the air. This is done with a variety of techniques – most of which are not legal. They do this quite a bit when selling horses in Europe. This may make the horses look impressive to the untrained eye, but it's unfortunate. To someone with a trained eye for horses, it does not cover up their innate abilities, or lack thereof. It just takes more time to establish what the horse's natural instincts are really all about. I finally started asking the sellers not to do that for me, because it only took more of my time and they were hurting themselves. I didn't need any of that prep to know what I wanted to buy.

After watching several horses which lacked the ultimate scope and quality that we were looking for, Mike did a typical Mike from Brooklyn thing. He yelled to the owner, "Are you going to show us a Real F**king horse or what?" The stable owner quickly realized that he had real horsemen on his hands and that the usual tricks were not going to work with this set of buyers. After a brief conference with his riders, the sliding door opened and a big, impressive looking bay horse came into the ring with a young man riding. The horse had a big, rangy stride and appeared to have a great deal of scope.

As the rider jumped the horse over some jumps, we became quite interested. Then all of a sudden, just as the horse was passing the sliding door to the barn, he propped and stood straight up in the air walking on his hind legs like a man and waving to us with his front legs. Then the horse lunged forward, yanking the reins from his rider and stood straight up again.

The rider, who had been smacked in the face when the horse reared up, was looking very ashen and shaky – he was white as a sheet and had a bloody nose. Mike enthusiastically yelled out, "We'll ride this one!"

The horse was still stuck at the door to the barn and refusing to move when the rider dismounted. This poor boy was very happy to get off, as he slunk back to the barn in shame. We put my saddle on and Mike gave me a leg up. As soon as I was on, I quickly spun the horse in a tight circle until he lost his equilibrium. I had his nose pinned to my knee and was spurring him lightly in the shoulder to make him turn. After several such circles, I then kicked the horse forward really hard, ready to spin him again if he even thought about standing up. We rode around the ring pretty well, until the horse decided to do his act at the door again. With less enthusiasm, he ducked his shoulder and tried to stand straight up again, but I already had his head pinned to my knee. I was spinning him and spurring his shoulder. The Dutch guys who worked there were trying to "shoo" the horse away from the door, clearly terrified of this animal. I laughed and said, "I'm fine. Just stand back and leave me alone."

Mike immediately piped in, as he had seen this movie for years and knew that I am capable of turning the rogues around. In his typical New York City manner, Mike yelled, "Get the F**k away from her. She knows what she's doing. She's a F**king Animal."

Mr. Investor was in awe. I kicked the horse forward and away from the door. Within two minutes the horse was riding like a real gentleman. I praised him for moving forward and began jumping. The horse was completely obedient. He jumped beautifully and with a great deal of scope.

This is probably a good time to mention that in the 1980s and before, women were considered a lower form of life in the horse business and equated with amateur riders – particularly in Europe. Showjumping was a very macho sport over there. But I changed that view for every chauvinistic male there that day. To show off a little, I tied my reins in a knot and rode this horse down to the jumps with no reins at all, seeing the distance way before I turned the corner and then dropping the reins.

The horse was responding like a saint - ears up and happy to be getting along with me. I was his new best friend. He even cantered right past the door with no reins.

When I had finished, every man there had gained a new level of respect for women riders. The horse dealer said that I was the best rider he had ever seen. The young men, at first so contemptuous, were catering to me like I was the Queen of England.

Mike offered $5,000 for the horse, contending that the horse was worthless without someone who could ride him and that it was obvious that the owner didn't have anyone who could ride this horse. Unfortunately for us, the horse did not pass the vet exam, as he had horrible radiographs.

PAUL SCHOCKEMOHLE'S IN GERMANY

SAN FRANCISCO, CHANEL AND MATADORA

San Francisco as a Young Horse

After looking at a few more horses around Holland, Mike said that we needed to go to Paul Schockemohle's place in Muhlen, West Germany. Paul is the biggest horse dealer in the world and has produced numerous World Class superstars. Mike said that Paul had six hundred horses on twelve acres – all of them jumpers or jumper prospects. So we drove our rent-a-car to Paul Schockemohle's yard – a venture which would super charge my posture in the business forever after.

Paul's stable is like a well-managed factory. The best horses and the ones who are currently competing are up front. The further back you go in the stables, the greener and the lesser horses are stabled - until you finally get to the foals, yearlings and two-year olds.

I quickly realized that I needed to sort through the green horses, because the experienced horses were way too expensive for our budget. It was really quite a remarkable experience - one which changed my life for years to come.

Paul started out showing us some mediocre horses which were extremely well prepared and jumped way up in the air. However that didn't last long. Another saucy outburst from Mike yelling, "Paul! Where the F**k are the Real Horses? Come on Man! It's F**king Cold as Sh*t out here and you're wasting my time. What's the matter with you?" Things went more to our liking after that.

The next horse to come out was a big, handsome five-year-old chestnut Hanoverian stallion, with a blaze and white stockings. He was by "San Fernando" and out of "Garnet", who was by the fabulous "Graphit". The stallion's name was "San Francisco" and he was an impressive horse. He was owned by Franke Sloothaak. Franke is a German show jumping champion and was later an Olympic champion in 1988 and 1996. Franke rode San Francisco around and he jumped beautifully. This was obviously a really nice horse with a great deal of scope.

I rode San Francisco around and loved his jump, his ride-ability and his scope. We made a deal and agreed to buy him, pending the vet exam. We had flown Dr. Flynn there to vet any horses we wanted to purchase.

Paul brought out a few more horses, including a gray mare named Chanel. She was a really lovely mare and a very beautiful jumper. I rode her and liked her a great deal. I questioned if she had the scope to jump the biggest classes, but I knew she was highly marketable. I told Paul my thoughts on her, as well as my reservations. We came to a deal that I was happy with and we bought Chanel too.

Paul brought out another gray mare that we also liked enough to buy, but she didn't pass the vet exam. Paul could not stand that we would be buying only two horses, so he said, "Wait! I have a full sister to San Francisco, the stallion you purchased. She is four years old and not in good condition. She has not been handled much, so she can be very difficult to work with."

This is when I met the greatest horse of my career.

THE DISCOVERY OF MATADORA
A TRULY GREAT MARE

Matadora

Paul had a groom take us all the way to the back of his yard where the foals and extremely green horses were stabled, as well as those which Paul thought less of as prospects. Paul evaluates every single horse in the jump chute, right down to the yearlings. He keeps notes on every horse in little books which he carries around. Paul had books on everything from the babies to the adult horses. These notes included the breeding, as well as the scores Paul gave each horse for type, ability, temperament, technique, quality and scope.

Once Paul realized that I knew what I was doing, he just handed me all of the books on the young horses for me to examine. Paul figured that his assessment would save us both a great deal of time. I greatly respect and value Paul's opinion on a horse, but my own feeling, instinct and evaluation of a horse is the ultimate bar for me. I know what I want when I see it, because I know and understand horses. What other people say good or bad about a horse is irrelevant, if I have a strong instinct about that horse. I decide and commit immediately – whether it's on the racetracks of America or within the vast stables of Europe. I'm very upfront about what I want.

The groom led us up to a stall with San Francisco's sister, way in the back of Paul's yard. Suddenly a big, raw boned, really skinny chestnut mare lunged at the bars of the stall with her teeth bared. She was completely wild eyed and had her ears flat back. The groom said that I absolutely could not go in the stall. He explained that the mare was a vicious savage and that it took at least four really big men to catch her in a ten by ten stall. The groom then said that this mare had hurt a lot of people and sent some to the hospital. He refused to go in the stall.

So I picked up a little hay, opened the stall door and walked into her stall. I said, "Hey Girlfriend! What's up?" The big red mare studied me from the back of her stall with her huge brown eyes. Then she put her big fuzzy ears up and walked right up to me.

This mare knew that I was not afraid of her and therefore she had some respect for me. She had not met anyone who was not afraid of her, so she was extremely curious.

This big chestnut mare nibbled on the old, ratty hay I offered and let me gently pet her. I don't know what it was exactly, but I felt that I had just found my soulmate. I loved this mare on first sight – a big skinny, raw boned four-year-old mare with a long mane, ratty coat and no horseshoes. I could relate to her personality, so her nature did not bother me. I'm sure that plenty of my employees over the years would say that I could be a terror too. This mare and I had the same personality.

I slipped a halter on the mare and said, "Let's go to the jump chute Girlfriend and you can show me what you're all about." I led her to the chute which was built in an old chicken barn with a very low ceiling. It was a tough place to see horses, because I always felt that the low ceiling inhibited their jump. But when I watched this mare jump, I knew I had to ride her. In the jump chute she showed tremendous scope and an extremely powerful hind end. Her hind end was so powerful, that it often made her tip over her front end. Young horses with powerful hind ends frequently do this, until they are taught how to shape their own jump and control their power.

Many people would pass on a horse which jumps over their front end, but that is a mistake when seeking a jumper. The right gymnastics and proper training can fix this. The most important things which I look for are that the horses have the scope, a big stride, a powerful hind end, courage and a natural instinct to be careful and jump clean. Technique can be improved significantly with the correct training.

A young, timid boy got on the mare and rode her around Paul's indoor. She was so skinny that she looked ridiculous. Her back appeared way too long and her neck appeared way too short. Paul and his staff were literally laughing at me for even considering this mare.

It's not too often that the sellers laugh at a buyer for looking at a horse they own. They could not believe an "American" would fly all the way over to Germany and consider a cheap, ugly, savage horse such as this mare.

I didn't let any of that bother me. I saw a great big stride and plenty of scope when she jumped a few small fences – plus, she had an unbelievable hind end. She jumped over her front end with the boy riding, but he was jamming her at the jumps in a typical very forward German riding kind of way.

I said I would like to ride her and I got on. Mike Cohen had already flown home because he thought we were done shopping. Mr. Investor was still with me in Germany. When the one horse failed the vet exam, Paul had me look at this mare as she was a full sister to San Francisco. Paul is a tenacious seller and could not bear to let me leave with one less horse than planned. It turned out that I was lucky the other horse had failed the vet exam or I probably never would have been shown this mare.

At this point the four-year-old mare was just barely green broke. I rode her around the ring and she felt really good to me. She had a big stride and was very powerful. I jumped a few small jumps and played with her, sitting absolutely still and giving her some ground rail. I wanted her to take a little more time, unhurried, to form a better jump. Like magic this mare's front end began to work beautifully because she had the time to put it in the correct position. I got off the horse and found Paul in the barn. I asked Paul how the chestnut mare was priced.

Please note that Paul and his staff were still laughing at me for trying this big, skinny, ugly, vicious mare. They thought it was hilarious that an "American" would be interested in such a horse. Paul, always trying his best to get the most money, told me $17,000. I told him that price would have to include all shipping and quarantine fees to America.

In other words, I would give Paul $17,000 to deliver this mare to my doorstep in Virginia. That brought the mare's actual sale price down to about $6,500. Paul agreed. As my instinct about this mare was so strong, I bought her on the spot and made the same deal regarding shipping and delivery on San Francisco and Chanel. Free delivery for all to Paul's Virginia farm, Chestnut Lawn, which was fairly close to my farm.

Then Paul wanted to show me a few more horses while Dr. Flynn was vetting the mare. While I was watching other horses, Dr. Flynn came to me on three different occasions. In his completely diplomatic way, Dr. Flynn said "I'm sorry to interrupt, but I thought you should know that this mare is trying to kill me." He said, "Hock flexions, hock radiographs and a breeding exam will be out of the question." This did not faze me. I told him to do the best that he could and let me know what he thought.

Mr. Investor asked me why I would want to buy a savage horse, but I assured him that everything would be okay. I told him that this was a good horse, however misunderstood. By this point Mr. Investor trusted me completely and would go along with whatever I said regarding the horses.

It turned out that what Dr. Flynn was able to exam on the mare was fine, including the radiographs of her front feet. We paid Paul and I was now the proud owner of Paul's "savage" mare. I named her "Matadora".

She turned out to be the Greatest Horse of my career.

THE HORSES ARRIVE IN AMERICA

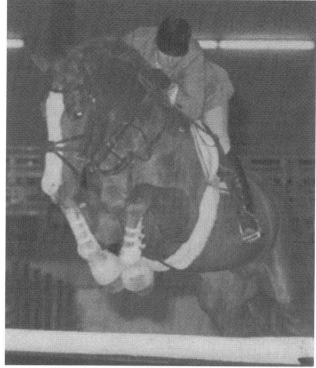

San Francisco as a Young Horse

Mr. Investor and I flew home after all of the excitement at Paul's yard. He had just purchased three horses for me. Mr. Investor was exhausted from the trip and said, "I'm tapped out like a pin-ball machine." Once again, I assured him that everything would be fine.

True to his word, Paul had all three horses delivered to Chestnut Lawn, Paul's farm in Virginia. It was less than an hour from my place, so I went to pick them up.

Chestnut Lawn was run by a superb horseman named Hans Hofschroer, who became a dear friend and a terrific business contact. Hans asked me if I had tried the chestnut mare, because I gather she had shown her excessive personality there and Hans was concerned. I told him that she was fine and picked up a little hay. I walked in her stall and said, "Hey Girlfriend! Are you ready to go home?" I slipped a halter on her and put her on the truck with Chanel and San Francisco.

I let the horses settle in for several days and become acclimated to their new surroundings. I had them newly shod, their teeth floated and I wormed them. Once they had settled in for about a week, I began riding my new prospects. San Francisco was very mannerly and performed extremely well. He showed that he had a good mind and wonderful scope.

Chanel rode and jumped beautifully, but she had a few surprises for me which did not show up until her first show – to be covered later.

Meanwhile, Matadora had already sent one groom to the hospital. Matadora had picked this girl up by her shirt, while grabbing a mouthful of skin on her chest too. Then Matadora began banging this poor girl against the wall. I heard the girl screaming and ran to the stall.

Matadora had the girl in her mouth, with the girl's feet a good foot off the ground. She was beating this poor girl against the wall with great vigor. I said firmly, "Matadora! Stop! Put the girl down!" Matadora looked at me attentively with her big, fuzzy ears pricked. I had her attention and she spit the girl out like she had a bad taste in her mouth. The girl hit the floor with a thud. Matadora had apparently broken this poor girl's arm. This was not the first employee that Matadora had savaged, so I now had to get up extra early every morning to feed her and turn her out in the paddock. I basically had to do everything with Matadora in the very beginning. She was intolerant of the staff and I couldn't afford to have any more people taken away to the hospital.

So Matadora and I became very close. Matadora never, ever attacked me, because she knew that I had no fear of her whatsoever. She felt that she had a human in the world who actually understood her – her soulmate. I loved her and she came to love me too. It all began with mutual respect and trust. I trusted Matadora completely and as I trained her, it quickly became apparent that she trusted me too. The most difficult thing would be keeping Matadora interested and challenged, because she was so highly intelligent and extremely courageous.

Everything was so easy for her. Matadora did not even begin to jump until the jump was four feet. She could just canter over three foot nine inches with no effort at all.

While I was training these horses at home and preparing them for the show ring, I had another huge problem. Apparently Mike Cohen, unbeknownst to me, had told Mr. Investor that he would triple his money on these horses within thirty days, as soon as I sold the syndicate. I wish I had known that up front and established a clear understanding of the reality of the project, because life soon became horribly stressful.

Mr. Investor would call me at eight o'clock in the morning - every single morning on the dot. He never missed a day. He'd call and make life threatening and very discomforting comments such as, "I'm going to burn down your barn and kill the horses if I don't get my money." Or, "You have nice teeth and I'm going to have them." You get the idea – very discomforting thoughts - most were unprintable.

Extremely stressful times and at this point I only had the horses for thirty days. It got to the point that I couldn't sleep anymore. I'd lie in bed frozen, just waiting for that threatening eight am phone call.

I'd tell Mr. Investor that I was doing my best to sell the syndicate, but it took a little time as I had to put together the entire proposal with these horses in it. I was almost there. The proposal was almost finished and would soon be ready to print out and begin marketing. However that was not fast enough for Mr. Investor.

Finally I could not take the stress anymore. I took it this long because I loved Matadora and believed that she could be a world class horse. The others were wonderful and very marketable, but I would not go through this abuse for them alone. It was all about Matadora for me. One night I was frozen in my bed and wide awake all night. I was terrified of the eight o'clock phone call by Mr. Investor.

So about four in the morning, I called Paul in Germany and told him exactly what was going on. (It was much later in Germany.) I was completely honest with Paul. I told him that I loved the mare Matadora and that I was afraid for my own life, as well as the life of the horses. Paul had met Mr. Investor in Germany when we were buying the horses. In fact when Paul and I were discussing business, Paul ordered an assistant to "Keep that guy busy, so we could talk." Paul knew exactly what Mr. Investor was all about and Paul had also gained respect for me as a horsewoman and a businessperson.

It was Mike's fault, because it is Mike who had promised this guy three times his money in thirty days without telling me. Mike had sold me out and Paul knew it. Mike had also made a commission on the horses, which Mr. Investor did not know about. After I had explained the entire situation to Paul, he told me to tell Mr. Investor to pick the horses up immediately. Paul told me that he would give me new horses which were just as good and that I did not have to pay for them until the syndicate was sold. He said he would ship them to me in America and that I could pay for them over three years. I told Paul how much I loved Matadora, but he insisted that he would give me horses just as good. So I lay in bed wide awake, shaking like a leaf and waiting for the dreaded phone call from Mr. Investor.

The phone call came right on time – eight o'clock sharp. I was wide awake and took the upper hand right off the bat. I told Mr. Investor to pick up the damn horses right away. I told him that Paul was going to ship me new horses that were just as good and that I did not have to pay for them until the syndicate was sold – in fact I had three years to pay for them. Mr. Investor immediately backed off and he promised that he would leave me alone. I told him to pick the damn horses up and I hung up the phone. What a relief, but my heart was broken at the thought of losing Matadora.

It took about twenty minutes for Mr. Investor to storm out of his house in New Hope, Pennsylvania and arrive at Mike Cohen's door step. It took another ten minutes for Mr. Investor to unleash all of his anger and rage onto Mike. Sure enough, at eight thirty sharp an extremely shaken Mike called me. I could feel the terror in his voice over the phone.

Mike said, "Jess, I want to come to Virginia and see you". I reiterated that he should pick up the horses, but Mike said he was getting in the car and heading to Virginia right now.

Late that afternoon I rode the three horses for Mike and told him exactly what I thought they were. He had not seen Matadora in Germany because he had already left, but he said that she was definitely the one with the most stride and scope. Mike wanted me to sell the three horses to a company called Amvest, which I had told him about. Amvest would buy the horses from Mr. Investor and then Mr. Investor would need to pay monthly payments to Amvest. It was a high interest scheme, but it worked for getting Mr. Investor off of my back temporarily.

Mr. Investor arrived in Virginia and we went to meet the elderly gentleman in charge of the equine division of Amvest – a wonderful, knowledgeable horseman named Harry Distan. Harry was a three-piece suit kind of guy and a perfect gentleman of the highest order.

I told Mr. Investor to wear a suit and not to say a word. I told him that I would do all of the talking. All he had to do was sign his name on the papers and he would have his money back. I explained that he would be getting monthly bills until I sold the syndicate, but at least he would have his money back for now. Mr. Investor followed my instructions extremely well. He looked quite handsome in his suit and was very mannerly in his composure, although a tad rough around the edges. I did all of the talking. Mr. Investor signed the papers and Harry Distan handed him a check. Mr. Investor's respect for me grew even more and for a short while, life was good. Everyone was happy. Mr. Investor had his money, Mr. Distan had a new deal and I no longer had to worry about the eight am phone calls.

I could now train the horses in peace and work on selling my syndicate – a $1,500,000 raise with a onetime payment of $100,000 per unit, which included all of the expenses on the horses. It was a deal for only the very rich who could afford to invest in a venture as risky as horses. But I felt really solid in the stock I had presented in the syndicate.

I loved the ones from Paul and I had gone back to Europe and bought a few more talented horses with money which I had borrowed against my farm. I had a super group of horses for this offering, with Matadora being my personal favorite.

This feeling of utopia lasted for thirty days. It ended abruptly when Mr. Investor received his first bill from Amvest, which included at least twenty two percent interest. Once again Mr. Investor was on the rampage. We were back to the eight o'clock morning phone calls and they were more terrifying than ever. The calls were too brutal and horrifying to put into print.

I had to think my way out of this, because I was not going to lose the horses – especially Matadora. I had to do something, because I could not live like this anymore.

MY NEW CLIENT OUT OF FLORIDA
THE FABULOUS MARE IN THE CARDS

In the Cards and Scott Hofstetter - Green Conformation Hunter at The Palm Beach Shows

Amazingly I got a phone call from a man about a junior hunter I had advertised. It was a truly lovely horse named "Tennyson". I invited this gentleman to come with his daughter from their home in Florida to try the horse at my place in Virginia. Tennyson was not a really expensive horse, but he was a perfect horse for this man's daughter at her stage of riding. I knew this horse was a saint and would never let them down.

I should point out that this gentleman asked me to pick them up at the airport in Charlottesville, Virginia. I said that I would be happy to do that. What I didn't expect was for this gentleman to personally fly his own airplane to Charlottesville. I had to go to the private plane section of the airport to find them.

This man was very tan and fairly young – maybe mid-thirties. He was not what I had expected. He arrived with his shirt mostly unbuttoned and his suntanned chest adorned with several gold chains. This was a young guy who had made a lot of money somehow, because he reeked of new money. This was not inherited or old money. This man had earned every dime of it – somehow.

During our initial meeting and small talk, I asked him about his profession. I was curious as to what type of work he did. He said that he sold insurance and the job caused him to fly his plane to the Caribbean quite often. Okay - well selling insurance on the islands obviously paid much better than I had realized. One learns something every day.

This man's daughter was a very polite, well-spoken teenager. A lovely girl. We went to my place and I showed them Tennyson. Of course Tennyson was a saint and perfect for the girl, so now it was time to discuss business with Dad. This gentleman told me that he would like to trade a young mare in foal that he owned, along with some cash to pay for Tennyson. I told him that I obviously needed to see the mare and said that I would fly to Florida within a couple of days – one day trip back and forth. He told me that he would pick me up at the airport in Florida and to call him when I was coming.

So I caught a commercial flight to Florida and arrived at the airport. When this gentleman said that he would pick me up at the airport, I had assumed that he would be driving a car. Not the case. He arrived in his little airplane and told me it was a short flight to his farm in Palm Springs.
Oh My God!!!

As tenacious as I was about doing business deals, I had to ask myself if this was a good idea. I thought I was going to die for certain. I ended up climbing into the smallest airplane I have ever seen, with this man as the pilot – no one else on the plane. This gentleman had the same attire – shirt unbuttoned to his navel and lots of gold chains. I was honestly terrified. I've flown all over the world, but little planes scare me because they seem to crash more than any other planes. I have seen model airplanes bigger than this tiny, fragile plane.

To make it worse, this plane had open sides so I felt like I could fall right out of the damn plane. But business is business, so I sat there shaking as he took off. By some miracle we arrived safely on a runway which was on this man's farm in Palm Springs. I knew I had to find another way home. I met this gentleman's wife who was lovely and once again met the daughter.

We went out to his stable to see the 3-year-old mare in foal to "Garibaldi II", which he wanted to trade in on Tennyson. I liked her right away. She was a very pretty, classy looking Hanoverian mare – chestnut with white stockings and a blaze. She was unbroken, so I could only see her jog, but she seemed very sweet. She was a beautiful mare and a lovely mover, so I did the deal right there. He gave me the extra cash for Tennyson and I said that I would organize the shipping. I also suggested that we drive back to the airport so we would be able to talk more about his goals in the horse business.

I named my new mare "In the Cards", because that is how this entire adventure felt. The mare had a lovely foal for me and later became a very fancy conformation hunter. That mare never let me down.

On the way back to the airport, this gentleman asked me about the other horses that I had in my stable. I told him all about the jumper prospects I had bought in Germany and my plans for the syndicate. I also told him about Mr. Investor and my eight o'clock am phone calls.

When he stopped the car he said, "I'll buy the horses so that you can syndicate them. How much money do you need?" I told him the money involved and the need to give Mr. Investor some profit so that he didn't kill me. He said that was not a problem and wired the money the next day.

So now I had Mr. Investor happy and off my back, but I had a new crazy situation to deal with. I made In the Cards part of the syndicate, so as to add to the breeding element of the project. I also went back to Paul's and bought some two-year-old fillies to breed for two years and then train as four-year olds – just as they do in Europe.

So I was busy bringing the horses along and selling my syndicate, which was going pretty well. I would fly to any wealthy businessperson I heard of and ask for only fifteen minutes of their time. Then I would promote the hell out of the syndicate and attempt to dazzle them with my brilliance. Occasionally some of the men and a few of the women agreed to invest. I started out on those trips looking really sharp, with my business suit and briefcase. I always flew home exhausted, drained and looking totally bedraggled – carrying my heels to give my feet a break and dragging my briefcase through the airports. Selling syndicates is the toughest thing I have ever done in the business. The absolute toughest.

Then I threw two big parties for the investors, along with every other wealthy person I could think of to invite. These parties were held in the evening, with a full bar available. The bartender was in a suit and the food was catered by lovely ladies in uniforms. I also had a very talented piano player with a rented piano who sang all of the old hits – mainly Frank Sinatra kind of music. It was perfect for this age group and they had one heck of a good time. Thank God for credit cards, because that is how I made all of that happen.

We were outside and I had the lights on in the outside ring. Then I had good looking, clean cut men such as Bert Mutch, in jacket and tie, lead the horses out under the lights.

I was adorned in a black evening gown, as this was a fancy, high class affair and I needed to raise a very serious amount of money. I spoke about each horse's breeding, as well as the huge investment and performance potential which each horse offered. Several people had already committed and I had raised about $500,000 per party.

As the Grand Finale of this showing, I had one of my men lead out "In the Cards" with her newly born filly running by her side. I announced that this was our very first offspring from our extensive breeding program and what a beauty she was!

All of the horses really helped me that night, because they came out of the stable under the lights looking like gorgeous, proud, majestic creatures.

That said, the new filly stole the show. She was a very pretty bay filly with white markings and was strutting around her mother like a ballerina. The crowd went crazy.

Then I said, "We still have to name this beautiful filly. Any ideas?" That's when a Doctor from Florida pulled me aside. He was already one of my biggest investors. He said that he would give me an additional $50,000 for the syndicate if he could name the baby. I gave him the obvious and immediate reply, "What would you like to name her?" The Doctor said "Born Lucky", because his mother had always said that he was born lucky. And so this beautiful, precious filly was christened "Born Lucky" from that moment on.

MY NEW TRACTOR TRAILER

Just after buying my new tractor trailer and driving it home

As I now had too many horses to ship to the shows in my Imperatore van, I decided to buy a tractor trailer. I called Ray Little in Maryland, as he was the go-to guy for the really nice big horse trailers at that time. I ordered a 17-horse trailer painted in my colors – silver and navy blue. It had my name and Showstock Stables, Ltd detailed on each side. I also bought a good used truck from Ray to pull the trailer and had that painted to match.

Ray called me when it was finished and I got someone to give me a ride up to Ray's place in Maryland. The entire rig looked great and I gave Ray a check. Now came the issue of getting this monstrosity of a tractor trailer home. I had never driven a tractor trailer before, but I figured that I would know how by the time I had driven it all the way home. Ray gave me some pointers and showed me how to work the ten gears – five on the floor with an overdrive. Ray showed me how to read the dashboard and gave me a number of handy tips.

Then we went for a little test drive around Ray's farm, which started out pretty rocky. Ray wanted to make sure I wouldn't crash this thing and kill myself before his check cleared the bank. I was going about 5 to 10 mph, but I was comfortable with that speed at this point in time. When we stopped, Ray hopped out of the truck and wished me luck.

My new tractor trailer, when I had delivered it home

Then I began my two-hour drive home - which actually turned out to be more like six hours because I was driving so slowly. People were honking, shouting unprintable curses and giving me very nasty gestures while storming past me, but I just kept my eyes on the road. I had all that I could handle just to do what I was doing. I even stopped at a huge truck stop and filled it up with diesel. I had no idea what I was doing, but I was figuring it out. I have to say that the other tractor trailer drivers there were really nice and very helpful with things like parking or showing me where the gas tank was. I never hesitated to ask these guys for help whenever I got in a bind, which was quite often throughout my tractor trailer driving career.

The really scary thing for me was crossing bridges, because I was so high up in the cab that I could not see the railing. It felt like a strong wind could knock the trailer right off the bridge and into the water. I never got over my phobia of driving the damn thing across bridges, but I just had to deal with it if I wanted to get anywhere. The other thing I could never figure out was how to back this long ass trailer up, which is also when other tractor trailer drivers were a huge help. They got me out of many a pickle during my tractor trailer driving days.

The longer I drove this rig towards home, the more comfortable I became. I was soon driving up to 35 - 45 mph and starting to relax. I got this rig all the way home and was quite proud of myself. I hadn't killed anyone and I hadn't hit anything. I made sure I had a big parking area behind the indoor ring so that I could turn this thing around. Backing up was out of the question.

And so it was. I drove this tractor trailer across the entire country for over two years, going from home to a horse show, back home and then to another show. I became quite competent, relatively speaking, and was keeping up with the other trucks on the road at 55 or 65 mph.

I never could back the rig up or get out of tight places, so thank God there always seemed to be some guy around who knew how to do that. At the horse shows, a horseman named Hank Hulick always took the trailer as soon as we unloaded the horses. Hank was the stabling manager at the big shows. He'd drive that trailer all over the showgrounds several times, and then park it very proficiently. Hank had a hell of a good time with my rig.

One really embarrassing incident happened when I was leaving the Southampton Horse Show. It was very muddy and it was an extremely tight turn out of the gate to get out of the showgrounds. I couldn't make the turn and was trying to back up a little, grinding gears like crazy and trying the turn unsuccessfully - again and again, over and over. What a mess. There was a whole line of other tractor trailers behind me trying to leave the show too. This went on for at least ten minutes.

Finally, JR from JR Horse Transport opened the door of the cab and asked me if I would like some help. I said that I would love some help, as I'm obviously an idiot and don't know what the hell I'm doing. JR got in the cab and within 30 seconds he had that rig safely out of the gate. I was so impressed that I told him we should get married immediately. Then I drove home from there, avoiding tight places at all costs.

On really long trips to the shows, sometimes I would take another driver with me so that we could switch off. There was a sleeper in the cab of the truck, so a driver could rest up in the sleeper. I had a great big black fellow working for me named Ricky. Ricky was super help, so I taught him how to drive the tractor trailer. It wasn't long until Ricky was driving it a hell of lot better than I was. I also taught Bert Mutch how to drive it, and he drove the rig really super as well – plus he was constantly washing it and keeping it in tip top shape.

So I decided that it was in the best interest of everything and everyone one on the road if I just let Bert and Ricky drive the tractor trailer from now on.

There's a reason that you don't see a lot of women tractor trailer drivers. It's really hard damn work – especially when you get to the show and have to unload a ton of equipment, hay and feed, plus all of the horses. Then I had to ride a truckload of horses after that. So those guys could drive from now on and I'd concentrate on the horses. Thank God. What a relief.

THE FABULOUS CHANEL

As I have mentioned, I purchased Chanel in 1985 on my first buying trip to Paul Schockemohle's place in Muhlen, West Germany. Chanel was a gorgeous 16.2 hand gray Holsteiner mare by "Calvados I", out of a "Cor de la Bryère" mare. She was a seven-year-old at the time, but as she had taken the time to be the mother of two fabulous foals, she was relatively green for that age.

Chanel was a very sweet mare with a dished face, as well as a beautiful eye and expression. She was also wonderfully soft and a joy to ride. Best of all, Chanel had an absolutely exquisite, extravagant, spectacular jump. Over time Chanel developed quite a large, loving fan club in America.

That said, my lovely new mare came with a little bit of baggage which Paul had neglected to mention. Chanel was wonderful at home, along with Matadora and San Francisco, so I decided to take all three to a small, local schooling show to see how they would react in a new environment.

Matadora and San Francisco jumped right around the couple of schooling hunter classes I entered them in and were wonderful. They were very brave - not the least bit spooky about anything, plus they jumped and covered the ground with ease. They had fabulous minds for the show ring, so I was thrilled as I looked ahead to our promising future together.

My pretty girl Chanel was quite good in the schooling area with the other horses, but when it came her turn to enter the ring, Chanel was not having any part of it. She made quite a scene. I was not expecting this so I was honestly blindsided. Chanel stood straight up and was waving to the crowd. She was quite adamant about not entering the ring – all of this with a lot of little kids and people scattered all around. I was fearful she would hurt someone, but the people moved away quickly. As with any horse who tries to rear and break bad, I spun her in a few circles with her nose pinned to my knee. When she began to give in, I assertively kicked her forward and into the ring. I rode her around that little schooling hunter course like my life depended on it. Chanel came around and jumped well on course.

After her good behavior, Chanel was well praised. However I was not ready to trust her yet. I entered her in several little hunter classes after that, until she was calmly walking in the ring on a loose rein and with her ears up.

Chanel went in almost every hunter class at that schooling show, but by the end of the day she was entering the ring happily and willingly. Chanel received more praise and was a happy girl who I hoped had found the most agreeable path forward from that point on.

After working with these three horses for a couple more months at home, I took them to another show in Culpeper, Virginia to compete in the schooling jumper classes. Once again, Matadora and San Francisco were wonderful.

Chanel entered the ring after a little encouragement and everything seemed as though it was going along smoothly. That was until Chanel eyed the water jump in the ring. I quickly learned that Chanel did not want to jump water jumps or liverpools – or even go anywhere near them. Nor did she want to walk through puddles or streams, or go near a pond. Therefore these were exactly the things I did with her from then on.

I ordered several liverpools and water jumps from Harry Gill, as selling these was something Harry did on the side. I had liver pools and water jumps all over my ring at home, so that the practice and education may begin. I started out with these liverpools very small and narrow and let Chanel follow another steady horse over the water. Each time she jumped water, she was praised effusively and given a piece of carrot. Making the liverpools and water jumps a little wider and a little higher each day, I worked through this problem with Chanel at home and she overcame her phobia.

As it was still an unknown how she would react at the horse show with the natural obstacles, I came up with some more effective training tactics. I felt that Chanel needed to overcome her overall phobia about water, well beyond just water jumps and liverpools. Whenever there was a stream or a puddle of water in the woods or running between the stalls at the shows or anywhere else, I would walk Chanel back and forth and up and down across each body of water. I never missed one. I did this until it became a non-issue, praising Chanel the entire time. I would then trail ride her and cross every stream I came upon regardless of the size.

Initially I had Chanel follow a steady older horse who was undaunted by water, but eventually Chanel would happily walk through, across and up and down any stream and bank I came across. My next test was the big pond. After an initial lead from a solid, older horse, I had Chanel swimming in the pond every day. I now felt ready to take her back to the horse shows.

As a point of interest, I strongly believe in trail riding show horses to give them exposure to anything and everything which they may not have seen before.

The same goes for riding all over a showgrounds and allowing the horse to see everything possible. Anytime a rider is able to help a horse confront and conquer their fear of something, whether it's a stream, a fallen tree, a tractor, a tarp or a jump, the bond of mutual trust becomes stronger and the horse's self-confidence grows radically. It is essential to give these horses all the time they need to walk up to the object they deem spooky and sniff it all over, becoming comfortable with the object. This may take a matter of minutes or it may be a matter of hours, but one can never, ever lose their patience or rush it.

Again, a good steady older horse is a wonderful guide for a youngster and helps tremendously with this process. Also leading the horse up to the object by hand and placing carrots on it works exceptionally well and is something I also believe in doing. Whenever I hit a minor roadblock, I back up to the step before and solidify my foundation of training. Once the horse has walked right up to the object, places their nose on it and sniffs it without fear or hesitation, you are ready to move on to the next "windmill". This should be done with encouragement, compassion and lots of praise – even empathy, as we all have our own fears and should attempt to relate to those of horses, animals and other humans.

Horses can overcome their fears just as we can, but it takes a great deal of patience and understanding from the rider. This is how great bonds are formed, which shall carry over into terrific success in the show ring. Some horses are brave about everything from the start, such as Matadora and San Francisco, but others need more exposure and confidence building. I also believe it is important to give horses a break from training and schooling in a ring.

A relaxing walk with loose reins on the trail or in the woods does wonders for their mind. I only ask the horse to walk and I leave the reins completely loose on these rides. This relaxes and refreshes a horse so that they do not become sour or resentful towards their work and training. I would trail ride a couple of times a week with each of the horses, often in a western saddle with a hackamore bridle so they could nibble on grass and leaves if they so pleased.

Chanel

At the shows there were always puddles of water around the barn area and often a stream of water draining off between the stalls. These puddles were either from rain or from the large number of people bathing their horses with a hose. I made sure that I walked Chanel through every drop of water, every puddle, every trench and every stream on the show grounds at every single horse show. Chanel always received a great deal of praise for doing this and she became quite happy about going through or over water. She even began enjoying her swimming time in the pond.

Chanel was a mare who wanted to be encouraged, but never forced. That is probably why she was not able to overcome her phobias in Germany. Their macho, strong, somewhat forceful ride did not suit the dainty, sensitive Chanel. She said, "No thanks Guys. I'm out of here." The more they fought with her, the more she dug in her toes. When the beautiful Chanel wanted to be tough, she was really, really tough, but we worked through and past all of that.

Chanel was a lady and insisted on being treated like one, which included asking her politely and gently. I'd talk to her constantly saying things like, "Come on Girl, Good Girl, Come On, You're OK, I'm right here with you."

Chanel took some hand holding in the beginning, but with each phobia she conquered she gained more and more confidence. She actually became quite proud of herself once she was no longer afraid of a situation.

Then after, Chanel and I happily jumped all of the big water and liver pools at the top shows in the country, including Palm Beach, Tampa, Farmington, Commonwealth Park, Southampton, Lake Placid and many more.

Chanel went on to win quite a bit for me and I actually went back to Germany and purchased both of her offspring from Paul. They were two gray geldings by a stallion named "Sylvester".

They were both extremely talented horses, although not really appreciated in Germany. I named Chanel's sons "All in Silver" and "The Silver Shadow". We shall cover them later, as they deserve their own chapter.

In addition, Chanel gave me two beautiful gray embryo transplant babies – one by San Francisco and one by The Silver Baron – both fabulous horses, which I shall cover in another chapter. Embryo transplant is a process where the fertilized egg is taken from the selected donor mare, in this case Chanel, and then placed in the uterus of a surrogate mare who is on the same cycle. The surrogate mare than carries the foal to term and raises the baby as their own.

I used wonderful, kind draft mares as the surrogate mares, as they made fabulous mothers and did a superb job of raising the foals. In the minds of those draft mares, those babies were their own and they cared for them lovingly, while the donor mares were out pursuing their careers. I was always amused to see these stunningly gorgeous embryo foals by the sides of these big, heavy, sweet draft mares. God Bless those draft mares – they were wonderful surrogate mothers.

Matadora also had two embryo transplant babies for me which were wonderful. They shall have their own chapter as well. In total I produced four outstanding embryo transplant babies with many thanks to Chanel and Matadora, as well as the kind draft mares who carried the babies to term and raised them with the very best of manners.

CHANEL'S MARVELOUS OFFSPRING

All in Silver, by Sylvester and out of Chanel

When it comes to horses, I am a big believer in families. If certain bloodlines are working for me, I seek them out. As Chanel was such a lovely mare, I was extremely interested when Paul told me that he had Chanel's two sons in his barn – one four-year-old gray gelding and one three-year-old gray gelding. I wanted to see them right away.

Both of these prospects were by a jumper stallion in Germany named "Sylvester". When the 17 hand, dark gray four-year-old was brought out for me to see, he had just been green broke.

He was a big, gangly Holsteiner who didn't always know what to do with his front legs as he jumped the little jumps. Paul seemed unimpressed with this horse and actually made fun of his jumping style.

However this big rangy colt had a fabulous hind end, a wonderful mind and showed a great deal of scope. I liked him right away. When I rode him, I could feel that he had tremendous power, a huge stride and a surplus of talent and scope. In addition, he had a really sweet, willing disposition and a fabulous temperament. He had a very kind eye and expression as well – to me, he was a lovable horse.

As I played with this youngster over some little jumps, his front end immediately improved by virtue of giving him a very quiet ride and the time to sort out his front end. I also gave him a little more ground line, so that he could better establish where to leave the ground.

As I've said before and as was the case with Matadora, often a green horse with an extremely powerful hind end will lose the ideal form and style with their front end. This is because their hind end overpowers their front end. Although many people would walk away from a horse like this which jumped over his front end, it has never bothered me. I know that this can be corrected with proper training. I believe the hind end is the most important thing, as that is what produces the power and scope. Their front end will catch up with proper training and experience. Once again, it's about understanding the horse.

I had already established a very reasonable price with Paul, so when I got off of this big youngster, I purchased him on the spot. I never regretted this decision, as this horse became one of my top horses. I named him "All In Silver".

Once home, I began to develop All In Silver and he came along beautifully. I began showing him in the small divisions and brought him along with great success up through the divisions.

As All In Silver was doing so well in America in bigger divisions, I flew him and a few other horses over to Germany to show. All In Silver was seven years old at this time and was absolutely wonderful competing in Germany. I ended up selling All In Silver to a buyer in Italy, but that is another chapter.

Chanel's three-year-old was a very pretty 16.2 hand gray gelding. He too was very green, but a very talented horse. Although he did not have quite the scope which All In Silver showed, he had enough scope and several good things going for him. I purchased him as well and named him "The Silver Shadow".

After developing The Silver Shadow at home, I began showing him and working his way up the divisions. I sold The Silver Shadow at the Palm Beach shows to Paul Valliere, one of the country's top horsemen, for one of his clients.

The Silver Shadow in Palm Beach with Molly Ashe Cawley

Paul Valliere continued to train The Silver Shadow and he ended up showing quite successfully in the Grand Prix classes with Buddy Brown riding. On this same Florida circuit, I also sold Paul Valliere a lovely 6 year old, 16.1 hand bay Thoroughbred mare named Terra Cotta, who I had been showing in the preliminary divisions. Terra Cotta also jumped her way up to the big classes with Paul Valliere training.

Terra Cotta and Molly Ashe Cawley in Palm Beach, Florida

Aside from the fabulous All In Silver and The Silver Shadow, Chanel also produced two beautiful embryo transplant babies for me in America. As I explained previously, this is a procedure where the egg is fertilized within the donor mare – in this case Chanel – and then that egg is transferred to a surrogate draft mare to carry to term and raise. This allows the showing mares to continue competing, while still enabling them to produce offspring.

Chanel's first embryo baby was a beautiful gray filly by San Francisco. I named her "Shabu". Shabu later had a lovely gray filly of her own named "The Pearl", who was by another one of my stallions, "The Silver Prince". Once in training, it was clear that Shabu was going to be a winner. She was very careful and fast, with plenty of jump. Shabu also had an exceptionally kind and honest disposition. I was winning in the high preliminary divisions with Shabu when a lovely gal from the Midwest fell in love with her. Shabu went very well for this girl and I felt they were a good match.

I sold Shabu to this gal and she called me in a couple of months to tell me how fabulous Shabu was and how well she had been doing with her in the Amateur jumper division. Then she added that she wanted The Pearl, Shabu's daughter, as well – so one big happy family. It's wonderful when things work out so well.

The Wonderful Shabu and Jessamy at a show

Chanel had one more beautiful gray embryo transplant filly for me named "Baronelle". Baronelle was by The Silver Baron and turned into a lovely mare. I sold her to some wonderful people in North Carolina and she did extremely well for them. So not only am I very grateful to Chanel for being such a wonderful horse herself, I am extremely grateful to her for giving me such sensational offspring.

In her later years Chanel went on to be a winning amateur and working hunter for a wonderful lady in Tennessee. Chanel also carried a child around in the equitation and jumped the big water jumps in the USET Equitation classes.

My girl had come a long way, which shows the importance of a solid, but patient and compassionate foundation in the beginning of a horse's training. That goes for the training of any animal.

THE WONDERFUL FAMILY OF SAN FRANCISCO

San Francisco and Jessamy

Upperville Grand Prix in Virginia

San Francisco was one of the first horses I purchased from Paul Schockemohle on the 1985 trip to Germany, along with Matadora and Chanel. San Francisco was a very handsome 17 hand, five-year-old, chestnut stallion with a blaze and white stockings. He was owned by Franke Sloothtak, one of Germany's top riders, who was riding horses for Paul at the time. San Francisco was by a winning Grand Prix stallion which Franke had ridden in Germany named "San Fernando". He was out of a fabulous mare named "Garnet", who was by the famous stallion, "Graphit". San Francisco, Matadora and Godiva were full brother and sisters with identical breeding.

San Fernando - Ridden here by Franke Sloothtak in Germany

Once back in America, I began the development of San Francisco into a top horse. As I did with the other horses, San Francisco started in the schooling jumpers, followed by the preliminary jumper divisions. Once he had established a solid foundation and was competing with success, I moved him into the Intermediate jumper division which was a stepping stone between the high preliminary jumper division and the open division.

San Francisco was confident, brave and jumping the Intermediate division with ease. After several months in the Intermediate division we made our way into the open jumper division and the Grand Prix classes. San Francisco was a six-year-old by then.

San Francisco won the very first Grand Prix class in which he competed, beating the talented team of Anthony D'Ambrosio and "Nimmerdor". I was extremely proud of San Francisco for that feat, as green as he was at the time. San Francisco continued his winning style right up to his sale to a client in Florida. I also used San Francisco as a breeding stallion and he produced several outstanding young horses. Many of San Francisco's offspring went on to become top horses as well. They too were brave, good-minded horses which jumped in excellent style with scope to spare. They also became winners in the show ring.

Almost all of San Francisco's offspring were chestnut horses with white markings, although he sired Shabu, the outstanding gray mare out of "Chanel". As I've mentioned, Shabu was an embryo transplant foal.

Early in their careers I realized how good San Francisco and Matadora were and went back to Paul's place in Germany to purchase their dam, "Garnet". I also purchased their full sister, "Godiva", who was only a yearling at the time. I was building a large breeding program and Garnet became my top broodmare. I had been buying a number of two-year-old fillies from Paul which I bred to San Francisco, as well as my other stallions once I had them in the stable.

This is what they do in Germany and much of Europe. They breed two-year-old fillies and then breed them back as three-year olds. The fillies each produce two foals. When the second foal is finally weaned from them, the fillies begin training to be show horses as four-year olds. I would go to Paul's and evaluate his two-year-old fillies in the jump chute, as well as by type, bloodlines and temperament. I picked out young fillies which I believed would not only produce wonderful foals, but would later become highly competitive show horses as well. I had great luck and success with this endeavor and produced many fabulous mares.

San Francisco and Jessamy competing in a Grand Prix in Palm Beach, Florida

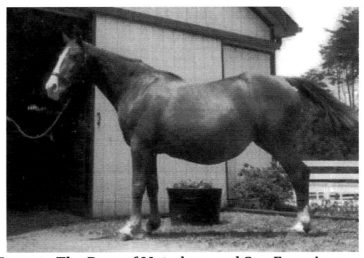

Garnet - The Dam of Matadora and San Francisco
Godiva, Tiburon, Pacifica and The Baron

Garnet was twelve years of age when I purchased her and she was in foal to "San Carlos", another son of "San Fernando". She foaled in America at Chestnut Lawn and the colt was an impressive chestnut individual with a lot of white markings. Garnet really stamped her foals. I named this colt "Tiburon" and showed him in the young jumper divisions when he was four years old.

Tiburon was also a fabulous mover and jumper, with an outstandingly good temperament. I sold him to a very good client in Pittsburgh, Pennsylvania who had great success with him and kept him for his entire life.

Tiburon, by San Carlos and out of Garnet

I also bought a yearling filly from Paul who was a full sister to Matadora and San Francisco. She was a well-built chestnut filly with a blaze and white stockings. I named her "Godiva". After producing one lovely foal, Godiva went on to be an excellent showjumper.

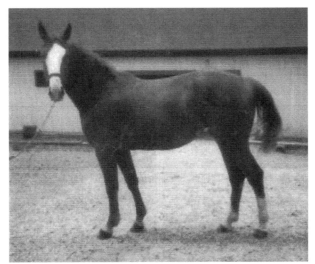
Godiva as a yearling, just after I purchased her in Germany

Godiva at the Palm Beach show with Kevin Maloney riding

When I took horses back to Europe to show in the early 1990's, I sold Godiva in Germany to a good rider there.

Another one of Garnet's babies which became quite famous was a filly named "Pacifica". I had purchased a fantastic gray three-year-old stallion in Germany from Paul. I named him "The Silver Baron".

I shall discuss him in detail later, as he became one of the greatest young Grand Prix prospects in the World at that time.

Once The Silver Baron had arrived, I bred him to Garnet and she produced the lovely gray filly which I named Pacifica. Pacifica was a big mare with a fabulous jump and scope to spare. I showed her with great success as a youngster and sold her to a professional in Pennsylvania named Chuck Waters. Chuck had bought over forty-six horses from me and had done extremely well with them. When Pacifica was a four-year-old, she won the International Jumper Futurity with Chuck. She went on to be a winning Grand Prix horse in the years to follow, as did her full brother "The Baron", who I also sold to people in Pennsylvania.

Just a note here to say thank you and God Bless to our broodmares, who give us so much and make all horse related sports possible. Garnet had never worn a saddle in her life. Instead Garnet had been a broodmare her entire life and had produced one champion after another.

Anyone who is involved in breeding will tell you that the mare is just as important as the stallion in producing outstanding foals – perhaps even more so.

I kept Garnet until her last day and am always grateful for all the talented horses she produced for me. Garnet was a real sweetheart and I loved her to the end.

MATADORA

THE HAPPIEST DAY OF MY LIFE
Matadora and Jessamy winning a class at Southampton Show

Leaving out two strides to the last fence in the jump off

Matadora began winning in the Preliminary and Intermediate Jumper divisions straight away. She was so brave and had so much scope, Matadora jumped for fun. She had a huge stride, was exceptionally careful and could run, jump and turn with the best. Matadora could leave out two strides in a jump off and make it look easy, all with her big ears up and alert. No course, no matter how difficult, was a problem for Matadora.

I felt like I could jump any course and win any class with her. She was the horse of my lifetime and we had a special bond. I have won many classes in my career, but the win which gave me the most joy was my first Grand Prix with Matadora. It was held at Commonwealth Park in Culpeper, Virginia – a place which had offered big prize money and superb competition in the Grand Prix classes during the 1980s and 1990s.

There were well over thirty top horse and rider combinations in that class, with the great Rodney Jenkins riding three of the entries. Rodney had been America's winningest rider for decades on both the hunters and the jumpers. When the riders walked the course, they all seemed quite concerned about various parts of it. The course was big and deceptively tricky, with very difficult distances. Plus it was a night class under the lights, which makes things even more difficult due to the reflections and shadows on the jumps.

As I walked the course I listened to the other rider's comments and concerns, but for some reason I was perfectly calm. I believed in my mare, regardless of the fact that she was a green six-year-old. I honestly believed that Matadora could jump anything and that we had a special partnership. She proved me to be right that night.

As the class progressed, everyone was accumulating faults on course in varying degrees. Even Rodney, who was riding three horses in the class, only went clear on his gray stallion "Aerobic". As a point of interest, Aerobic was supposedly the most expensive jumper ever sold in Europe at that time.

Matadora and Jessamy winning a Grand Prix

When my turn came, I rode Matadora in the ring and she marched in there like she owned it. She had no fear or reservations. Matadora jumped the course so easily, I almost felt badly for the other horses and riders. After the first round, only Rodney on Aerobic and Matadora and I were clean with no faults whatsoever.

So now Rodney and I had to jump off to decide the class. Rodney went first and had a very smooth, fast and clear jump off round. The crowd was cheering as they assumed that he would be the winner. But Matadora had yet to go. She walked in that ring with her big ears pricked forward and her mind on the task ahead. I gave her a big pat and we started out with a good gallop to the first few jumps. Our turns were tighter than Rodney's turns had been, but we still had the last line to conquer.

There was a very tall vertical coming home, which continued to a big oxer. There were about nine strides in between the two jumps. I turned and galloped to the vertical and then allowed Matadora to keep up her pace to the huge oxer. She accomplished this in seven strides. She jumped a foot over the oxer and galloped through the timers to beat Rodney's time by over two and a half seconds. Matadora knew she had done well. As I was rubbing her neck with praise and easing her to a walk, she pricked her ears and seemed quite cocky. When she walked out of the ring and past Aerobic, I could almost hear her say to him, "That's how it's done!"

A green six-year-old mare and I had just beaten the sensational Rodney Jenkins on an expensive and talented stallion. The Girls prevailed and the crowd went wild, standing and cheering.

I couldn't stop praising Matadora as we rode in for the award ceremony. A year and a half before, Matadora had been a green broke, skinny, scruffy mare who was recognized only for her savage ways. Now this big, strong beautiful mare had just beat one of the best horse and rider combinations in the world. It was the happiest night of my life.

Matadora showed not only how talented she was, but the fact that she and I were true soulmates. I love all my horses and all of my animals, but I have never loved a horse as much as I loved the great chestnut mare Matadora. I was so happy and so proud of her, that I could not sleep that night. Matadora was the greatest horse of my career and the love of my life. She was a once in a lifetime Superhorse.

The Great Mare - Matadora

CHIEF DE EQUIPE
INTERNATIONAL TEAM TO BERMUDA

Carla and I awaiting the start of the International Competition in Bermuda

In the latter part of the 1980's I was very fortunate to have a terrific girl named Carla working for me. Carla was originally from Bermuda and her mother was still quite active in the Equestrian world there. Carla's mother had been contacted by the equestrian authorities in Bermuda and asked if she would be able to help put together an International Invitational Showjumping Event. This event was for a wealthy Bermudian sponsor. Needless to say, Carla and I were contacted immediately regarding the task of turning all of this into a wonderful reality.

I was the Chief de Equipe for the team and needed to supply the horses, equipment, and grooms, as well as manage the transport of the horses from America to Bermuda. In addition, I had the responsibility of organizing the riders and horses once we were on the ground there. I put together half a dozen very good, solid and honest horses which I felt would do a wonderful job in Bermuda.

I also looked ahead to the possibility of these horses being sold after the event in Bermuda, as they were very kind horses and suitable for junior and amateur riders. We arrived in Bermuda and allowed the horses to settle in for a couple of days and become comfortable with their new environment. The International riders then arrived and I began the task of suiting each rider to the horse most appropriate for their riding style.

My top rider on the team was the great Bruce Davidson of Olympic medal fame. Bruce represented America in this competition. Although Bruce was a multiple Olympic medal winning event rider, he was such a sensational talent that he could ride anything beautifully and with the utmost of style. Bruce was just as good on a jumper.

Bruce Davidson on Sharky in Bermuda

Bruce is a class act in every possible way. I had brought a talented bay Thoroughbred horse named "Sharky", who was a tad more sensitive than the other horses. However he was the perfect ride for Bruce, as Bruce is such a soft, sympathetic and extremely capable rider.

There was a Canadian gal there who also rode quite well and I put her on another very nice Thoroughbred horse which I had brought. The other two riders were rather big guys – one gentleman from Spain and the other gentleman from Italy. I mounted these fellows on two very steady big Warmblood horses which I had brought to Bermuda with the idea that I may need some really solid packers on the trip.

The competition was beautifully done, the grounds were lovely and the weather was gorgeous. It was a very pleasant, friendly and festive time for all involved. The horses were pampered not only by their riders and grooms, but by the adoring public. The horses were enjoying their trip to Bermuda as well.

Needless to say, the ultra-talented Bruce Davidson representing the USA was the big winner in this competition. Bruce rode beautifully and his Thoroughbred Sharky was flawless. He was followed by the Canadian gal and then the other riders – all of which did an excellent job. All of the horses were wonderful as well. I was absolutely thrilled with each rider and every horse. There were several festivities surrounding the Competition which were enjoyed by all. Bruce and the other riders signed many autographs and were adored by the crowd. It was also wonderful exposure for the residents of Bermuda who don't often get to see an International competition.

However my work had only begun. Carla and I had several interested parties in all of the horses. These were people from Bermuda who wished to try them for a possible purchase. I told Bruce that he was not only my Number One Rider for the Competition, but he was also my Number One Ace Sales Rider.

Bruce is such a wonderful, kind and generous person, he said that he would be delighted to ride the horses and show them to potential customers. This began our Bermuda sales venture. We actually had a wonderful time, as the people of Bermuda are fabulous and very friendly. It was the most enjoyable sales tour I had ever been on. Bruce agreed.

**Bruce Davidson winning
International Invitational Competition in Bermuda**
(Abroad, the winning ribbon is red – not blue as it is in America)

Carla and I worked our tails off to have the horses looking their very best, but it was all worth it in the end. We sold every single horse that we had flown there - all to residents within Bermuda. These people were so excited to own the very horses which they had watched compete so successfully. There were many fabulous parties for all to enjoy and we were sorry when the time came to go back home. Leaving Bermuda felt like leaving a paradise, but we had horses waiting for us at home. I am extremely grateful to the people of Bermuda who showed us such tremendous hospitality, as well as to Bruce Davidson and all of the riders and grooms who did such a fantastic job. I am especially grateful to the horses who performed so admirably and, in the process, found themselves wonderful new homes. I am looking forward to another trip to Bermuda.

ALL THE GOLD

FOUR-YEAR-OLD COLT IN GERMANY

TO THE SHOW HUNTER

HALL OF FAME

After I had purchased Matadora, San Francisco and Chanel from Paul Schockemohle in 1985, I went back to view and buy horses at his place and throughout Germany multiple times per year. On one trip Paul showed me a lovely two-year chestnut stallion who had recently been approved for breeding by the Breed registries in Germany. The horse's name was "Grand" Grand was by Paul's favorite stallion at the time, "Gepard", and out of a very good mare named "Wedda", who was by "Wettstreit". Paul was extremely excited about this handsome young colt and believed that he would be a top Grand Prix horse. He insisted that I watch Grand in the jump chute, despite the fact that I was not looking for a two-year stallion.

I watched Grand in the jump chute and liked him very much. He was a lovely mover and he jumped in truly superb style. I asked Paul what he wanted for this two-year stallion and he said $80,000. I then gave Paul my honest opinion, as I always did and which I believe he appreciated. I told Paul that I did not see $80,000 in this two-year-old at that time. I also told him that I believed the horse would make a wonderful show hunter in America, but did not have the scope to be a top showjumper. I was proven to be correct over time.

I have always believed that the horses with Grand Prix scope do not jump out of their skin in flawless style over three and a half foot or even four-foot jumps. A hunter needs scope and stride, but too much scope will make the horse casual over hunter size fences and consequently not a top winning hunter.

For the next couple of years, I continued to buy many horses from Paul and throughout Germany and Europe. Paul has a huge horse auction at the end of each year called the PSI Sale and Paul wanted me to attend. This is an extremely extravagant affair, with wealthy people dressed to the nines in tuxedos and evening gowns. There are white tablecloths on the tables, an open bar and wonderful delicacies – all being served by top notch waiters and waitresses in formal attire.

The PSI sale is an extraordinary extravaganza, packed with extremely wealthy horse buyers from across all of Europe, Japan and America, as well as several other countries. The PSI sale is absolutely a first-class event. It is along the lines of our top Thoroughbred sales in Kentucky and Saratoga. The price tags on the horses at the PSI sale are beyond exorbitant, so I knew that I would be unable to buy anything there, but I wanted to see this spectacular show at least once.

I was accompanied by a wonderful German fellow named Heiner, who was my driver and translator when I went throughout Germany seeking horses to buy. All Heiner wanted in return was for me to help him with his horse.

I did ride Heiner's horse for him with terrific results. Heiner was thrilled with how his horse went after I rode him – plus I gave Heiner pointers on how to keep him going well. Heiner was so grateful, as I was grateful for all that he had done for me. I usually did not need Heiner when I went to Paul's place, because everyone spoke English and Paul always made sure that I had a driver and accommodations organized near his place. Paul was wonderful and quite smart in this way, as he knew how to make it easy for American buyers.

Paul recognized how difficult it was for foreign buyers in a different country with the language and cultural barriers. Paul always had everything perfectly organized for me on every trip, from a driver to a room in a charming, cozy country Inn.

Paul had everything organized for me at the auction as well, including a lovely table right up front in the auction. I checked into the very fancy hotel which Paul had arranged. Heiner would pick me up each morning and we would go to look at the PSI horses the two days before the sale.

During this time, I saw my friend "Grand" again. He was now a very handsome four-year approved stallion and had been competing in the young horse divisions throughout Germany.

As those young horse divisions are judged on style and smoothness, much like our American show hunters, Grand did very well. I watched him ridden before the auction and rode him myself for a few minutes. I jumped a few jumps and Grand jumped them with beautiful technique. However I still believed that he was a fancy hunter – not a Grand Prix horse.

Then came the night of the auction. After everyone had their share of drinks and wonderful food with the band playing and entertaining the entire time, there was a drum roll. This is when Paul Schockemohle and his Dressage horse partner Ulli Kasselmann enter the auction house on a red carpet amid much fanfare and applause.

They were wearing suits and looked very stately and handsome. It reminded me of an American president entering Congress for the State of the Union address. The atmosphere was that electric and with the aura of prestige and true significance. After each giving a short speech about the wealth of talent in horseflesh available on this evening, Paul and Ulli went to their high seats on the stage overlooking the auction arena.

The auction then began. The big, boisterous German announcer took his place at the podium. He was also wearing a suit. After setting out the rules of the auction in German, he was ready to begin. This is another reason that I needed Heiner, because everything was in German and the bids and sale prices were stated in German marks at that time. I needed Heiner so I knew what the hell was go going on.

The first horse was led into the ring and the announcer's voice boomed over the loudspeaker with details about the horse's specifics, breeding and show history – all in sensationally glowing terms. Then the auctioneer started the bidding off quite high, as is often the case in high class auctions.

**From the left - Paul Schockemohle, the Auctioneer and Ullrich Kasselmann
PSI Auction**

Playing around with the numbers, the auctioneer quickly found a place to start receiving legitimate, real bids. At this auction, as with all high-class auctions, there were a number of men in suits searching the crowds for bids and yelling them out to the auctioneer.

This is when some "shilling" takes place, which is when the price is elevated by non-existent bids with the purpose of raising the numbers for the real bidders. This happens at all auctions, regardless of what is being sold. The key to buying well at an auction is to allow the initial shilling to take place and remain calm, until the legitimate, solid bids start being called. Most of the horses I liked went so far out of my price range within the first sixty seconds, I realized that I probably would not be leaving there with a horse. Paul was having one hell of a good night.

About mid-way through this auction, Grand entered the ring. He looked gorgeous and was as cool in temperament as ever. As with all of the other horses, the auctioneer immediately started out with an excessively high number.

The shilling went back and forth and finally started the price at the minimum reserve which Paul would accept. I sat there quietly throughout all of this, with my hands folded on the table.

I waited and waited until all of the initial bidding and nonsense was over and we had reached what was apparently the end of the real bids – about $33,000 in American currency. Things got quiet and no one was moving. I gathered that the European buyers had also figured out that Grand was not going to be a top Grand Prix horse. After all, they had watched him compete all year. Paul looked over at me. It was deadly silent for a moment and they were ready to "No Sale" my friend Grand. Just then I nodded and raised my hand. The hammer fell immediately. With one bid, I had just purchased what would become one of the greatest show hunters and hunter sires that America had ever seen for $33,000, which is a song when one considers what he became.

I decided right then to name him "All The Gold". I was brought a huge bundle of red roses and an enormous bottle of champagne. Paul was so happy that he came over and kissed me. The roses and champagne were given to anyone who bought a horse, but not everyone got a kiss from Paul. Heiner loved the champagne and I gave him the roses to give to his wife. Everyone was happy.

Paul was well aware that I knew what I was doing and that I was going to make this horse a star in America. I did not let him down. Heiner and I went back to the stable area and visited my new Champion. All The Gold was as cool as ever. He looked at me with his big, warm brown eyes while munching on a mouthful of hay. I pat him and said, "Everything is okay now Buddy. You never have to be a showjumper again. You are headed to America to take the hunter world by storm." All The Gold did just that. He was everything that I thought he would be and he did not let me down.

All The Gold arrived in America towards the end of the year. I wanted him to settle in, regain all of his condition and become happy with his new home. In early December, I began riding All The Gold.

In January, I shipped him to the Palm Beach Horse Shows in Wellington, Florida to begin his career as a First Year Green hunter. I didn't do any warm up or smaller divisions with him. I knew that this exceptionally brave horse did not require any of that.

I just rode All The Gold straight into the first-year green division and won the very first class we entered, as well as several others after that. Everyone already loved him. All The Gold was on his way to becoming an American Superstar.

Paul showed up in Florida and was amazed at what I had accomplished with this horse. He honestly could not believe it. Paul had laughed at me when I told him that I was going to name the young stallion "All The Gold". He thought that was hilarious. But Paul was not laughing now.

All The Gold with Bert Mutch

Grand Working Hunter Champion at the Detroit Horse Shows

During this time, I had a very large string of jumpers - from talented prospects, all the way up to Grand Prix horses. Wellington, Florida is so huge and spread out, that it became very difficult for me to ride all of the jumpers in different rings and then commute to the hunter ring to ride All The Gold.

Plus, I'd have to wait around for the jog order and ribbon presentation, which was a hassle. I decided to have one of my good friends, Allen Smith, ride All The Gold in the First Year Green division. Allen was a super rider and had ridden horses for me before. Allen also won on All The Gold. We had an outstanding time in Wellington and now it was time to move on to the horse shows in Tampa, Florida.

Allen was not going to the Tampa shows, so I had my young and talented friend Scott Hofstetter ride All The Gold at Tampa. I had given Scott several rides on good horses after he had won the Maclay Finals on the wonderful "Keep the Change". Scott had always done a fabulous job. Scott won a ton of classes at Tampa with All The Gold. Some of the classes were at night under the lights, but that only made All The Gold better. He was fearless and he was a winner. When we came home from Florida, I let the horses relax and unwind in Virginia. It had been a long circuit and they had been sensational. Now they deserved a break.

One day out of the blue, Bert Mutch drove up my driveway. Bert was a Superstar as a junior rider. He was the son of renowned horseman Ronnie Mutch. Bert had won the Equitation finals, as well as countless other classes as a junior. Many of these Superstar junior kids feel a little lost when they break out of the juniors, because they are now head to head with the top professionals competing for rides on the nicest horses. It is another world for these young people. It can be a very disorienting and scary time if they do not have a support system to help them with the transition into the professional world. Bert had been riding horses for Rodney Jenkins on the farm, but something had happened and Bert was now looking for another position.

Bert was always an extremely handsome, clean cut, well turned out, well-spoken and very polite guy. He was a class act and had been well raised by his parents, Ronnie and Sue Mutch. But it had not always been an easy time for him. Superstar junior riders like Bert are put under unbelievable pressure to win at such a young age. It can be emotionally damaging for these kids and they need some support - especially when they are no longer juniors and don't have the haven of those junior divisions to excel in. It's a whole different world when a rider is competing against the pros.

I happily greeted Bert and was surprised when he asked me if he may have a job cutting grass. Bert was obviously going through a little slump. As it turns out, Bert loves to cut grass. (Cutting grass must be some kind of a man thing which I accept, but do not pretend to understand.)

I told Bert right up front that I had three barns full of really nice horses – way more than I could ride myself. If he was going to work for me, he needed to ride horses because I was not going to stand by and watch his talent go to waste. I also told Bert that I needed him to help deal with the customers during horse sales, because I knew that all of the girls would love him. I promised Bert that he could cut grass to his heart's content in the evenings. We made a deal.

The next morning Bert showed up extra early looking as handsome and clean cut as ever, holding his cup of steaming hot coffee. He enthusiastically broke through my kitchen door and exclaimed, "Good Morning Boss!" Bert did that every morning thereafter and I always loved him for it. I'd be exhausted and stressed on the phone at my desk, but Bert would inspire me to get going. He was a joy to have around.

Bert rode all the sale horses and did a really fabulous job. As expected, when clients came to buy horses, which were usually for young girls or amateur women, the girls and women all fell in love with Bert immediately.

It was impossible for these girls and women not to fall in love with this handsome, charming, polite young man, so I did the smartest thing I could do. I got lost. Bert would come and get me when it was time to discuss the money with the father or husband. That was my forte. Consequently Bert and I sold a ton of horses together.

But Bert was too talented to just ride sales horses, so I started putting him on some of my nice prospects and most importantly, I put Bert on All The Gold. That was a match made in heaven - eventually. As I had done with the riders before, I did need to explain to Bert that the warmbloods, especially All The Gold, needed a constant, really strong leg right up to and throughout the jump in order to get the very best jump out of the horse.

A rider could never, ever take their leg off of All The Gold, or it would be like taking your foot off of the gas pedal of your car. All The Gold was very quiet and kind, but he was also extremely lazy. It was part of his charm, but it also drove me crazy sometimes. I had to keep him really sharp at the shows in order to win. All The Gold almost never jumped at home.

Our very first show together, Bert was trying to ride All The Gold like one of his fancy Thoroughbred junior hunters. He was disappointed when he didn't win, because he knew the horse had won at Palm Beach. Once again, I explained that riding warmbloods, particularly All The Gold, was an entirely different ball game than riding the Thoroughbreds. However if ridden properly, the warmblood horses could win consistently due to their natural talent. With the exception of warmblood dressage horses, the warmbloods are bred to jump.

As point of interest, I needed to explain this to all of All The Gold's riders. The horse needed a constant and consistently strong leg from start to finish. He also would not jump his best from a weak, hunter gap – so often used with the Thoroughbreds. He'd slap at the jumps, which was not a winning act. All The Gold's riders had to learn to ride him up to the base and allow him to back himself off of the jump. That's when All The Gold's spectacular jump came out and wowed everyone.

When the riders listened to me and adapted their style, they consistently won. Bert listened and adjusted his style. After that Bert started winning with All The Gold right away, regardless of how tough the competition. Bert and All The Gold were tough to beat.

After winning all over Virginia and surrounding states, I decided to ship my horses to the Detroit horse shows. They no longer exist, but they were fabulous and great fun at the time. I miss them. The Detroit shows were very well managed and it was a beautiful setting. Everyone there always seemed very polite and happy. I wasn't crazy about the fourteen-hour drive to get to the Motor City, but I absolutely loved those shows once I arrived. So Bert and All The Gold came along to Detroit.

As the first-year green division was so easy for All The Gold by now, we entered him in the Working Hunter division. Four-foot jumps were no problem for this brave, athletic stallion and he jumped them in exquisite style. Bert gave All The Gold a super ride and they ended up Grand Hunter Champion at the Detroit shows.

While Bert was showing All The Gold, there was a sweet young lady named Sarah Steffee who was paying extra attention. I wasn't sure if she was in love with the horse or with Bert, but it turned out that she loved All The Gold from the minute he had first walked into the ring at Detroit. Sarah asked if All The Gold was for sale and I told her yes, he is for sale to the right person. Sarah asked if she may ride him, so the next morning Sarah and her wonderful mother Billie Steffee came to my barn at the show. Sarah gave All The Gold a little ride in the schooling area and was absolutely in love.

While Sarah was riding, I explained the significant tax benefits of owning a breeding stallion to Billie Steffee. I told her that I had bred All The Gold to several mares and it did not change his kind, sweet disposition one bit. All The Gold was a saintly stallion who needed no preparation for anything.

All The Gold never needed any schooling or lunging – not even a hack in the morning. He was as dead quiet, brave, sweet and honest as he appeared all the time.

Billie and Sarah wanted to buy All The Gold right away and they purchased him right there in Detroit. I advised Billie that she could build up a big breeding business around this one stallion. I was right and Billie thanked me forever after. She said that everything I had told and taught her had come true. Billie was in heaven. She loved All The Gold and he made her life a joy.

Leaving the Detroit shows, the plan was that All The Gold would come back to Virginia with me for the breeding season. This would allow Sarah to get started with him at my farm under my supervision and that of Bert.

Sarah stayed at my farm and with guidance from both Bert and me, she became a fabulous match with All The Gold. They were winning in the Amateur Owner division and made an outstanding pair.

At the same time, I was teaching Billie Steffee all about the breeding business - how to manage a stallion's breeding book and how to handle the collection and shipment of semen to outside mares.

All The Gold had some fabulous babies for me, which were all christened with Premium Foal Awards by the Oldenburg registry. All of the babies were beautiful movers and jumpers, with exceptionally kind, quiet and honest dispositions. These babies went on to become famous show hunters all across America and Canada and dominated the International Hunter Futurity for years to come.

All The Gold was the first stallion to have his babies exceed $200,000 in earnings at the International Hunter Futurity. All The Gold was awarded The Grand Performance Stallion in 1994, 1998, 2001 and 2003, with top placings by offspring in 2004 as well.

All The Gold was then placed in the Show Hunter Hall of Fame for his amazing achievements in the show ring and as a sire.

He also has a walkway named after him at the gorgeous Horse Park in Lexington, Kentucky. People still remember All The Gold decades later. He was a phenomenon.

Billie Steffee kept All The Gold until he passed away at a very old age. All The Gold gave Billie a wonderful life while she owned him and she loved him dearly right up to his last day. They gave each other a wonderful life.

Billie made a loving tribute to All The Gold in The Chronicle of the Horse after his passing. I have posted it below. I cried when I first read this and I could still cry today. My four-year-old colt purchased out of the PSI sale in Germany became a Hall of Fame Legend. I was extremely proud of him.

One of my many All The Gold babies

I was also extremely proud of the beautiful job that Billie Steffee did in managing his career, as I had been her initial guide into the world of breeding and managing stallions.

All The Gold became Billie's whole life. He gave Billie much joy every day, as well as the support system she needed when hit with personal tragedies such as the pre-mature death of her beautiful young daughter Sarah. All The Gold was Billie's horse, no question about that, and they were there for each other right up until the end.

Heartbreakingly, Billie passed away not too long after All The Gold had passed. Billie wanted to be with her horse. A legend gone, but his youngsters would carry on his legacy for years to come. Billie and All The Gold could watch them proudly from above.

All The Gold

He said goodbye with a few days left in summer and just before the rain. It was an honor to know him.

April 22, 1982 – September 19, 2011

All The Gold

Elite Hanoverian stallion and champion hunter All The Gold died Sept. 19. He was 29.

Jessamy Rouson imported All The Gold (Gepard—Wedda, Wettstreit) from Germany in 1986, and Billie Steffee of Craighead Farm in Novelty, Ohio, purchased him soon after.

Steffee recalled first watching him in the regular working hunters at the Detroit Horse Show. "I had never seen a horse jump like that and bought him shortly after that performance," she said.

In 1990 and 1991, he took home championships and reserves in the regular working hunters during the Arizona Winter Festival. All The Gold won back-to-back grand circuit championships at the Winter Equestrian Festival (Fla.) in the regular working division in 1992 and 1993. He was also reserve champion in the amateur-owner, 18-30, division in the same years. Steffee retired All The Gold in 1993 and moved him to the breeding shed full time.

In 2003, All The Gold became the first stallion whose get exceeded $200,000 in earnings in the International Hunter Futurity. He was awarded the Grand Performance Sire title and was High Point Stallion in 1994, 1998, 2001 and 2003. In 2004, two full siblings, Gold Digger and Gold's Gone Fishin' (All The Gold—Silver Surf, The Silver Prince) claimed the 3-year-old grand championship and the 4-year-old reserve grand championship, respectively, at the International Hunter Futurity in Lexington, Ky. In 2008 and 2009, All The Gold was second in the U.S. Equestrian Federation leading hunter sire rankings.

All The Gold retired from stud duties at Craighead Farm at the end of 2007. His offspring are still competing in hunter/jumper shows, eventing and dressage. Most recently, at the 2011 IHF International, Play Mister For Me (out of an All The Gold mare) was Best Young Horse.

At home, All The Gold was affectionately called "Goldie."

Sarah Steffee, Billie's daughter, said: "It has been such an honor to know him. He brought out the best in all of us."

THE SILVER BARON
A WORLD CLASS STALLION

The Sensational Stallion - The Silver Baron

On one of my trips to Paul Schockemohle's place in Muhlen, Germany, I showed Paul a video of "The Officer", my chestnut Thoroughbred Grand Prix horse. The tape had The Officer jumping several double clean rounds in multiple big Grand Prixs. Paul was very interested in The Officer and wanted to buy him. So we eventually negotiated a deal with which we were both happy.

As with all trips to Paul's stable, I was looking at several horses. One of the horses Paul had shown me was a three-year-old gray stallion by the good Grand Prix horse "Domino", out of a wonderful mare by "Furioso II". This young stallion had just failed the stallion testing in Germany because he was built very base narrow. This means that he had a very narrow chest and his front ankles practically touched – not ideal for a breeding stallion. If he were to stay in Germany the stallion would have to be castrated, as he would not be recognized for breeding by the breed registries. Paul wanted me to look at the stallion because he believed that despite his conformational flaws, he would be a good stallion for me in America.

The stallion was quite weedy at this stage, but he was a beautifully headed horse. With the exception of being base narrow, he was otherwise built quite well. He stood about 16.2 hands.

I knew that he would grow and fill out with time as he was only a three-year-old. I watched this young stallion being ridden and jumped over a few small jumps. I liked what I saw so I decided to ride him myself.

The stallion had a big floaty stride and a lovely way of moving which I really liked. I jumped a few jumps and he jumped light and airy with plenty of loft, scope and style. He seemed very careful and very brave at the same time, which is a difficult combination to find.

I got off the horse, gave him a pat and told Paul that we should sit down and work out a deal on "The Officer". I told him that I would accept this gray three-year-old stallion as part of the deal. After much discussion, Paul also added Chanel's three-year-old gelding who later became "The Silver Shadow".

With these two young horses as part of the deal, we came to acceptable terms. Paul now owned "The Officer" and I owned the two gray three-year olds. I named the three-year-old stallion "The Silver Baron". And so it was. "The Officer" flew to Paul's place in Germany and "The Silver Baron" and "The Silver Shadow" flew to my place in Virginia.

I felt that I had consummated a good deal for myself, but I did not yet realize that I now owned what would become one of the greatest young Grand Prix prospects in the world.

"The Silver Shadow" turned out to be a wonderful horse too. I sold him as a young horse to trainer Paul Valliere. He ended up in the Grand Prixs with Buddy Brown and was fabulous. However, "The Silver Baron" turned out to be a phenomenon. This is his story.

When The Silver Baron arrived in America, I wanted him to settle in at the farm and regain his condition. He needed weight and muscle, all of which he would develop under a steady, patient and caring program at my place. After about a month, I began to ride and train him lightly. I don't believe in doing too much with three-year olds, as they are so immature physically and mentally. I like to put a solid foundation of the basics on them and then allow them to grow into four-year olds. I find that four years of age is an excellent time to begin the horse's more serious education. The Silver Baron was wonderful at home, so I decided to take him to a horse show at Commonwealth Park in Culpeper, Virginia when he was a four-year-old. I showed him in the Hopeful Baby Jumpers, which is a wonderful division to introduce youngsters to jumper courses.

The Silver Baron marched around those courses like a made horse and jumped in exquisite style. It would not be long until we began inching our way up the divisions to the schooling jumpers and then to the Preliminary Jumper Division.

Once The Silver Baron was jumping around the Low Preliminary Division with ease and his usual extraordinary confidence, I moved him into the High Preliminary Division.

The Silver Baron as a four-year-old

The Silver Baron had gained admirers right from the start of his career in America because he was a phenomenal jumper and rode so softly and beautifully. Plus The Silver Baron had turned into a beautiful horse. When he began jumping the bigger jumps in the High Preliminary, people really took notice. I had a tremendous amount of interest in him, but I had syndicated him at this point and really wanted to bring him along. In addition, I was using The Silver Baron as a breeding stallion and he was producing absolutely gorgeous foals.

One point of interest here is that the gentlemen from the German Oldenburg Registry flew over once a year to inspect and paper foals in America.

These were the same gentleman who had turned The Silver Baron down as breeding stallion when he was a three-year-old in Germany. But a lot had changed since then.

When these gentlemen saw The Silver Baron and how beautifully he had developed, they were extremely impressed with him. Then I showed them videos of The Silver Baron competing at the shows with his exquisite, light, lofty, smooth style, and they were completely taken back.

They were also beside themselves when they saw his beautiful foals. From that point on, The Silver Baron had a score of ten, which is the highest mark, in every single category with the exception of a somewhat lower score for his narrow chest. The Silver Baron was now an Approved Premium Stallion in the Registry. All of his foals won Premium Foal Awards as well.

People came to watch The Silver Baron whenever he walked in the ring. By this point I had turned down a lot of money for him, but I was planning on re-syndicating him for $1,200,000. David Broome had even flown over to see The Silver Baron as a four-year-old and had offered me a tremendous amount of money, but I knew this was a once in a lifetime kind of horse.

After The Silver Baron was very solid and confident in the High Preliminary Division, I eased him into the Intermediate Division – just one step below the big Open Division.

One show after another, The Silver Baron just kept getting better and better. Regardless of their size, he was handling the courses with sensational style, scope, ease and courage – all while riding as softly and smoothly as ever. He was now recognized as one of the top young Grand Prix prospects in the world.

Our next show was the prestigious Southampton Horse Show in New York. Mike Cohen came along, as he always loved that show. The most extraordinary part of the Southampton Show is riding in the big grass Grand Prix field. It is beautifully maintained all year just for this event. The grass field was surrounded with spectator tents for the very wealthy and the VIPs. There was a bar and wonderful food available to all of those who purchased an exorbitantly expensive table within the tent. People came very well turned out.

The Silver Baron and Jessamy competing in Farmington, Conn

The Southampton Horse Show was a huge and festive social event in New York. One could expect to see celebrities and dignitaries, as well as powerful business people. If you won at Southampton, you were immediately recognized as having done something very special. There was a tremendous amount of prestige involved with winning at the Southampton Horse Show.

Mike and I both wanted to show in the Grand Prix field, as that was the place to be. We carefully planned our week with the culmination being the Sallie Hansen Open Jumper Gambler's Choice.

This was a big stake class with really large and impressive jumps. Each jump was numbered according to the degree of difficulty which it poised for the horse and rider. Each jump could be jumped in either direction, but could only be jumped twice. If a jump was knocked down, no score was awarded for that effort. The feat was to cleanly jump as many high numbered jumps as possible within a minute.

The horse and rider with the highest score were the winners. Riders and trainers huddled together to figure out the best course for them to gain the most points. These were mostly very experienced horses and riders, so this was not going to be an easy class.

The Silver Baron and Jessamy at Raleigh, NC Show

The Silver Baron and Jessamy showing in Palm Beach

Mike and I figured out the course which we felt would suit us the best in order to jump all the high numbered jumps. This involved some roll back turns and galloping between the jumps.

We then went to the schooling area to get our horse warmed up and ready. The Silver Baron didn't need much to get ready. We jumped a few jumps until he was feeling really comfortable and confident. Then we went to the ring.

When The Silver Baron and I walked through the in-gate and onto the expansive grass Grand Prix field, The Silver Baron acted like he owned it. After walking a short twenty second tour, The Silver Baron and I began our course according to plan. Our plan was to jump all of the highest point jumps twice and we had worked out a way to do just that.

The Silver Baron ballooned over the jumps with ease and then would roll back and jump the obstacle again in breathtaking style. At the end of the course there was a very big Joker fence - over six feet high and made of huge cylindrical poles. This fence was optional. If you jumped it cleanly, you gained two hundred more points. If you knocked it down, you would lose two hundred points from your score.

I let The Silver Baron catch his breath for a moment and gave him a big pat. I then picked up his beautifully smooth canter and headed down to this imposing jump. The Silver Baron jumped it with loft, style and a good foot to spare. It was as though he was saying, "Is this all that you've got for me today?" It was a stunningly beautiful showing. When The Silver Baron and I galloped through the timers, we were the winners of the Sally Hansen Gambler's Choice Stake.

I was so proud of my young stallion and praised him effusively all the way out of the gate. He was quite proud of himself as well and walked out of the ring like he was the Boss. People swarmed around to congratulate us and Mike was so happy that he lost his Tareyton again.

After several carrots and the Awards Ceremony, The Silver Baron went back to the stables for a nice Vetrolin bath.

And so, a Superstar was now recognized. The Silver Baron had beat some very expensive horses with significantly more experience than he had, but he was as cool about it as ever. This stallion was an absolute Class Act in every possible way and everyone knew it by this time. The Silver Baron was "The Young Horse to watch".

**The Silver Baron and Jessamy winning
The Sally Hansen Gambler's Choice at Southampton**

THE SILVER BARON'S EXCEPTIONALOFFSPRING

IF YOU WANT THE BEST, BREED TO THE BEST

FOR WINNING HUNTERS, JUMPERS AND DRESSAGE HORSES

FOUR EXTRAORDINARY GRAY STALLIONS BY THE SILVER BARON

LEADING MONEY WINNING SIRE AT INTERNATIONAL JUMPER FUTURITY (IJF) FOR THREE CONSECUTIVE YEARS.

SHAREEF
OUT OF WINNING GRAND PRIX
MARE "MATADORA"
WINNER OF THE IJF
FIVE/SIX YEAR OLD STAKE
GOLD CUP - DEVON, PA. 1995

SAMBUCCA
OUT OF "BLACK GOLD"
A FULL SISTER TO
"ALL THE GOLD"
TOP PLACINGS AT THE IJF

THE SILVER BARON
FROM THE PROMINENT
DOMSPATZ-FURIOSO II LINE
WORLD CLASS GRAND PRIX
HORSE AND SIRE

THE SILVER CARD
OUT OF "GOLD CARD"
(WHO IS BY "ALL THE GOLD")
IJF 4 YEAR OLD RES. CHAMPION
GOLD CUP - DEVON, PA 1994

THE SILVER FROST
OUT OF "FROSTY MORN"
(WHO IS BY "OMMEN")
TOP PLACINGS AT THE IJF

THESE SIRES HAVE PRODUCED SEVERAL PREMIUM FOALS
WONDERFUL MOVERS - PHENOMENAL JUMPERS - BEAUTIFUL TYPES
EXCEPTIONAL DISPOSITIONS AND BLOODLINES
SEMEN SHIPPED NATIONWIDE

MISS JESSAMY ROUSON

SHOWSTOCK ASSOCIATES
BOX 81
KESWICK, VA 22947
804-979-0898

PERHAPS AMERICA'S FINEST AND MOST CONSISTENT SELECTION OF
QUALITY HORSES

SHAREEF AND CAPTIVA

The Silver Baron produced some phenomenal offspring. I had two embryo transplant babies by The Silver Baron, out of the great mare Matadora. There was a 17-hand gray stallion named "Shareef" and a 16.3 hand chestnut mare named "Captiva". Both of these horses dominated the International Jumper Futurity. (IJF), as four, five and six year olds. The IJF was held in Devon, Pennsylvania during the prestigious Devon Horse Show.

Shareef was Reserve Champion at the IJF as a four-year-old. He was Reserve Champion to his full sister Captiva as a five-year-old and he was Champion at the IJF as a six-year-old. Captiva was right behind him as the Reserve Champion six-year-old, followed by Sambucca. The Silver Baron's offspring had won the top three placings in the International Jumper Futurity.

Shareef and Captiva were winners all the way up the divisions and became very successful Grand Prix horses. Shareef was a very kind horse and an excellent breeding stallion as well, who produced some exceptional offspring of his own.

I sold Shareef to a foreign client who was a student of George Morris. He did quite well with Shareef also.

Shareef and Jessamy - Champion six-year-old at the International Jumper Futurity

IF YOU WANT THE BEST, BREED TO THE BEST
FOR WINNING HUNTERS, JUMPERS AND DRESSAGE HORSES
SHAREEF

OUTSTANDING 17 H. GRAY OLDENBURG STALLION BY THE SILVER BARON—LEADING MONEY WINNING SIRE—INTERNATIONAL JUMPER FUTURITY (IJF) (HELD AT THE GOLD CUP, DEVON, PA), FOR THREE CONSECUTIVE YEARS. SHAREEF IS OUT OF WINNING GRAND PRIX MARE MATADORA AND OFFERS THE PROVEN BLOODLINES OF DOMSPATZ, FURIOSO II, GRAPHIT, SAN FERNANDO, THE SILVER BARON AND MATADORA.

PHENOMENAL JUMPER

WONDERFUL MOVER

BEAUTIFUL TYPE

EXCEPTIONAL DISPOSITION AND BLOODLINES

CHAMPION 1995 IJF
FIVE/SIX-YR.-OLD

WINNER 1995 IJF
FIVE/SIX-YR.-OLD
STAKES CLASS

RES. CHAMPION 1993 IJF
FOUR-YR.-OLD

SEMEN SHIPPED NATIONWIDE

STANDING WITH:
MISS JESSAMY ROUSON
SHOWSTOCK STABLES, LTD.
KESWICK, VIRGINIA
804-979-0898

OWNED BY
GOLDENSONG FARM, INC.
AND
SHOWSTOCK ASSOCIATES

PERHAPS AMERICA'S FINEST AND MOST CONSISTENT SELECTION OF QUALITY HORSES

Captiva and Jessamy - Champion Five-Year-Old at the International Jumper Futurity

Captiva was Shareef's full sister - an embryo transplant foal by The Silver Baron, out the great Matadora. Captiva was Champion five-year-old at the IJF, followed by her brother Shareef as Reserve Champion.

Shareef was Champion six-year-old at the IJF and Captiva was the Reserve Champion six-year-old. Both Shareef and Captiva were very kind horses with a tremendous amount of ability. Captiva followed Shareef into the Grand Prix ring and became a winner herself.

I sold Captiva to a client in North Carolina of top rider and trainer, Aaron Vale. She went on and did extremely well for them as well.

As a point of interest, I would like to thank my good friend Mary Donner for showing up at the International Jumper Futurity and saving my tail when I found my one groom face down in the dirt, stone cold drunk first thing in the morning. I called Mary and she showed up to help me immediately. I was at the Futurity with a truckload of stallions and two mares. Only a superwoman like Mary Donner could have held that situation together and allowed me to go on and be Champion and Reserve. So thank you and God Bless you Mary for saving the day.

Also of interest is the fact that Mary Donner now owns the old Lotus Farm in Spring Valley, NY. This is where I went to ride for Mike Cohen when I was fourteen years old. She has done a beautiful job with the place and it is absolutely charming. Mary calls her beautiful farm Springvale Farm. Mary is an excellent horsewoman and a dear friend.

Whenever I visit Mary, I stay in my old room where I lived when I was fourteen years old. Lots of memories on that farm.

THE SILVER CARD

The Silver Card and Jessamy competing at Raleigh,

"The Silver Card" was a 16.2 hand gray stallion by The Silver Baron and out of "Gold Card", who was by "All the Gold". He was a fabulous mover and jumper as well. The Silver Card was a winner at the International Jumper Futurity and then went on to be a winner in the Grand Prix division. The Silver Card was also an approved stallion with the Oldenburg Registry and produced several lovely premium foals. They all went on to make a name for themselves.

As I mentioned, The Silver Card was a big winner at the International Jumper Futurity. I have a little story about this angel which I feel I should share. The award presentations for the Jumper Futurity were to be given the following day with much fanfare - just before the Gold Cup. My boyfriend at the time suggested that I lead my gray mare Shabu into the famed ring at Devon for the award ceremony. He was concerned about me leading a stallion in there alone. I insisted that I wanted everyone to see The Silver Card, as I was promoting him as a breeding stallion. I also wanted to get a win photo of him for the Chronicle of the Horse, a widely read equine magazine, also to promote him as a breeding stallion. Then my boyfriend said that maybe he or my groom Nacho should come with me into the arena and lead the stallion. I assured him that I would be fine.

The day of the awards ceremony, I was nicely dressed in a pants suit with a little jewelry and a touch of make-up, just trying to look nice for the win photo in front of 20,000 people. It was muddy that day, so I had to wear paddock boots which I had shined the night before.

My turn came and I proudly led The Silver Card to the end of the arena where several important and dignified people were standing to present the awards. The Silver Card was immaculate for this event. I felt as though I looked pretty good too, with the pants suit, a little make up, a little jewelry and my hair clean and fluffed.

When I got to the presentation site, the photographer asked me to walk up a step so that he may take a better photo of the ceremony. I then made a huge mistake. I turned my back to the stallion in order to lead him up a step. This did not end well. As soon as I turned my back to The Silver Card, he stood straight up on his hind legs and slapped his front hooves on my shoulders, as though he was trying to mount me. I fell face down in the mud – fancy pants suit and all – in front of 20,000 people. How embarrassing was this scenario? I got up a tad shaken and said to the dignitaries, "Well, I guess he liked my perfume."

Now the stallion was loose in the arena and all of these dignified people were scared to death of him. They were completely horrified and no one would catch him, so my loyal groom Nacho walked into the grand Devon arena at the Gold Cup and promptly removed the problem.

Covered in mud, I had to walk out of that damn arena with my award in front of the huge crowd. No win photo that day.

I hate to admit it, but my boyfriend was right. I should have led Shabu into the ring for the awards ceremony. No one would have known the difference and I would have had a nice day. Big lesson of the day – never turn your back to a stallion.

Having learned this lesson the hard way, it turned out that I had another lesson to learn with this stallion. I was at the big horse center at the Lexington Horse Show in Virginia. I had just had a good class in the coliseum on The Silver Card and it was time for the awards ceremony.

I had learned my lesson and decided to ride The Silver Card into the coliseum for the award. I was sitting on The Silver Card at the entrance to the ring, when he suddenly stood straight up on his hind legs and wrapped his forelimbs around a tall pillar at the in-gate. He was trying to mount the pillar. When I tried to pull him off to the side, he whacked me in the face with his head. This momentarily knocked me out, so I tumbled off from way up high.

I hit the ground really hard and broke my collar bone. Once again, The Silver Card was loose and scaring the hell out of everyone. My boyfriend ran in the ring to catch him and ran right over the top of me. What a day.

The pain was terrible and stayed that way for the next several weeks. There is really nothing one can do for a broken collar bone except take pain pills and give it time to heal. After this event, I decided that it was much easier to win on The Silver Card than to lead or ride him into an awards ceremony. That was the end of The Silver Card going into the ring for any award presentations.

I'd show The Silver Card and when he was done, Nacho took him immediately back to the barn. I'd pick up my damn ribbon riding a civilized gray horse, or sometimes no horse at all. He wasn't going to fool me again.

I sold The Silver Card to some wonderful clients in Pennsylvania - Mr. and Mrs. Dan White. They also did extremely well with him and kept him until his passing. They always said what a sweet stallion he was, so it must have been my breeding operation that made him behave that way – or perhaps he really did like my perfume.

All I know is that it's really difficult to breed and show a stallion at the same time. The only stallions I have ever had who handled that really well were All The Gold and The Silver Prince. They were two of those rare saintly stallions. The Silver Baron and his offspring were stallion through and through and did not let anyone forget that they were all Man.

SAMBUCCA

Sambucca was a gorgeous 16.2 hand steel gray stallion by the "The Silver Baron", out of a full sister to "All The Gold" named "Black Gold". I had purchased Black Gold from Paul Schockemohle in Germany when she was a yearling, as I was already having success with All The Gold.

Sambucca did very well at the IJF and placed just behind Shareef and Captiva. He went on to jump the bigger classes quite successfully. I sold him to Mr. and Mrs. Gorman for their daughter Laura. They had great success with him as well in the mid-west and across the country.

THE SILVER FROST

"The Silver Frost" was by the "The Silver Baron" out of a mare named "Frosty Morn", who was by the Dutch Grand Prix stallion "Ommen". The Silver Frost was an extraordinary jumper who jumped in exquisite form and was exceptionally kind and quiet. He was extra careful – perhaps to a fault. Due to The Silver Frost's over careful nature, he was not moving up the jumper divisions as quickly and confidently as his siblings. I questioned if he would have the heart to jump the biggest of the big and I decided that this horse's forte was jumping in extravagant style around four-foot jumps. In other words, I made The Silver Frost a hunter and a winning one at that. I sold The Silver Frost to some lovely people who continued with great success in the hunter ring. I did have a couple of offspring by The Silver Frost which were fabulous as well.

SOMETHING SPECIAL

FROM A GREEN COLT IN HOLLAND TO WINNING SHOW HUNTER IN AMERICA

Something Special showing in Palm Beach with Scott Hofstetter

On one of my many trips to Europe, I saw a bay three-year-old Dutch stallion who I liked very much. He needed some weight and condition, but he was a lovely horse and a beautiful mover and jumper. Best of all, this young stallion was graced with the most wonderful mind. He was a total gentleman at all times and was quiet, brave, cool and unflappable.

When I purchased him, I believed he would turn into a very fancy show hunter. I named him "Something Special". After some training and conditioning at home, I started Something Special in the pre-green hunter division as a four-year-old. I won a great deal with him at the Virginia shows and he was usually Champion. As a five-year-old, it was now time to take Something Special to the winter circuit in Palm Beach, Florida.

As I had so many horses to ride, I gave the ride on Something Special to my friend Scott Hofstetter. Scott had been riding a few horses for me and always did a fabulous job – plus he was the nicest guy to work with. Scott loved Something Special and did a terrific job with him as well, winning up a storm. Something Special was admired by many and the time came when one of his admirers stepped up and purchased him.

Something Special went on to be a winning Amateur Hunter for his new owner and was dearly loved. That is what one hopes for when selling horses. I always tried to make sure that the horses were sold to people who would love and care for them. Something Special had a stellar career in the hunter ring and was adored.

LIONNE D'AIR

A VERY SCOPEY, BUT VERY STRONG WESTPHALIAN MARE

Lionne D'Air and Jessamy competing at Southampton, New York

On one of my trips to Germany, I went to Paul Schockemohle's place and saw a very rangy 17 hand, attractive and athletic bay Westphalian mare who showed a tremendous amount of scope and quality in his indoor arena. She was extremely careful – almost to a fault.

This was a very strong mare and clearly not a ride for just anyone. I watched her jump and was impressed with her scope. Paul had said that she did not have a great deal of experience, but she certainly appeared to have the scope needed for the Grand Prix ring. I rode her and got along with her very well. Paul was thrilled.

I named this mare "Lionne D'Air", which is French for "Lion of the Air". I thought it was a fitting name given the intricacy and power of her way of going. Lionne D'Air was a mare who was really strong and really spooky at the same time – an extremely difficult combination. I don't believe that this mare was one of the smartest horses I have ever come across.

If a horse is naturally strong in the bridle, one focuses on holding them together and in as neat a package as possible. However if a horse is spooky, the rider needs to continually be riding them up into the bridle and forward towards the jump to give them the necessary encouragement and confidence.

Lionne D'Air would hold herself off of the jumps, because she was so careful and spooky. At the same time, she was unbelievably strong and pulling the rider to the jump as hard as she could. I realize that this sounds like a contradiction of terms, but that's what she did. Lionne D'Air would pull to the jumps as hard as she could, while spooking and hawking the jumps the entire time. As I've already stated, this mare was not the brightest bulb in the room.

Lionne D'Air had as tough a mouth as I have ever encountered and was one of the most difficult rides of my career - if not the most difficult. That is saying a lot.

I started her in the schooling jumper classes to build her confidence, but even as she became relatively brave in those classes and was moving up the divisions, I always entered a schooling jumper class in the morning to thaw her out and keep her confidence level up. That was a daily chore with this mare.

I tried endless different bits on this mare and never really found a perfect match. Lionne D'Air would just run through the sharper bits and cut her mouth, so they were no good. A gag bit, as shown above, worked fairly well for a while. I often used an elevator bit on her as well and alternated between those two bridles.

Lionne D'Air and Jessamy competing

Then I became even more creative and added fuzzy Velcro attachments to the side of Lionne D'Air's bridle, so that the bit wouldn't rub her jaw and so she could not see behind herself and spook – just as racehorse trainers often use blinkers. I used a drop noseband because when she pulled like a train, she would open her mouth as wide as possible and resist. Lionne D'Air was a very sweet horse on the ground, but an extremely tough lady to ride on course.

Lionne D'Air definitely kept me thinking. The tack shops loved me because I was always in there buying something new to try on this unbelievably strong mare. I'm quite strong and have ridden countless stallions and other tough horses, but this mare's strength in the bridle made those horses seem like lead ponies.

**Lionne D'Air and Jessamy competing
Southampton, New York Horse Show**

Despite the difficulty of riding Lionne D'Air, we won quite a bit as we moved up the divisions and into the Grand Prix ring. She was a competitive horse because she had tremendous scope and was extremely careful and fast. The jump offs suited Lionne D'Air well because she had already been around the course once and had become comfortable with the jumps. A strong, fast ride around a shorter course was not a problem for her. Hence we were often very well placed in some big classes at very prominent American shows.

That said, the American riders were wary of the strong ride that Lionne D'Air required. This made it extremely difficult to sell her in America, so I began to make plans to fly and show a plane load of horses in Europe. The European riders, particularly the German riders, would appreciate this mare's talent – plus the good ones were strong enough to ride her. We were Europe bound within a few months.

Lionne D'Air and Jessamy competing in the Grand Prix at Southampton, New York Over the double liverpools

THE TALENTED KEY TO FORTUNE

FROM BAVARIA TO A WINNING GRAND PRIX HORSE

**Key to Fortune and Jessamy competing
South Hampton Horse Show in New York**

Beginning with that first trip to Germany in 1985, I continued to go back to Germany and Europe up to eight times per year looking for good horses. On one of these trips I ventured to Bavaria in the south of Germany. I had heard of a farm there which had several horses and decided to take a look. It was a rather muddy and bleak yard, but it did have an indoor ring and several horses in the stables.

The weather was still miserable, which is why almost every European stable has an indoor ring. I began looking at several horses in the indoor – one after another.

Nothing had really caught my eye until a skinny, rangy black 16.2 hand, seven-year-old mare came into the ring. She was by "Ramiro", a top sire of showjumpers. Her condition was quite rough and she was very green, but I found her interesting. They told me that this mare had a few foals and was now in work to become a showjumper. She was long bodied, decent headed, had a huge stride and a lot of Thoroughbred blood. She looked and moved like a horse which had scope. This was confirmed after a few small jumps and I asked to ride her. I liked what I felt and believed that I could develop this skinny mare into a good horse. Plus she was a very sweet, kind mare. I bought her that day.

Once this mare arrived in America, I began the long process of conditioning and training her at home. She was turning into a very promising mare, so I named her "Key to Fortune". After establishing a solid foundation at home over a few months, I began taking Key to Fortune to the shows. She began in the schooling jumper divisions and was always brave and willing to please. The bigger the jumps got, the better she became. By the time we had worked our way through the preliminary and intermediate divisions, Key to Fortune had become a very competitive horse.

After building a very solid foundation in the lower divisions, I moved Key to Fortune to the open jumper division and eventually into the Grand Prixs.

Key to Fortune had tremendous scope, an excellent jumping style and was quite rideable. The bigger the course, the better she jumped. This now sleek black mare became a consistent ribbon winner in the Grand Prixs and caught the eye of Leslie Burr Lenehan, one of America's top riders.

Key to Fortune and Jessamy competing

Leslie had Mr. and Mrs. Luis de Hechavarria as clients at the time and they were looking for a promising horse for their son Paul. Leslie tried Key to Fortune in the indoor at my farm during the winter and liked her very much. Arrangements were made for Paul to come and have a ride to see how she suited him. Key to Fortune was wonderful for Paul, so the sale was consummated.

Leslie won a great deal on Key to Fortune in Palm Beach the next year. Paul flew in to ride on the weekends and also did extremely well with her. Their success continued beyond Florida and into the regular show season at some of America's biggest shows

Key to Fortune and Jessamy competing in a Grand Prix

Commonwealth Park, Virginia

After a year or so, Leslie called me and told me that Paul de Hechavarria was going to college and needed a lower key horse to take with him. Key to Fortune was an athlete and a competitive horse, but Paul wanted something which would fit into his busy college schedule – a horse which only needed to be ridden whenever Paul had the time. I traded Key to Fortune for an older saint of a horse who could and would do everything that Paul wanted. Everyone was very happy with the trade and I was happy to have Key to Fortune back. I was organizing a trip to Europe to show my horses and was glad that Key to Fortune could be a part of that trip.

**Key to Fortune and Jessamy competing at Farmington,
Before shipping to Germany**

The American dollar had been very strong against the German mark in the mid-eighties, making horse buying not only a joy, but a super deal. However things had changed. The dollar was falling significantly in the later eighties against the mark. It was now time to sell in Europe – not buy. I put together a load of horses and flew them to Germany to show and sell

EUROPE BOUND

Lionne D'Air and Jessamy competing in a Grand Prix before Shipping to Germany

And so it was that I began my plans to stay and show in Germany for the summer with the hope of making a good showing and selling my horses.

I planned to take Lionne D'Air, Key to Fortune, All In Silver and Godiva – a nice selection for the European market. My only companion on the trip was my Great Dane, Tuxedo.

I'm really good friends with the Hofschroer brothers, Hans and Ernst, as they both worked for Paul Schockemohle and I knew them well. Ernst was one of the top sales managers at Paul's farm in Muhlen, Germany. Hans managed Chestnut Lawn Farm in Virginia, which was Paul's quarantine stable as well as his American breeding and training facility. Consequently, I saw both Hofschroer brothers frequently – either Ernst in Germany or Hans in Virginia.

Both Hofschroer brothers were living back in Germany at the time that I shipped the show horses there. I stabled the horses with Ernst at his lovely place. I was also in constant touch with my good friends Hans, his wife Maggie and their wonderful children. During the time that Hans had been in Virginia, we did a lot of business and I sold many horses for him – plus all my imports went to Chestnut Lawn for quarantine. This great friendship continued when Hans went back to his place in Germany. Hans would ship me horses from Europe to sell in America, which worked out exceptionally well for both of us.

Once the horses settled in nicely at Ernst's place and were back in work, we made plans to show at a big National show in Drestedt. As an American guest I was allowed to bring two horses to the show. I took Lionne d'Air and All In Silver. I was second with Lionne d'Air in a big class there and caught the attention of rider Rene Tebbel.

Rene is a top German rider who was short listed for the German Team World Championships in Stockholm at the time. Rene felt this may be a promising horse for him, so he asked if he may ride her in a class. I told Rene that she was strong for me, but of course I was just a girl. Surely with a man like him, the mare would do extremely well. Renee rode Lionne d'Air very well and bought her shortly after. However, Hans and Ernst told me that the "I'm just a girl" line was not going to work anymore – not in Germany anyway. Everyone got to know how strong and tough that mare was to ride, and gave me credit for riding her well.

At this same show, I rode All In Silver in a big night class which had sixty-eight top horses and riders entered. This was a big course which ended with a choice of jumping either a very high vertical called a "Joker" fence for extra points, or jumping a somewhat lower fence. All In Silver was truly phenomenal under the lights and was jumping out of his skin. Although he was only seven years old at the time, he jumped the tall Joker fence with style, ease and confidence. The crowd adored him and the horsemen paid attention.

All In Silver and I ended up second to Dirk Hafemeister, riding the German Olympic horse "The Freak". Dirk is a German rider and an Olympic champion. Dirk had won a gold medal in the show jumping with the West German team at the 1988 Summer Olympics in Seoul, riding the wonderful mare, "Orchidee." (Ludgar Beerbaum had ridden "The Freak" to win the team gold medal at the Seoul Olympics in 1988. Both The Freak and Orchidee came from Paul Schockemohle).

The most memorable part of that fabulous evening was when they played the American National Anthem for me during the award presentations. I was so moved I had to fight back tears. I was missing America.

I was extremely proud of All In Silver and received many accolades from the adoring crowd. He had beaten so many top horses – older horses which had much more international experience than he had at that point. All In Silver was extremely impressive and people took notice. I signed a bunch of autographs after the class. It was a wonderful, fun night.

I showed All In Silver very successfully at the Wiesbaden and Hamburg shows as well. He generated many fans and there were multiple interested parties. Ernst had contacted a big owner and sponsor of showjumpers in Italy named Mr. Gianpaolo Rolli. Ernst told him that there were some horses he needed to come and see in Germany.

Mr. Rolli came to Ernest's place with his rider and tried All In Silver and Key to Fortune. He bought them both that day.

Once I returned to America, I sent Mr. Rolli a video of a Thoroughbred jumper named "Voo Doo". This horse was owned by my good friend Olin Armstrong, the fabulous rider from Virginia. I told Mr. Rolli that this was a very talented horse, but also an extremely difficult horse to ride and manage as the horse had multiple quirks.

I advised Mr. Rolli that he really should come and see the horse himself, but as Mr. Rolli was afraid of flying, he wanted to buy Voo Doo solely off of the video.

I then suggested that Mr. Rolli speak with Olin Armstrong so that he could understand this horse's peculiar idiosyncrasies and know everything that he needed to know about the horse. That phone call did not go well at all, which was actually pretty funny. Apparently Olin was unable to understand Mr. Rolli's thick Italian accent and Mr. Rolli was unable to understand Olin's southern Virginian accent – despite the fact that they were both speaking English. Olin and Mr. Rolli both called me and asked me to handle the entire deal as it was impossible for them to understand each other. And so, Mr. Rolli purchased Voo Doo and this complicated Thoroughbred horse found himself on a plane to Italy. It all worked out well in the end.

These were not the only horses I sold in Germany. As previously stated, I also sold Paul Schockemohle my Thoroughbred Grand Prix horse "The Officer". I sold Godiva to a good German rider there as well, who bought her off of Ernst's farm.

CONGRATULATIONS

GIANPAOLO ROLLI
OF ITALY
ON THE PURCHASE OF
ALL IN SILVER
17.0 H. GREY HOLSTEINER GELDING

TRAINER
ERNST HOFSCHROER
AND RIDER
RENE TEBBEL
SHORT LISTED FOR GERMAN TEAM
WORLD CHAMPIONSHIPS
IN STOCKHOLM
ON THE PURCHASE OF
LIONNE D'AIR
17.0 H. BAY WESTPHALIAN MARE

WINNING GRAND PRIX HORSES AND PROSPECTS

MISS JESSAMY ROUSON

**SHOWSTOCK ASSOCIATES
SYNDICATES
CISMONT, VIRGINIA
804-979-0898**

HORSES OF QUALITY FOR THE DISCRIMINATING BUYER

The Officer and Jessamy in a Grand Prix, shortly before I sold him to Paul Schockemohle in Germany

TUXEDO
MY INTERNATIONALLY LOVED MASCOT

Tuxedo as a puppy

I need to mention again that my number one partner and best friend throughout the entire European business venture was my beloved Great Dane puppy "Tuxedo".

I had gotten Tuxedo as a small eight-week-old puppy in Palm Beach, shortly before we went to Germany. He slept snuggled next to me every single night at the Palm Beach Polo and Country Club. He also followed me all day at the horse show. I never needed a leash for Tuxedo, except for the one-time Tuxedo marched across the busy main hunter ring on his way to the food stand. He had decided he was hungry and needed to take the shortest route to the food. Very understandable. However I did get my ear chewed off by the announcer and horse show management. They couldn't stay angry for too long though, because everyone loved Tuxedo.

Tuxedo flew to Germany with the horses once I had made the decision to show and hopefully sell in Europe. Tuxedo grew quite a bit throughout our stay in Germany. While we were there, Tuxedo had to learn how to climb the stairs in the little country inns where we stayed. This took a great deal of time and patience, but once Tuxedo had figured it out, he'd go up and down stairs for fun. He was so proud of himself. Tuxedo was always by my side. He even slept with me in our little twin bed in the German Inns. This did get me kicked out of a few hotels, but it was not a matter which was up for debate. Tuxedo stayed with me always.

One truly wonderful thing about Germany was that Tuxedo was allowed in all of the restaurants and food courts. People would fawn over him and feed him constantly. Even the Inn owners would feed Tuxedo wonderful food early in the morning before we went to the shows, as well as in the evening when we came back to the Inn. I never had to buy Tuxedo food while we were in Germany, because all of my new German friends fed him all day long. If Tuxedo was off his leash at a horse show, he knew exactly which food stands he wanted to visit. He knew which ones had the best sausages and which vendors would pamper him the most. Tuxedo was a huge celebrity in Germany. He was adored, loved and spoiled to no end. Tuxedo could not have been happier.

Ever since Tuxedo was a little puppy, he carried around his Teddy Bear which I had given him for comfort when he was a tiny baby. Tuxedo also slept with his Teddy Bear every night. All three of us were in the twin bed in the German Inns.

Tuxedo with his Teddy Bear

Tuxedo never outgrew his Teddy Bear or sleeping with me on the bed. We slept really well, although all the rich food Tuxedo had eaten during the day did cause me to get up and have some middle of the night walks with him. I was wondering where all of his fans were at three o'clock in the morning.

These small, cozy German Inns always had a little bistro type restaurant and a bar. I was expected to show up with Tuxedo after the show for a drink at the bar with all of his fans - then again during our dinnertime after I had tidied up. Tuxedo not only received free dinners for himself, he usually managed to find sponsors for my drinks and meals as well. Everyone who saw Tuxedo wanted to be near him and they would do whatever that took - including paying my restaurant tab.

Tuxedo - the Majestic Dog who was loved by all

At the German horse shows, the wealthy women went absolutely crazy over Tuxedo. When we arrived at the show each morning, there would always be a gathering of wealthy women who were horse owners. They all wanted to walk the beautiful, handsome Tuxedo around the showgrounds. This sometimes ended up in petty spats amongst these women.

They would squabble over who was going to walk Tuxedo around the show while I was competing. I attempted to ration the Tuxedo walking duties fairly in an effort to make everyone happy and keep the peace amongst these classy ladies. It was a tough job, but every loving fan got to spend some time with Tuxedo. He was quite proud of himself over all of this adoration.

Mrs. Hafemeister, Dirk's mom, usually won the battle. This determined and classy German lady came to the show extra early each morning. She would wait for me to arrive in my little rental car with Tuxedo perched up in the back seat. She immediately jumped up, took him out of the car and began pampering him.

Mrs. Hafemeister took Tuxedo to every food and sausage stand at the horse show and occasionally would allow the other women to walk with him a little bit. She became Tuxedo's official horse show manager while he was in Germany.

Even the vendors loved Tuxedo. They didn't want money for Tuxedo's food – they just wanted to be the vendor who had the food that Tuxedo enjoyed the most. This was a big selling point and wise marketing strategy. Tuxedo was a huge celebrity and was loved and followed daily by his fans. He really needed a stage handler, which is why I chose Mrs. Hafemeister for the job. She was always there when we arrived at the show and she was always back with Tuxedo when I was ready to leave for the Inn. Such a wonderful lady. Tuxedo and I adored her.

When I adopted Tuxedo as a puppy, I adopted his Dad as well. He was a beautiful older Boston Great Dane named Badger and the sweetest, gentlest and most loving dog imaginable.

Badger and Tuxedo could be trusted with a baby bird or an infant child – they were that kind. Badger lived out his life very happily in my house and on my farm, sleeping on my bed with Tuxedo at night. Badger had his own couch in the office during the daytime. He passed away at fourteen years old, which is quite old for a Great Dane. I miss Badger and Tuxedo to this day.

I had several Great Danes over the years – actually up to twelve at one time. They were all exceptionally spoiled and lived in my house. I had to break down and buy a California King sized bed in order to accommodate everyone.

Badger offering a handshake

I think it is important to give an honorable mention to the one Great Dane who started me on the Great Dane love affair, which dated back to 1980. He was a black Great Dane named "Walter". I got Walter when he was barely eight weeks old. He slept in the bed with me and went absolutely everywhere that I went – including California and all of the horse shows across the country. Walter had a huge fan club and never needed a leash at the shows. He stayed by my side constantly.

Walter waiting patiently for me, outside of the Ladies Room at the Upperville Horse Show

THE SILVER PRINCE

THREE-YEAR-OLD IN GERMANY TO

THE TOP CONFORMATION STALLION IN THE COUNTRY

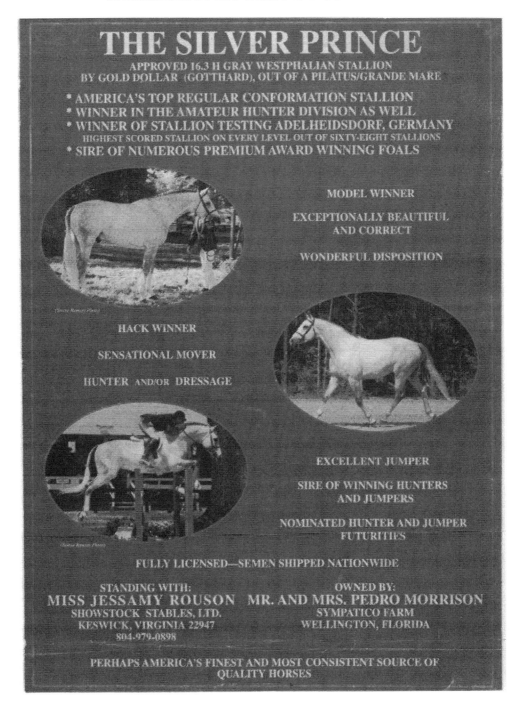

While I was on a buying trip in Germany, I had been told about a nice 16.3 hand, three-year-old gray stallion. This young stallion had just won the stallion testing at Adelheidsdorf, Germany by beating many top stallions. He was by "Gold Dollar", who was by the highly successful and renowned sire, "Gotthard". His dam was of the fine "Pilatus" and "Grande" bloodlines. I said that I would like to see this young stallion, so I contacted the woman who owned him. It was already quite late, but she insisted that I come and see the horse that very evening.

It was probably midnight by the time we arrived at the small, rundown farm. It was in the middle of nowhere and surrounded by cow fields. The woman who owned this stallion turned out to be quite a character. She was a disheveled lady who had obviously been hitting the bottle with conviction long before our arrival. Her hair was ruffled and flying around wildly. She looked as though it had been a very long day for her – or perhaps a long life.

Her husband was completely passed out in a drunken stupor on a pile of hay. She led the stallion out with a short rope shank and into the indoor ring. She apparently had no help whatsoever.

As it was clear that she would be unable to jog the horse, I asked her if I may watch the horse move freely while loose in the indoor. She unhooked the shank and sat down next to her husband. Then she immediately began swigging on a flask from her jacket pocket. This was clearly going to be the extent of her showmanship at this late hour. The stallion and I were on our own.

While the owners drank, I watched this horse and could see that this three-year-old stallion was a truly lovely individual. He was a gorgeous horse with virtually perfect conformation. He looked like a true model horse and it was very easy to fall in love with him. This stallion had the sweetest, kindest, gentlest disposition one could possibly ask for - a real pet.

When his owner turned him loose, he was a sensationally beautiful mover and carried himself in a perfect hunter frame. He had "winning conformation hunter" written all over him. I asked this woman what she wanted for her three-year-old stallion and she drunkenly stated an extraordinarily exorbitant price. Given her inebriated state, I didn't think this was the time to negotiate. I asked if I may come back and see the horse in the morning. Arrangements were made and I got a room at the closest local Inn.

The next morning, I went back to the farm and asked if I may see the stallion ridden. The woman said that she did not have a rider, but that I may ride him if I would like. She said that he had not been ridden since the stallion testing several weeks ago. Having no idea what to expect, I tacked the horse up with my saddle and a bridle with a soft rubber bit. I led this kind three-year-old stallion to the indoor and hopped on – ready for whatever may happen on a fresh, young stallion. To my sheer delight, this colt was absolutely stone quiet and displayed exceptional manners. A true gentleman. He had a big, floaty stride and was a sensational mover. I loved him immediately. I then asked the woman if I may jump him over a small jump. She said that she did not have any jumps on the farm. She did show me a photo of the stallion jumping at the stallion testing which looked good, but I wanted to see for myself.

I again brought up the issue of the price to see if we could negotiate something with which we could both be happy. This crazy lady then proceeded to raise the price substantially even more from the night before. We were talking in the six figures for a three-year-old. This was an old, hard headed German woman who loved the young stallion which she had bred and was obviously not that anxious to sell him. I realized that I needed help in dealing with her if I wanted this horse. I called my dear friend Hans Hofschroer and told him the story.

I told Hans that I was putting him in charge of the deal. I wanted him to go there and make arrangements to watch this horse ridden and jumped over fences, so I may at least have his opinion. I told him that he needed to deal with this crazy woman and establish a realistic price. For this I would gladly pay Hans a commission.

So I flew back to America and left the deal in Han's capable and competent hands. Hans called me a couple of days later and it was clear that this woman was driving him crazy as well. But Hans is a tenacious German horseman and businessman who does not give up. After two weeks of visiting this woman and haggling with her, he called me with the best price that he was able to establish.

The stallion passed the veterinary pre-purchase exam with no problem whatsoever and I sent Hans the money. Hans handled everything. A few weeks later my gorgeous three-year-old Westphalian stallion was in America and on my farm in Virginia. He had received glowing reports of superb behavior from all of his shippers and he arrived as the complete and total gentleman I had seen in Germany. I named my beautiful new stallion "The Silver Prince".

As it was almost the end of the year and The Silver Prince was only a three-year-old, I allowed him to settle in and become acclimated with a few light rides. The Silver Prince was a horse who seemed to be naturally broke and was an exceptionally easy horse to ride and train. The hunter ring was waiting for him.

I called the Legendary Robert (Bobby) Burke and asked him to stand The Silver Prince for me in the model classes at the shows. Bobby was a fabulous horseman and few could show a horse off as well as he did.

**The Silver Prince at Upperville Horse Show
Being handled by the great Robert Burke**

The Silver Prince was so quiet that he did not need any time on the lunge line. However Bobby would show up very early each morning of the show. He was dressed like the dapper gentleman that he was with a starched shirt, tie and jacket, along with perfectly creased slacks. Bobby would then proudly ride The Silver Prince all over the showgrounds, visiting with his many friends. Bobby loved The Silver Prince and the stallion loved Bobby – particularly their morning rides together as everyone doted over both of them. It wasn't long before everyone was calling them the "Two Silver Princes". Bobby looked younger every day that he worked with this horse. It was a joy and an honor to watch the bonding of Bobby and The Silver Prince. Few horses have as handsome, classy or legendary a handler.

I had the outstanding Olin Armstrong ride The Silver Prince in the show ring. Olin is a fabulous and very natural rider who gets along wonderfully with virtually any horse. Olin and The Silver Prince were an especially great team.

I believe that Olin and the stallion enjoyed each other too. Olin would ride The Silver Prince in the classes, but it was always Bobby who jogged him and stood him on the line. No one could have done it any better. I had an outstanding team. I started The Silver Prince out in the First Year Green Conformation Division at the Virginia shows. He was a winner and a Champion right from the start. The Silver Prince almost always won the model and the hack, as well as most of the over fences classes. He was Champion everywhere. It soon became apparent that three-foot six-inch fences presented no challenge for The Silver Prince, so when appropriate he showed in the Working Conformation Hunter Division. Again, he won virtually everything.

From the very beginning, The Silver Prince covered most of my mares as well as a large number of outside mares. This began with the very first breeding season. The Silver Prince's breeding book grew quite rapidly because he was the leading conformation stallion in the country. Using shipped semen, The Silver Prince was able to be bred to numerous mares from coast to coast. Oftentimes he had to be collected two or three times a day to accommodate his book of mares, plus all of my mares. In the breeding shed The Silver Prince was as much of a gentleman as he was in the show ring. The only other stallion who I had which was this quiet and gentle while breeding was "All The Gold".

Just as All the Gold's offspring went on to be big winners, so did the offspring of The Silver Prince. They were all lovely movers and jumpers, plus they were all extraordinarily quiet, brave and unflappable. This meant amateurs could ride them as young horses.

The Silver Prince and Olin Armstrong competing at the Upperville Horse Show

Foals from my stallions
(Gray foals are born chestnut, brown or black)

The Silver Camp

By the Silver Prince, out of French Camp, by San Francisco

The Silver Prince made me a small fortune in stud fees, along with the sale of his wonderful offspring. He was an extremely popular stallion across the entire country.

My friend, the excellent horseman Gene Estep, told some wealthy customers in Wellington, Florida about The Silver Prince. They were extremely interested. Their names were Pedro and Carla Morrison. The Morrison's bought The Silver Prince shortly after and he began a new career in Florida. Carla rode him in the Amateur hunters and did very well. They would occasionally show him in the Conformation Working Hunter division with a professional and The Silver Prince continued his winning ways.

As sad as it was to see The Silver Prince leave, I consoled myself that I had so many sensational babies by him – many of which became extremely famous. I enjoyed raising, training, showing and selling The Silver Prince's offspring for many years afterward.

TWO YEARS OLDS FROM MY BREEDING PROGRAM

VISITING WITH ONE OF MY MARES AND FOALS

I loved the offspring from all of my stallions. It started with "San Francisco" and "The Silver Baron". Then came "All the Gold". Next was "The Silver Prince" and by then I also had all of The Silver Baron's stud colts ready to breed. They were "Shareef", "The Silver Card", "Sambucca" and "The Silver Frost".

The babies were a joy and I handled them with love and kindness from the very start. They were introduced to a halter and taught to lead nicely next to their mothers after just a few days of age. I'd rub on them and get them very happy and comfortable with human contact. Once they were old enough, we trimmed their feet. When they were yearlings, I jumped them in the jump chute and evaluated them just as Paul did with his offspring in Germany. I too had my little books of scores on each baby, with the breeding and full description included.

All of this was very helpful, but no one can teach a foal good manners better than their own mother. Those mares knew how to school their foals and they also knew when it was time to wean them. There are many differing opinions on the proper time to wean a foal, but I always felt that the mare and foal knew best as to when they were ready to wean from each other. I found that when the foal was around six months of age, he or she was ready to explore the world and the mother had much less interest in watching their every move.

I'd watch them and when they appeared to be weaning themselves, I put all the mares in one field and all of the babies in other nearby fields so they could see each other. I always separated the colts from the fillies. I found this to be the least traumatic way of weaning foals. There was no panic or screaming when I weaned my foals, because I always let the mothers tell me when they were ready. By this point the foals had grown baby teeth and had already started eating grass and some grain on their own, so they no longer needed to nurse for their nutrition. In my opinion this is the best way to wean mares and foals with the least amount of trauma, stress and frantic behavior. By six months of age there was none of that. Mothers know best, so I don't believe humans should question their wise judgement. At least I never did.

Teaching a baby about the halter

BOYSIE II

SECOND BIGGEST MONEY WINNER IN EUROPE

Boysie II and Jessamy

All of my career I have discovered young horses and developed them towards their full potential – be it Thoroughbreds, Warmbloods, or even some Quarter horses. I was always looking for that "Diamond in the Rough" horse which I could train, show, promote and eventually sell in order to make a profit and keep my business running. Of course I have always ridden and trained many older horses which had come in to my stable to be sold, but I had personally only purchased young horses to develop towards the show ring. But one can never say never.

In the early 1990's, I was sent a horse named "Boysie II" who had been the second biggest money winner in Europe after the great "Next Milton". Both Boysie and Next Milton were top British horses. Boysie was a sixteen-year-old, 16.2 hand chestnut Hanoverian gelding with a great deal of thoroughbred blood in him. Despite his previous greatness in the show ring, Boysie had gotten into the wrong hands and had turned into a really bad stopper in the triple combinations. He would always stop at C, the third part of the combination, and usually throw his riders into the dirt.

For this behavior Boysie had been beaten unmercifully, which only made his stopping problem and confidence level even worse. In fact, one of Boysie's eyes was horribly scarred from being hit in the eye with a whip. This scar significantly impaired Boysie's vision in that eye, yet he managed to never miss a thing. Somehow Boysie saw and sensed everything.

I rode Boysie when he came in and I really liked what I felt. Despite being sixteen years old, Boysie had tremendous scope and was extremely careful – he did not want to touch the jumps. Boysie jumped as light as a feather and as easily as a deer. In fact Boysie jumped exactly like a deer, never using his head or neck. Boysie's back was flat as a table, just like a deer. He never jumped with a round bascule. Hence Boysie did not take the prettiest of jumping photos, yet he could jump huge courses with the utmost of ease, defying all odds. I had a really good feeling about him despite his unorthodox style, his age and his bad history. Plus Boysie became an exceptionally sweet horse to be around.

I did not jump big jumps and I did not ask Boysie to jump a triple combination. I was well aware of his problems, but I felt that I could turn him around with some time and understanding. Boysie needed an understanding friend and a lot of tender loving care – my specialty. I had recently sold the majority of horses I had been competing, so Boysie would give me a project with which to have some fun. I got off of Boysie, feed him some carrots and headed to the telephone to call his owner.

The owner was a motivated seller and knew that she had an old horse with a major stopping problem, as well as some serious vetting issues. Boysie was a very sound horse, which is a tribute to how tough he was after a lifetime of jumping huge jumps, but his scarred eye would stop any veterinary pre-purchase exam. I made the woman a very low offer and she took it immediately. I was now the proud owner of Boysie with all of his problems and baggage. I would get to work the next day, beginning to make Boysie my friend and gaining his trust. I believed that if I could do that, I could have a happy and winning horse again.

Boysie's problem, which no one seemed to understand, was that he had so much scope, his arc and center of gravity were way past the center of the jump. Hence when Boysie got to the third part of a triple combination, he would be right up against it and was unable to jump out.

The key to Boysie's success would be accomplished by getting his arc back where it belonged, over the center of the jumps, and re-building his confidence. I began with very small gymnastics, so as to build Boysie's confidence. The jumps were barely two foot high. I set up three single rail mini verticals with snug distances between them to encourage Boysie to rock back and jump off his hocks, as opposed to lunging forward at the jump. I then put two rails to form a V on each vertical to help Boysie focus on the middle of the jump and the top rail. I tightened those Vs up as we went along. I also had a rail on the ground between each vertical. This was so that Boysie would have to restrain his arc and be sure to land a tad shallow from his usual style in order not to step on the rail.

This placed his arc and center of gravity in the correct position over the middle of the jump. The rails on the ground and the V rails on the jumps really help a horse get his or her arc over the center of the jump. I always used very generous ground lines on the verticals to encourage a good front end. Each and every time that Boysie went through this little exercise, he received a surplus of praise and fuss after the last jump, as well as several treats. I wore a waist pack filled with cut up carrots, so I was immediately ready with his treat.

It didn't take long for Boysie to enjoy his little exercises, because he received more praise and treats than he had been given his entire life. Soon this was fun for him and he looked forward to our work together. Boysie would nicker whenever I came in the barn or whenever he saw me, which was such a wonderful feeling. We were forming a really close bond and becoming great friends.

I only did a little bit each day, with a couple of days per week designated for solely walking Boysie on the trail with a loose rein so that he could totally relax. As Boysie gained confidence, I'd sneak the jumps up a little establishing his confidence at each level. Boysie was learning how to create his center of gravity over the middle of the jump and was extremely pleased with himself. It was not long before he was happily and comfortably jumping through the verticals beautifully and with great confidence at four foot six inches high. We were ready to go to a show and see what we had.

Boysie was wonderful at the shows in the schooling jumpers and would receive an enormous amount of praise from me after each triple combination. His ears were always up and he was happy and confident, not to mention pretty proud of himself.

I never, ever hit Boysie. Never. Our entire program together was based on forming a bond of confidence and trust through positive reinforcement. Personally I believe that this is how every horse and animal should be trained – using positive reinforcement for each bit of progress along the way. This produces a happy and competitive animal.

As a point of possible interest, it makes me absolutely crazy to watch horses try their hearts out and the riders won't or don't praise them. What the hell is that about? Do these riders think the horses owe them something? The horses owe them nothing. The people owe the horses everything, because the horses do all of these insane things for us out of the generosity of their heart. These riders and trainers need to learn and understand that very important fact.

A horse does not care what you paid for him. They only care about the bond that they form with a person. If someone gave too much money for a horse, that is not the horse's problem – it is their problem. A horse does not set his own price tag. It is all on the humans and their sometimes unfortunate misjudgment and ignorance.

That said, let's get back to Boysie. As Boysie had won too much money to enter the preliminary or intermediate jumper divisions available at that time, I had to find a place to jump bigger jumps without stepping right into the Open Jumper division. So I jumped Boysie around some open speed classes slowly, not even trying to win a ribbon. Those classes enabled Boysie to jump bigger courses, but they seldom had a triple combination. Generally there were only double combinations in the open speed classes.

Once Boysie was jumping the Open Speed happily and with great confidence, I began doing the mini-prix classes with him. Boysie jumped the triple combinations beautifully and confidently in these classes and began becoming a competitive horse again. He was enjoying himself and very happy.

Not only had I fixed the arc and center of gravity problem, but I had gotten Boysie's confidence back. Even more importantly, I had gotten Boysie's heart back.

I picked my shows and classes carefully, but Boysie became very competitive in the big classes. He was second in the Rhode Island Jumping Derby, which was quite a big class with many top horses and riders at the time. Boysie went on and won a lot for me after that in the big division and I showed him until he was twenty years old.

I could have sold Boysie several times, even at his old age, but Boysie and I had made a deal. Boysie would perform for me to the very best of his ability, and I would care for him and love him forever. We both kept our promises and had several joyous years together.

When Boysie finally passed away, I buried him in a place of honor on my farm. I felt as though I had lost my best friend and the reality is that I had – Boysie had been my best friend. I was devastated. I missed Boysie's nicker whenever I walked in the barn and I missed fussing over him every day. We had a special bond which is difficult to duplicate.
This is just another little story about how love, understanding, compassion, proper training techniques and empathy can turn an animal around, no matter how old they are.

Whoever said that you can't teach an old dog new tricks was no part of a trainer and did not belong with animals. You can teach any animal new tricks with positive reinforcement and proper training techniques – regardless of their age.

GLORIOUS TRIP TO RUSSIA

The Intourist Hotel in Moscow

In 1992 I was in Ocala, Florida competing with my horses on the winter show circuit. The hotel where I was staying gave a complimentary copy of USA Today to all of the guests. One particular day there was a bold headline saying $499 TWA round trip airfare to Russia. I thought Wow – that is intriguing. How often does anyone get to see Russia? The Soviet Union had just broken apart. Russia was to be an independent and democratic society led by Mikhail Gorbachev up until 1991, and then by Boris Yeltsin until 1999. The Russian and American relationship was very good at that time, thanks to the friendship between President Ronald Reagan and President Mikhail Gorbachev.

When I returned home to Virginia, I bought two roundtrip airline tickets to Russia. A good friend named David came with me. David is a writer and was the perfect companion for this trip, because he is highly intelligent and curious about new places. I didn't know what to expect in Russia and thought that it would be wise not to go alone. It was a direct flight from Washington D.C. to Moscow. We planned to spend five days in Moscow and five days in St Petersburg, (which was previously called Leningrad.)

The flight was uneventful and took about the same amount of time as it does to fly to Europe. Upon arrival at the Moscow Airport we were met by our guide – a wonderful Russian woman named Maria who spoke flawless English. Maria turned out to be a truly fabulous guide who really knew the history of her country.

We had a driver named Ivan who resembled an old KGB guy straight out of the movies. In fact I think Ivan actually was an old KGB guy. Ivan drove a car which looked as though it was one of the earliest models ever made – like something out of the "Untouchables".

Everything on the trip had to be planned in advance to the day - including our guide and driver. The Russians did not want Americans or Europeans traipsing around their country unattended. We knew this was going to be a different kind of experience because the government was always watching - always.

At that time the concession stands in the airport used an abacus as opposed to a cash register. There were gypsies in the airport begging for coins, along with their small children. All of the cars at the airport were very old, with the exception of the fancy black limos which drove the Russian oligarchs and top government officials around. Things looked fairly bleak, but fascinating.

David and I had our driver Ivan take us to the Intourist Hotel, where we had been told to reserve rooms in advance. The Intourist is right by Red Square and the Kremlin, so we were in the center of everything. The hotel was quite old and the rooms were bare bones minimum – no frills whatsoever. David, who had once worked for the CIA, said that there were cameras in all of the rooms – particularly the ones with foreigners.

Our car with our driver Ivan in Moscow

The hotel had herds of gypsy children outside, all begging for coins from the tourists. The children would come up in groups with no adult in sight. I was told that the parents sent the kids out to beg, as they were cute and more likely to gather donations from the tourists. The Russian people on the street would brush these kids aside and continue walking. I saw one man who was obviously in a hurry, swat the children away with a rolled-up newspaper as though they were a swarm of annoying flies. Of course the tourists were suckers, because the kids were so cute and they all spoke English quite well.

One of the first things I noticed about the Russian people was how well educated they are – at least in the two cities I visited. Many spoke superb English, right down to the numerous street vendors.

The street vendors would come up to us with books about Russia which were written in English and displayed gorgeous photographs. Each major attraction had its own book, so I ended up buying several. These vendors also had copies of famous Russian artifacts, as well as artwork from the local artists – all of which was fascinating. I bought all kinds of souvenirs and the street vendors loved me.

I bought Russian nesting dolls with all of the Russian leaders going back to Lenin, who was the tiny one at the end of the puzzle. I bought statues and artwork on the street by fabulous local artists.

It was truly impressive how much intellect and talent there was in Russia. I loved the people.

Moscow is a very busy, hectic city - quite similar to Manhattan in that way. The buildings in Moscow are very, very old. In America we think a building that is two hundred years old is a very old building, but there were buildings and churches in Moscow which were hundreds and hundreds of years old – several from previous centuries going way back in time.

Maria took us for a walk around Red Square, which included seeing St Basil's Cathedral, the Kremlin, Gum's Department Store, Lenin's tomb and the Tomb of the Unknown Soldier, with its constantly burning flame. St Basil's was built in the 1500's. Given its unique architecture, St Basil's Cathedral is probably the most recognizable of symbols for Russia.

Our driver Ivan, and our guide Maria

As part of Russia's program of state atheism, the church was confiscated from the Russian Orthodox community and has operated as a State Historical Museum since 1928. It is a property of the Russian Federation. Although St Basil's was being restored while we were there, I can say that it is a truly beautiful and unusual cathedral - both inside and out.

We also went on a tour of the Kremlin – at least the 1st floor of the building. I assume the government officials were on the upper floors.

The Kremlin was also a beautiful, old structure and very impressive. We were not allowed to take photos inside, but I have a few shots from Red Square. The Kremlin also has a cathedral which was magnificent.

We also toured the first floor of the KGB Headquarters. Many photos of spies were on display, including American spies and their actual spy craft – real James Bond stuff. They actually had photos of a captured spy who was tied to two bent over young sapling trees. Once this enemy was securely tied, they would let the saplings loose. As the trees sprang back, they literally tore the human in half. Just inconceivably horrible acts and they had photographed it all. They had umbrellas which were actually a gun or a poison dart and pens filled with poison. Fascinating artifacts from the past, but we were not allowed to take photos. They were very serious about that at the KGB Headquarters.

The Kremlin in Red Square, Moscow

Lenin's mausoleum was in the middle of Red Square with the body of Lenin embalmed for the ages. The public was allowed to quietly walk in the mausoleum and solemnly view the display of Lenin's body. Lenin was a very small man in stature. Again – no photos allowed.

We also explored Gum's Department store in Red Square which is huge, but was quite barren inside – the sign of a struggling country and a poor population.

After we had explored the buildings and sights of interest on Red Square, we went to the main shopping street in Moscow – Arbat Street. Arbat Street was once a very elegant cobblestone street in Moscow, but it is now Moscow's biggest shopping area.

On Arbat Street, one could buy everything from souvenirs to really superb original watercolor and oil paintings. The street had many local artists, cafes and several performing artists which were all wonderful. It was great fun as the Russian salesmen and women all spoke English and one could haggle over the prices of items. I was a wonderful customer for the vendors on Arbat Street and they were thrilled.

The Changing of the Guards at Lenin's Mausoleum

The Tomb of the Unknown Soldier

The Kremlin Palace in Red Square - Moscow, Russia

The Kremlin in Red Square, Moscow

Gum's Department Store in Red Square, Moscow

St Basil's Cathedral in Red Square, Moscow

Arbat Street, Moscow – Moscow's main shopping area

One day we went to the Moscow Olympic Stadium and saw some young horses in training. These horses were all Trakehners, between three and seven years old. We met the top rider at the stable and looked at some horses in the huge indoor stadium. I got on one four-year-old horse which was appealing, but was priced exorbitantly high. These guys must have thought that all Americans were filthy rich. The horses were lovely and more hunter types than jumper types. However, they were way overpriced. It was a fun visit though and great to see the Olympic arena which was built for the 1980 Moscow Olympic Games.

Jessamy riding a young, green horse in the Moscow Olympic Stadium

Jessamy riding a young, very green horse in the Moscow Olympic Stadium, jumping one of his first jumps ever.

One evening we saw an incredible performance of the Nutcracker at the Bolshoi Ballet. The Russians are world famous for their magnificent ballerinas and dancers. They did not disappoint. The Bolshoi Ballet was founded in 1776. The building is an exquisite work of art onto itself, with its royal balconies, lush seating and ample stage. It was a sight to behold. Upon leaving the performance at the Bolshoi that night, of course I bought the vendor's book on the Bolshoi Ballet with gorgeous photographs of the building inside and out. I also bought a beautiful watercolor of the Bolshoi Ballet from a very talented local street artist – one which I thought was truly outstanding. I paid twenty-five dollars for the painting and have it hanging in my house to this day. That piece of artwork is one of my favorite belongings, as it brings back the wonderful memory of the performance that evening and my visit to Russia.

Watercolor purchased of the

Bolshoi Ballet - Moscow, Russia

This wrapped up our five-day tour of Moscow, so we went on to St Petersburg and checked into the lovely Astoria Hotel. We had a fabulous young guide named Peter, who was highly intelligent and spoke flawless English. Most of the buildings in St Petersburg were not as aged as those in Moscow. It was a port city and had a European air about it. But there were some very old churches which were breathtakingly beautiful. The artwork in these churches dated back centuries and was absolutely gorgeous. For a country which had banned religion, I was astonished that these were the most beautiful churches I had ever seen.

We spent a full day going through the Hermitage. The Hermitage had been a monumental palace and was turned into a magnificent art museum with works from the old masters. Many famous paintings can be found within that museum.

We also stopped at another stable and visited with the horsemen and women there. As was the case in Moscow, we also saw a number of lovely Trakehners in St Petersburg. The riders were anxious to learn and were thrilled to have an American rider with whom to speak. Of course, they all spoke perfect English.

Probably the most impressive thing of all in St Petersburg were the palaces and the churches. We went to the Summer Palace which was truly majestic and beautifully opulent. The ballroom in the Summer Palace was painted with real gold. It was quite incredible. This was opulence like I had never seen before or since.

St Petersburg, Russia – Statue of Peter the Great

Due to the enormous breadth of income inequality in the past decades, it is no wonder that the starving masses overtook the royals on the throne, hence making Lenin their new leader. It was the beginning of Communism and The Soviet Union. Now here I was in Russia, just after the end of Communism. It was a remarkable time to see this magnificent country.

The Majestic and Opulent Gold Painted Ballroom in the Summer Palace, St Petersburg

Another really beautiful thing about St Petersburg were the canals which surrounded and crisscrossed the city. St Petersburg has as many canals as Venice, Italy. Of course, there was wonderful shopping on the streets as well, with beautiful artwork by local artists, fabulous books and many souvenirs.

This wrapped up our five days in St Petersburg, making a total of ten wonderful days in Russia filled with a lifetime of fabulous memories.

The glorious hand painted dome in St Isaac's Cathedral

The Winter Palace, also called The Hermitage, in St Petersburg, Russia

I loved the country and I loved the people. They were wonderful, but that was in 1992. I cannot vouch for how things are over there right now.

We flew home and went back to business as usual, but I was so glad that David took all of these terrific photographs so that I may share the memories with all of you.

ANIMAL HAVEN
THE FIGHT FOR NO KILL SHELTERS

Jessamy Rouson and some friends in the haven of her caring arms.

I have loved and rescued animals my entire life. As a very small child, I remember going to the animal shelters in New York City with my parents in order to pick out dogs and cats for our personal pets. I would always pick the oldest, saddest and loneliest of animals. I wanted the dogs and cats who really needed someone to love them, because I had a surplus of love to give. I related deeply to these animals in a very heartfelt way. Whenever I found a stray dog or cat on the street, I would bring it home and hide it in my room so my father wouldn't know. Once I brought a homeless mother kitty and her entire litter home.

Saving strays was working out pretty well until one day my bedroom door was left ajar and an army of cats and kittens came merrily parading into the living room – right in front of my father.

He went crazy and yelled and screamed, but he loved animals too, so he eventually settled down. I told him that I was going to find them good homes, but they could not live out on the street – it was not right. I did find these strays some wonderful homes at school, but we kept a few as well.

More problematic was when I felt the next-door neighbor was abusing his collie. It was a beautiful sweet dog and this old man was extremely rough and abusive with him, even hitting the dog repeatedly with a stick. So I climbed over the chain link fence between our yards and took the dog. This rescue didn't last for very long, as my father insisted that I give the dog back - but at least I was able to tell the neighbor how I felt about his treatment of this lovely collie. Hopefully he would take better care of him going forward. I told him that I would always be watching - always. I was about six years old then, but I really did try to be diplomatic with the neighbor. I watched him with the dog every single day. That old man had to be good to his dog, or I would climb the fence and take that dog again in a heartbeat. That happened a few more times until the old man finally got it. He now knew that I could see into his house from his picture window in the kitchen, as well as into his yard. He had to be nice to that dog or I was coming to get it.

These neighbors were a big Italian family and they were always fighting ferociously amongst themselves in Italian. I didn't know exactly what was going on, but it was clear that they were a dysfunctional family. As almost every household on Staten Island was dysfunctional, including mine, I really didn't care as long as the dog was OK.

The old man would bring my father fresh tomatoes which he had grown in the yard, in the hopes that my father would control his animal rescuing daughter. It didn't work, but they were good tomatoes.

From fourteen and on I was deeply involved in the horse business. I would always take care of any dogs or cats who showed up at Lotus Farm or later, on my farm. I would get them to a vet for anything that they may need, including having them spayed and neutered. I even cared for orphaned deer or any injured wildlife which may show up.

I usually took the wildlife to the Wildlife Center, which was much better equipped to care for these animals. Wonderful people in wildlife work.

It wasn't until 1998 that I realized how horrendous and horrific things were at the local animal shelters in Albemarle and Louisa Counties in Virginia – shelters which were close to my farm. I had decided to go to the Albemarle shelter to adopt some old, tough tom cats to live in my tack rooms and barns, because we had a growing mouse and rat problem. I always fed my barn kitties very well and they never had to kill anything, but just by virtue of having cats on the property, the mice and rats would quickly relocate to the nearby woods. It was a win, win solution and no animal or rodent was hurt or killed.

I do not believe in poison or lethal traps for these rodents, because the rodents will leave of their own free will once they see cats in the house or on the farm. Poison is a horrible death. Many pets die because they had gotten into poison their owners had put out to kill other animals. I am strongly against any poison for any purpose – including lawn pesticides, which can also harm animals. I believe in 'Have a Heart' traps, which catch the animal unharmed and you can let them go in the woods. Most SPCAs or Animal Control Officers have Have a Heart traps.

My kitties had beds, food and water in a heated and/or air-conditioned tack room and soon became the Bosses of the Barn. Several lived in my house as well. There were dog/cat doors on the tack rooms and the back door of my house, so they had their choice of accommodations.
They staked out their own territory and took their jobs very seriously. Kitties are extremely organized creatures.

In all the years that I had lived in Virginia, I had never gone into the local animal shelters. I always seemed to have a surplus of animals, but old age had taken most of my cats and I wanted some kitties that no one else would want – the old tough survivor type tom cats with the big, grizzled cheeks, and the hardy old momma cats. These older kitties were always overlooked by adopters who were drawn to the cute, adorable little kittens.

The same with the dogs. Everyone wanted a cute puppy and the older dogs suffered as a result. Personally, I love the senior animals, because they are so wise and have a story to tell. Plus they are usually housetrained. I see that gray muzzle and I absolutely must have them. I don't know what comes over me.

What I did not realize at that time was the staggering number of animals being euthanized at the shelters – thousands per year. Albemarle shelter cremated their euthanized animals.

In the case of the Louisa Shelter, the euthanized animals were just thrown out onto the land fill like garbage. I had no idea that any of this was going on, or the vast extent of the numbers.

And so it happened that I walked into the Charlottesville/Albemarle SPCA in 1998 in search of some kitties who really needed homes. I was there picking out the oldest and toughest cats - the ones with signs that said, "Do Not Touch – Animal will Bite and Scratch". I knew I was in the right place. This is exactly what I was looking for in Kitty Patrol. These were my type of barn cats and I loved them.

Suddenly a huge cart of dead animals was wheeled down the center aisle of the shelter by a worker. These were dog and cat corpses, with their heads and legs hanging out from under the tarp which covered them so insufficiently. Their eyes were glazed over and their bodies and tongues were limp. It was horrible and I went absolutely crazy. I loudly exclaimed, "What the hell is going on here? Who is in charge of this establishment?" One of the exhausted employees pointed to a small, hunched over man named Mike. They said he was the shelter manager and the person in charge. Apparently Mike had been there for many long, hard, tedious years and he showed it. He was completely numb to the killing of these animals.

I walked right up to him, introduced myself and asked again, "What the hell is going on here? How many animals are you euthanizing?"

This weary old man said flat out that at least twenty animals per day were euthanized to make space. He said that Animal Control brought in animals by the truckload every single day and that he had to make room.

Now that I realized that more space was the only thing that could save these animals, I went on an immediate mission. I was quickly told that Virginia law only permits the adoption of two animals per month per person, to avoid puppy mills or other animal abusers or hoarders. It's a good law, but two empty cages were not going to save all of the animals currently in the shelter.

I got on the phone and called every single friend, employee and acquaintance I had in the area and begged them to come and adopt two animals. I promised that I would take the dogs and cats to my farm and would pay the adoption fees, but I needed adopters for the paperwork. Cars and pickup trucks starting flying into the shelter parking lot. God Bless my good-hearted friends. I would hand them two animals and ask them to do the paperwork at the front desk. Then we would take the dogs and cats to my farm.

We pulled about sixty dogs and cats out of the Albemarle shelter that day. The SPCA staff had never seen so many empty runs and cages. They were thrilled. They eventually realized that instead of me being a disruptive pain in the neck, that I was actually a savior – for them and for the animals. But this was just the beginning. I told them that I would be back almost every day until this problem was resolved.

I met all the animals at my farm and bathed all of the dogs. The dogs went in stalls in the stable with food and water bowls, along with a big, comfy bed. The kitties went in apartments I had on the farm with food, water, kitty litter trays and beds. It was an exhausting and expensive day, because I had to pay for all the adoption fees and necessary supplies. But at least these animals were safe and now had a shot of living out a good life.

At this time the shelter just had an intake form on each cage. Each form had an intake number, minimal information about the animal and the date the dogs or cats arrived at the shelter. These intake forms revealed how much time the animals had to be either adopted or euthanized. Stray dogs and cats had to be held for seven days in the event that an owner showed up. Dogs or cats with collars had to be held eleven days. (This is why micro-chipping pets is so important).

When the designated times were up, the animals could either be adopted or euthanized. Animals which owners turned in to the shelter and signed over could be adopted or euthanized immediately, so pet owners should think about that before they take their pet to a Kill Shelter and abandon it. If you are one of those people, you are a disgrace to humanity in my view.

Mike would walk down the rows of cages each night marking a big X on the forms of every animal to be euthanized the next morning. The animals with the big X on their chart were the first ones we yanked out of there. I had no serious education in animal rescue, but I was a very quick study. I knew what had to be done because the animals needed me, I became an expert almost immediately

The animals were not named and there was nothing to make the shelter a warm, inviting place for potential adopters. Mike absolutely refused to work with outside rescue groups or foster people, or to do any marketing of the animals whatsoever. The staff was perpetually in a sour, foul mood - understandable when one works around that much death. The SPCA was a heartbreaking place to work at that time and even to visit, if one had a clue as to what was going on there.

I went back there every day with new found volunteers for my cause. This mass slaughter had to be stopped. This killing was not going to happen on my watch, now that I was aware of it. Each day I studied the situation and came up with new ideas which would improve the dilemma at the shelter. For example, giving each animal an inviting sign with names for the animals and cute stories about them on their cages, instead of just a cold intake sheet.

I also said that all of the animals who were of age should be spayed and neutered before they were adopted and that the Albemarle SPCA should work with outside rescue groups and foster parents.

But Mike didn't want to hear any of it. He had been doing things one way for almost twenty years and that is how he wanted it to stay. I quickly realized that I had to meet with the SPCA board members in order to get some positive changes in place.

I also realized that I needed to raise public awareness of the problems at the shelters and of precisely how many animals were dying there. Albemarle is a very wealthy county and there was no excuse for this barbaric situation.

So I met with the SPCA board. They had to meet with me because I had the press and the public on my side. That's when we began to turn the Albemarle SPCA into a NO KILL shelter. I gave the SPCA board a precise and documented plan with multiple ideas on how to improve adoptions at the shelter and how to make the shelter a warm and friendly place for potential adopters. I raised some money through local corporate sponsorship in order to air SPCA television commercials which depicted the shelter as a warm, welcoming and loving place. I wanted to change the public's negative view of the shelter so that they would come and adopt or foster animals, or perhaps volunteer. I also told the Board that it was mandatory to work with reputable rescue groups and foster parents in order to make more room at the shelter to accommodate the daily intake of animals.

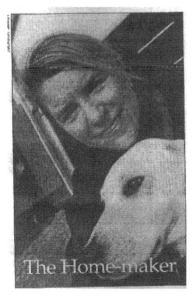

The Home-maker

With the Charlottesville/Albemarle Shelter, it was a case of very wealthy people on the board who hadn't been in the shelter for decades. They had no idea what was going on. They just thought it sounded like a good deed to be on the board of the SPCA.

Once I gathered the SPCA Board for a meeting at the shelter and made them aware of the euthanasia rate, they were horrified. I shared all of my ideas for improving adoptions and making more space, so the animals had time to get adopted. The major movement towards NO KILL at the Charlottesville/Albemarle shelter began and went into effect fairly quickly after that.

Mike was fired. In fact much of the staff was fired, replaced, fired and replaced until the board got what they wanted – a NO KILL Shelter with friendly, animal loving staff members. Board members dropped off the board like flies, as they could not stand the heat of public scrutiny. They were replaced with younger, more progressive and proactive board members. Things were moving along in the right direction beautifully.

I started that movement and am very proud of it. Thousands and thousands of animals have been saved and the Charlottesville/Albemarle SPCA is now doing amazingly wonderful things – way beyond my dreams. Charlottesville/Albemarle SPCA is now a NO KILL shelter and has been for many years.

Charlottesville/Albemarle SPCA is now rated as one of the top shelters in the country – plus they are taking surplus animals from the Louisa Shelter. This is something I had dreamed would happen one day. The Albemarle Shelter also has some outstanding vets and a vet clinic on the property now. All of the animals can be spayed or neutered right there before adoption, as well as receive any necessary veterinary care.

Dr. Anna Sims from the Charlottesville/Albemarle shelter does about thirty surgeries per day. She happened to be fostering my most recent adoption. My little Chihuahua/beagle mix, Missy.

Missy is a 17 year old dog which had been horribly abused and abandoned in an empty house - she was terrified of literally everything. But through Anna's wonderful foster care and then my loving home care, Missy is now an extremely spoiled and very happy little lady.

Missy

Initially I had to personally pay the SPCA adoption fees and pay to spay or neuter each animal at the veterinary clinic. I worked with several vets as there was such a large number of animals. I worked out the very best deal I could with them. I promised these vets that I would radically build up their business by sending the new adopters to them for the vet work on their recently acquired pets. I held true to my promise. The established vets were busy enough already not to really care, but they did what they could to help after I had a meeting with all of them. I wanted the entire community involved in this mission because it was a huge and overwhelming task.

One day I met a brand-new veterinarian in the area – Dr. William Hay. He had come to the shelter to introduce himself and was walking down the dog runs with an employee. Dr. Hay stopped by a very skinny dog which had absolutely no hair due to an atrocious case of mange.

The dog's skin was red and covered with pustules and sores. He was a sweet, fairly good-sized dog, but it was impossible to determine any type of breed due to his horrendous condition.

Dr. Hay turned to the employee and said, "I assume this one shall be euthanized?" I jumped up and said, "No way! That is my dog. My name is on his sheet to hold him until his seven days are up. Then I'm coming for him immediately." Dr. Hay was a little taken back, so I introduced myself and told him all about the rescue work of my Animal Haven. He seemed quite pleased with that and we instantly got along very well.

Dr. Hay had purchased the practice of a retiring veterinarian, but it was a little bit out of town and on the way to the airport. In fact it was called "Airport Animal Hospital". Not the easiest location to get a new veterinary practice going. He desperately needed some help and promotion to get off the ground. Bill Hay is an extremely nice man and he has a big, wonderful family to support. He is also a board-certified surgeon and a superb veterinarian. We worked out a deal on what Animal Haven would pay for spay/neuter services and I promised him a great deal of work for his new practice. I did not let him down. Very early the next morning, the young veterinarian Bill Hay and his brand-new office had at least a dozen barking dogs in crates and twenty meowing cats in carriers – all in his lobby.

I called Dr. Hay and told him to let me know when they would be ready to be picked up and gave him my credit card number. If I adopted puppies or kittens who were too young to spay or neuter, the adopters paid for the surgery fee in the adoption fee, but had to take them to Dr. Hay to have the surgery.

The adopters didn't have to pay anything at the vet, because Animal Haven paid the vet bill. These adopters usually became long time customers of Dr. Hay. His business was booming and is to this day. Dr. Hay had to hire additional veterinarians in order to manage his work load.

I had started out by adopting the dogs at the horse shows. I would lead dogs around the shows with a bandanna on them and try to find every good home that I possibly could. I rounded up as many friends as possible to help me show these dogs to people at the horse shows and we adopted a lot of dogs. The cats needed to be adopted off of my farm and I ended up keeping most of them. At that time, I owned two farms in Keswick, Virginia so I was able to house and care for these animals.

By now I had formed a 501c3 non-profit called Animal Haven so that I was able to collect a few donations to help with the frightening cost of rescue work. I lost over $100,000 of my own money saving animals, but it was worth every dime. I was also able to have the shelter animals transferred to Animal Haven, so there were no adoption fees or limits on the numbers I could take. (Animal Haven's registered name with the state of Virginia is "Showstock Animal Haven.")

I had navy blue Animal Haven tee shirts and polo shirts made up. The front said "Animal Haven – We Love Our Animals", with a silhouette of a dog and cat together. The backs of these shirts said, "Animal Haven, Open Your Heart - Save a Life." All of my volunteers and employees wore these shirts while adopting animals at the farm, horse shows or on adoptions outings. I also had to write and print up adoption contracts and keep all of the paperwork in huge books for the state records.

After a while I had tapped out the market for the dogs at the horse shows. I knew it was time to come up with another plan when my own dear friends would see me and run the other way as fast as they could, for fear of getting another dog. I started advertising the pets in the local newspapers and the Washington Post.

If I had some lab mixes, I would advertise "<u>Labs</u> – Beautiful, loving family pets, spayed/neutered and all shots. Adoption fee $85. Open Your Heart – Save a Life"

It was the same thing with shepherd mixes, hounds, beagles and everything else. I would pick the most attractive breed reasonably acceptable for these guys and write an ad in glowing terms about them.

People who read the classified ads saw purebred labs or other purebred dogs or cats for sale for $500 or more. Then they would see my ad with the same type of dog for $85, already spayed/neutered and all shots. Kitties were $65 with all shots, spayed and neutered. I received a ton of calls and had to pay someone just to handle the phone.

Long haired, fluffy cats I would call "Persians" or "Maine Coons" or "Himalayans", (or any other kind of exotic cat breed which I could reasonably match them with). I had a breed book for dogs and one for cats. If a predominant breed was not obvious while looking at the individual animal, I would go through the pictures in my breed book and come up with something which looked close to the mutt I had just rescued. I could barely pronounce or spell the names of some of these breeds, but they sounded important and people loved it. The phone rang all day long and well into the night with potential adopters.

Although tiring, this was a good thing because I was taking about fifty to sixty dogs and cats out of the shelters every week.
Rescue work is overwhelmingly exhausting, plus financially and emotionally draining. May God Bless anyone who rescues animals.

The local press and television stations got wind of what I was doing and absolutely loved it. I became a darling of the local press. I was on the front page of the Charlottesville and Louisa papers multiple times – always holding a dog or cat. The local television stations would show up with cameras unannounced on a slow day, whenever they needed a story. I was voted one of the "Distinguished Dozen" citizens in Charlottesville for my rescue work with Animal Haven.

All of this awakened public awareness which was a tremendous help in moving my goals forward towards No Kill shelter policies in Albemarle and Louisa Counties. Initially the public was unaware of the problems at the shelters, just as I had been unaware. When they read the newspaper articles or saw me on local television talking about the plight of shelter animals and my work with Animal Haven, everyone wanted an Animal Haven pet and tried to help. The public became very engaged.

Some people sent donations, which was a big help. Others volunteered and many adopted animals. A few trusted volunteers also fostered animals.

I had a surplus of volunteers - most of which were children. Various camps, organizations and schools would call and bring these kids out to my farm by the busload – literally a school bus would unload these children onto my property. I even had "special needs" children, which in this particular case meant that they were basically in a home for tough, out of hand and uncontrollable children. These kids came with professional supervisors and hence, were among the best behaved. Those supervisors were like military officers – they were never disobeyed, yet they were kind and professional. I also had young people who needed to do "community service" for some minor infraction of the law.

In the beginning it was sheer pandemonium. I had kids and loose dogs running everywhere on the farm and it quickly became a situation which I realized I couldn't handle alone. I was over my head. Fortunately, I had some wonderful middle-aged women who were volunteers as well. These women were fabulous, so I made a very intelligent decision. I put a couple of the adult women volunteers in charge of the children volunteers. These wonder women had been mothers and school teachers. There was nothing that they could not handle. Once I gave them the very official sounding title of "Animal Haven Volunteer Coordinator", with a matching polo shirt, they whipped things into shape in no time.

Almost instantly there were no more screaming wild children running with dogs on leashes and setting them loose. Suddenly we had lovely, clean cut, very polite children all dressed in Animal Haven tee shirts, quietly and happily walking dogs. These kids now brought their own lunch and had an official "lunch break", instead of bugging me every time one of them got hungry.

Of course the Volunteer Coordinators wore the Animal Haven polo shirts to show their authority. These women were magical in the results that they produced. I thank them to this day.

While I was getting the Charlottesville/Albemarle Shelter under control, I was contacted by other rescue groups showing support for my efforts. However the main purpose of their call was to tell me about the truly deplorable conditions at the Louisa Shelter, which was conveniently located right next to the Louisa land fill.

These rescue groups said that the conditions for the animals were so bad at the Louisa Shelter that they refused to go there. I couldn't believe these people. I said, "Isn't that what animal rescue is all about – getting animals in dire need out of bad situations?" I knew that I had to go to Louisa and see what was going on for myself.

The next afternoon I headed out to the Louisa Shelter with one of my adult volunteers. Nothing could have prepared me for what I saw when we entered the warehouse type building which was the animal shelter.

The dogs and cats were in very small, absolutely filthy cages set up on the concrete floor. These dogs and cats were standing and lying in their own urine and fecal matter, which was all over them. They had no food or water bowls and no bedding whatsoever – just the cold, disgustingly gross concrete floor.

The dogs were infested with fleas and ticks - many had mange. Most of the animals were extremely thin. The majority of the cats had ear mites, fleas and ticks. No vaccinations or wormers had been given to any of the animals.

The tall, older man in charge of the Louisa Shelter was unable to read or write, so no paperwork was provided. This man simply said, "Take as many as you want, because I'm going to kill them ALL at 4:00. Help yourself." He then sauntered off with a beer and went into a back room.

I had only driven my car to Louisa, so I was back on the phone calling every friend, rescue contact, volunteer, acquaintance and employee to come to the Louisa Animal Shelter immediately with as many crates, trucks, vans and cars as they could find. I told them to also bring leashes, collars, lead ropes – anything we could use to get the animals out of this horror show.

Within an hour, pick-up trucks, vans and cars were filing into the Louisa Shelter parking lot. We emptied the place out. There was not one animal left in the shelter. As we didn't have enough crates, we doubled some dogs and cats up in their carriers, but several had to ride loose in the cars. At that time, I had a relatively new black Mercedes 560 SEL sedan – a $90,000 (financed) car when I had bought it brand new. But that didn't stop me from loading fifty animals into that car.

Several were puppies and kittens which went in crates, but many were adult dogs and cats which had to ride loose on top of the crates, on the car floor, on the dashboard, or in my lap. I could barely see where I was going, looking out the windshield over the heads of so many dogs and cats.

However the most amazing thing to me was how intelligent these dogs and cats were, proven by how well they behaved. Somehow these animals knew that this was their one and only ride out of hell and away from a certain death. I had dogs and cats on top of each other in that car, but they all got along beautifully.

These animals knew this was serious and they couldn't be fighting with each other. They just stared straight ahead, grateful to see what their future may hold. They knew I was trying to save them and their manners were impeccable and appreciative.

Once we arrived at the farm, the work had just begun. I bathed and scrubbed all of the dogs with flea and tick soap and dip, as well as some of the cats. I wormed them all with ivermectin, which also kills ear mites and sarcoptic mange.

Sarcoptic mange is a fairly common, highly contagious skin disease found in dogs. It is caused by the Sarcoptes scabiei mite. These mites burrow through the skin causing intense itching and irritation. The scratching that results from mange is what causes the majority of the animal's hair to fall out. Although it looks horrible and some animals lose all of their hair, it is easily treatable with ivermectin. Ivermectin kills all of the mites and parasites in the animal. In a few months the dog's coats grow back and you have a beautiful, adoptable animal.

The dog I had rescued from Albemarle which had absolutely no hair, miraculously turned into a gorgeous yellow lab who was adopted by one of my very best volunteers. Despite the fact that he was now a beautiful dog, she kept his initial name of "Scruffy".

Back at the farm, stalls had to be prepared. Dogs had to be doubled up because the numbers were overwhelming - even with a twenty-stall barn. They also filled up my eight-stall barn. All my horses were in what I called "the Show barn", by the indoor ring. The kitties went in apartments and offices. It was a horrendously long day, but we had rescued, bathed, housed, fed, wormed and vaccinated every animal from the Louisa Shelter. At the end of the day we all looked even worse than the animals did when we picked them up. But the warm eyes of these dogs and cats portrayed their gratitude and forever loyalty. That loving look in their eyes made it all worth the monumental effort. They knew they were now safe, cared for and loved. I was so happy and proud for them.

The more animals which one has to adopt, the more creative strategies one has to come up with quickly. I'd tapped out the horse shows, but my classified ads in the local papers and the Washington Post were still a good source of adopters.

I began doing "Adoption Outings" at the PetSmart in Manassas, Virginia, as there was no PetSmart in Charlottesville at that time. Every Saturday I would get up at five o'clock in the morning and load up a van full of dogs and cats to drive one and a half hours to the PetSmart in Manassas. My volunteers, employees and I would stand out front of that PetSmart, all wearing our Animal Haven attire, holding at least two dogs each.

I had all the paperwork and adoption contracts in neat folders on a fold out table. I had a few deck chairs, a tablecloth, some flowers and a donation basket.

PetSmart allowed me to put the kitties in cages inside of the store with a sign for each one, and leave them there all week for adoption. The PetSmart staff cared for the kitties all week and were schooled on how to screen for good adopters. They did a wonderful job.

I did all of the paperwork involved in this venture which took endless hours, but I felt one of my greatest talents was in writing the signs for the cats. If I had a big, old neutered male cat, I'd have a sign that would say, "Hi! I'm Charles. I've been looking for love in all the wrong places and am now looking for the real thing. I want to settle down and I promise that I'll love you forever and always be loyal. I am now your man and very best friend. Let's go home."

Or a shy female kitty may have a sign which said, "My name is Melissa and I am very shy. I had a rough childhood but I am looking for one special person who I can trust and love forever. Are you that special person?"

These signs varied every week and we adopted an incredible number of kitties this way. Adopters would of course be thoroughly interviewed to make sure that they would be solid, loving pet owners. I was looking for good, forever homes for these animals – not someone who wanted a summer pet.

Of course any cats which bit and scratched the PetSmart help or the adopters immediately came home and became a part of the Showstock Stables' Kitty Patrol. They were replaced at PetSmart with cats who had manners, were not afraid of people and would not attack anyone.

I personally did the evaluations on all of the animals as to where they would find the best home for their needs. I also worked with the dogs on the leash, so that even the big, strong dogs would heel like gentlemen.

Initially right out of the shelter there were some big, strong, energetic dogs who would take the volunteers, children and adopters water skiing when they tried to walk them.

I needed to explain to these dogs that a good life was dependent on them being manageable and friendly with their new owners. I was always amazed by their high level of understanding and intelligence. They definitely got it and found themselves wonderful homes. These dogs knew that I understood them and they listened. Animals talk all the time, if one just listens.

Then came the exceptionally rambunctious and out of control dogs, which I knew would tear a nice apartment or house to shreds within minutes. My demolition squad. As I have always done with the horses, I looked at the animal's natural instincts in order to decide on a career where they would excel. I often adopted these extremely rambunctious and somewhat destructive dogs to law and drug enforcement officers. They became drug sniffing police or customs dogs to work airports or any job where the officer suspected a problem.

Several of these dogs became regular working police dogs as well. Police and drug dogs need tremendous stamina and drive. Those are the traits for which these canine officers were searching and which several of these dogs offered.

These dogs were not pure-bred dogs or of any particular type, but they showed an excessive drive and a desire to please. That is what the officers were looking for and many of these rescues became heroes. They lived in the loving homes of their canine police handlers. Then there were also the owners of vineyards and orchards, who needed energetic dogs to run around and keep the deer away from eating the vines or orchard produce.

Any purebred dogs which came from the shelter, I immediately sent to a highly reputable rescue group for that particular breed. Some rescues just specialize in one breed, which is fine. But I needed to specialize in mutts because they were in the majority and needed the most help. After all, we're all mutts of some sort.

These guys deserved a loving home as much as any other animal. Little dogs were extremely easy to adopt, especially if they were cute. These were always adopted at PetSmart immediately, but I also discovered another outlet. States like Massachusetts have very strong spay/neuter laws. Therefore the shelters there were always in need of puppies and small dogs – a refreshing change.

I contacted them and we organized the "Pups to Massachusetts" trips. I would have a volunteer drive the crates of puppies to Dulles Airport in Washington, DC, so they could take the short flight to meet the shelter volunteers at the airports in Massachusetts. That was a huge weekly program, so I put another very capable volunteer in charge of that. This program saved a countless number of puppies and dogs. The people in Massachusetts and New England were thrilled with them. They were always asking for more. I sent them some cats and kittens too, and they were also a big hit up north.

The most difficult thing about our adoption outings was dealing with the public. Fortunately most of the time the public consisted of wonderful animal loving people who came over to view the animals and hopefully adopt.

But occasionally we would get some wise guys. I remember one Saturday when I was standing out front of Manassas PetSmart, feeling like a complete idiot in my Animal Haven polo shirt. Two smart ass boys about eighteen years old wandered over.

They had been drinking beer and were on the verge of being rowdy. They were looking at the dogs and bugging my volunteers – especially the pretty young girls in their Animal Haven shirts.

My volunteers directed them to me, as they didn't know what else to do with them. These guys staggered over and asked a bunch of stupid questions, which I answered as nicely as I could. I always tried to be polite, because you never knew who may at least donate into our Animal Haven donation basket. These guys were smug, cocky and reeked of beer.

At the time I was holding two big black lab/hound mixes - or in other words, "Animal Haven Labs". These two dogs had been neutered recently, as all of my animals went right to the vet's office when they came out of the shelters. Every animal was spayed or neutered before any adoption outings and had all necessary shots and worming already.

One of the big black dogs was resting on a dog bed and the other was drooling and slobbering in the breeze, with his tongue hanging out and just as happy as he could be. These two characters liked the dogs because they were big and a tad obnoxious - just like them.

Then the dog on the dog bed started to lick his private parts where his stitches had recently been removed after surgery. These guys started laughing and popped open another beer. One of the guys said "Wow! I wish I could do that!" I looked him right in the eye and very serenely said, "You can. $85 donation and I'll hold your beer. Go for it."

The volunteers and surrounding crowd who had been watching this tentative interaction burst into hysterical laughter. This seemed to sober these guys right up. They apologized for their behavior and left me two $100 bills in the donation basket.

So you just never know what the public will bring your way. I adopted those dogs to a lovely young couple that afternoon who wanted the dogs to keep them company on their morning runs. These were the dogs for this fitness aware couple – they could run and jog with the best of them. This couple sent me nice cards and photos long after of their two "Animal Haven Labs". They loved them.

Rarely, but every once in a while, someone would be annoyed with the fact that I advertised the dogs by predominant breed as opposed to stating that they were a mix.

All the little old rescue ladies would say that I was a reckless maverick, but I saved thousands of dogs and cats and put them in loving homes. It helps to have a marketing strategy.

However every once in a while, some haughty woman would come from one of my classified ads and complain when she saw the dog. Okay. Fair enough. You judge for yourself. Here is one example. Below is a photo of "Newman", named for his two beautiful blue eyes. He came out of the Louisa shelter trembling in fear and afraid of his own shadow.

He was filthy and matted – a case of total neglect. He had been horribly abused, beaten and abandoned. Newman did not have a friend in the world. He was shy to an extreme and terrified of everything. This is normally the type which I automatically kept for myself, but Newman was so adorable I was sure that he could find some wonderful lady to love him forever.

I cleaned Newman up beautifully and prepared him for a showing to potential adopters – preferably nice little old ladies. I advertised Newman in the Washington Post as a shy but sweet young "Lhasa Apso/Terrier", neutered and all shots - $85. I know that was pushing the envelope a little, but I was trying to save lives. The phone rang off the hook. Two very prim and proper little old ladies drove all the way from DC to see Newman.

Newman

When these ladies arrived, Newman was hunkered down on a dog bed under my desk where he felt safe. He would only leave that spot if I was with him, or when it was bedtime and he slept in my bed. Newman was very comfortable with me, but was still extremely wary of strangers. I had Newman's bandanna on so that he would look extra cute.

I clipped Newman's leash on and encouraged him out from under the desk. Newman was happy because he thought that he and I were going for a walk. I said "Isn't he the cutest little thing you ever saw? But then Newman saw these two High Society, hoity-toity ladies. Newman cringed terribly and peed all over himself, leaving a big puddle and trembling like a leaf. I felt horrible for putting him through this and for thinking that he was adoptable just because he was cute. A huge mistake on my part.

To make it worse, these women were nasty about it and did not hold back their contempt. "That's no damn Lhasa Apso! I wouldn't give you $85 for that mutt who trembles and urinates all over himself!" All of a sudden I loved Newman more than anything on the planet and I was going to defend him to my death. I said, "I wouldn't adopt this dog or any dog to you hoity-toity bitches! You want a dog as a status symbol, not as a loving companion. Go back to DC and buy an expensive Lhasa Apso, because there is no amount of money which could ever buy Newman now. You don't deserve this dog. This is now my dog forever and I would like you to leave my house and property immediately."

And so it was. Newman was my dog to the very end, which was well into his late teens. He was loved endlessly and waited under my desk for me to come and take him out. He slept in my bed and snuggled up to me so that he felt secure. I could never apologize to him enough for even thinking that he could be anywhere but with me.

The day the vet had to come to the farm to put Newman to sleep, I was inconsolable. He had stopped eating for several days and it was time, but my heart couldn't let him go. I buried Newman in a beautiful spot under a lovely tree, overlooking the lake on the farm where Newman and I used to run and play.

I cried for three weeks and was completely devastated and useless. I cancelled all business appointments and horse viewings.

My employees and volunteers cared for the horses and the rescue dogs and cats, while I sat on Newman's grave crying. They didn't know what to do with me.

Newman

I hadn't been this heartbroken since I lost Tuxedo, my Great Dane and best friend who braved all of Germany with me. Some pain never goes away. Time helps, but the scars are deep and can easily re-open. I have a scar for every animal which I have ever lost. My employees and volunteers cared for the horses and the rescue dogs and cats, while I sat on Newman's grave crying. They didn't know what to do with me.

I learned a couple of very important lessons the day that I tried to adopt Newman to someone else just because he was "so cute". First, I now know immediately when an animal belongs with me. I do not go against that instinct anymore or try to intellectualize the reasons.

I've adopted hundreds and hundreds of dogs and cats - but the very old or shy or frightened or abused stay with me. Period. I am the only one who is able to really understand and love them as they should be loved. Very rarely a special person comes along and loves a shy or abused animal, but I watch the animal closely and allow the animal to make the decision as to adoption.

I saved too many dogs and cats to cover all of them here. I may need to write another book in their honor. But there were two extremely shy and terrified border collies which I would like to discuss. On one of my trips to the Albemarle Shelter, the great gal in charge named Beth told me that she had two purebred border collies which were completely and totally feral – meaning that they were like wild animals. These dogs had never been handled by humans.

Of course I asked to see them immediately, because Beth said that she would have to euthanize them if I couldn't take them. I loved Beth because she really appreciated what I was doing. She had been the one who had to euthanize many loving animals in the past and that takes a toll on a person who loves animals. Beth did not want to do that anymore and I had been the solution to avoiding that trauma.

Beth took me to the dog run where these two young border collies, apparently a brother and sister, were cowering in the corner. Their eyes were closed and they were huddled together trembling in unimaginable fear. They were so terrified that they were panting heavily. It was heartbreaking to see such beautiful creatures so traumatized. The border collies were matted and filthy. It was clear that these young dogs had to fend for themselves for their entire life. They were petrified by any human contact and the trip in with Animal Control was more than they could handle – they were dragged into the shelter with catch poles. I went in the cage and they were pressed against the wall in the corner shaking with fear. Their eyes were clamped shut.

I got down low on their ground level and tried to offer some treats and pet them gently. They did not open their eyes or take the treats, but they did not try to bite me. That was a very good sign.

I continued to pet them until I felt it would be alright to try and pick one of them up. They had no idea of how to walk on a leash.

Trembling in my arms with his eyes still shut, the male allowed me to pick him up. With urine running down the front of me and soaking my Animal Haven shirt, I carried him towards the door. I asked Beth to hold the door to the shelter open, because I was going straight to my car.

There were several potential adopters in the shelter during all of this. As I carried this trembling, urinating young Border collie out of the shelter, I said with a big smile, "This is exactly what I have been looking for!" Beth had to laugh.

I put that dog in the car and came back in the shelter for the female. She was even more timid than the male, but I picked her up and carried her to my car, urine streaming all over me again.

I drove right up to the barn when I got home and gently carried each of them to a stall which I had prepared in their honor. It was a big 12 by 24-foot broodmare stall, because I knew it would be awhile until they would be able to walk on a leash for exercise. These were feral animals. They huddled together in the corner of the stall trembling violently, with their eyes clamped shut.

They had food, water and big cushy beds, so I wanted them to settle in for the night and hopefully relax before doing any more with them. I took a shower and went to bed thinking about these dogs the whole time and wondering about the life they had led to date. They were going to be a huge project, but in my opinion, they were extraordinarily special.

The next morning I went to the barn to check on my new border collies. They were in the exact same place as I had left them the night before – trembling in the corner against the wall of the stall. They had not eaten or had any water. I went back to the house and got some broiled chicken which I hoped would entice these lovely, terrified dogs to eat. I squatted down and tried to feed them tiny pieces of chicken. They would not even open their eyes to look at it. Then I got a wonderful idea.

I went back to the house and got some more chicken and Tuxedo, my super cool, calm and world traveled Great Dane. I walked Tuxedo to the barn on a leash and brought him in the stall with the border collies.

Tuxedo gently and politely introduced himself and they were sniffing noses. I started to feed Tuxedo the chicken and closely watched the two rescues. With the ultra-cool Tuxedo there, the border collies opened their eyes. I squatted down and showed them how Tuxedo was happily eating the chicken. Then I offered a tiny piece of chicken to the male. Watching Tuxedo eat, the male Border collie tentatively took the chicken and ate it. I offered more and he took it gently from my hand.

Gandhi and Indira

Then I offered chicken to the frightened female who had just opened her eyes. She very tentatively took the chicken and ate it. This was a huge milestone, thanks to Tuxedo. They were very comfortable with Tuxedo and felt that they had finally found a friend. I fed the border collies and Tuxedo little pieces of chicken for well over an hour. The rescue dogs relaxed somewhat, so I very gently put leashes on them. Then I opened the stall door with Tuxedo leading the way out. Miraculously these dogs got up and very tentatively followed Tuxedo on their leashes. Within fifteen minutes I had the two happiest border collies walking beautifully on a leash and following the great Tuxedo.

Tuxedo was so cool and had been right by my side and sleeping in my bed ever since he was the smallest of pups. He told this brother and sister – "Everything is okay. She's with me".

The transformation was unreal, but these dogs came out of their shell and trusted me. I knew that I would have to keep them forever – I wouldn't even have trusted a rescue with them. They would become my personal, beloved pets. And so they did. I named them Gandhi and Indira, because there was something spiritual about them. They were wonderful dogs who slept together on a huge dog bed in my dining room. Eventually they went in and out of the house on the farm as they pleased, but always came right back to their bed.

They were very happy and excessively spoiled. They got to the point where they would accept guests in the house without being afraid. They were always concerned about new people, but were not afraid if Tuxedo and I were there.

I have neglected to mention that when I originally adopted Gandhi and Indira from the shelter, another pure-bred border collie was there as well. They were all captured by Animal Control at the same time and in the same area, so I believe this dog was the father of Gandhi and Indira. However this dog had been socialized and was friendly. I cleaned him up and named him Beau. He was quickly adopted by a wonderful woman police officer and had a happy life thereafter.

I always wondered what had happened to the mother, but I guess we'll never know. I worry about her to this day, because she obviously had these pups out in the wild. I was just lucky enough to get these two and give them a wonderful life. I loved Gandhi and Indira until their dying day, which was when they were into their late teens. Gandhi was the first one to go. It broke my heart and Indira's as well. She passed shortly after.

I could never bring myself to move their dog bed, because they had become such a fixture on that bed. Eventually other rescue dogs took to sleeping on the bed and that was okay. That is what Gandhi and Indira would have wanted.

The sensitive souls of animals need to be protected, cared for and loved. That is my mission in life. Everyone should do whatever they are able to help protect and defend the animals who share this planet with us so graciously. After all, it is their world too.

TURNING AROUND THE HORRIFIC LOUISA ANIMAL SHELTER

Jessamy with a pup on the way to a good life

The Louisa Shelter was a different situation than the Charlottesville/Albemarle Shelter and much more difficult. The Louisa Shelter was run by the County Board of Supervisors who really didn't give a damn about the shelter or the animals. So, I went to a public meeting of the County Board of Supervisors in Louisa where the public is able to speak and ask questions – sort of a Town Hall. People could stand up and state their opinion on anything from the roads, the schools, trash pick-up or anything else which may be on their minds.

The Board of Supervisors were perched up on a stage behind podiums, attempting to look very important. Their response to almost every issue was, "We'll take it under advisement." No promised action – just words.

I was very well prepared, with all of the facts and statistics regarding the horrors at the Louisa shelter in my briefcase. I wore a business skirt suit to the Town Hall and looked very professional. I stood up and introduced myself as Jessamy Rouson – President of Animal Haven. I explained what Animal Haven did in regard to saving the animals of Louisa. I discussed the wonderful changes my efforts had made at the Charlottesville/Albemarle Shelter and stated that we needed to do the same for the Louisa Shelter.

I discussed the deplorable and filthy conditions at Louisa, as well as the tiny cages. Then I discussed the horrific rate of euthanasia of the vast majority of the animals.

I described how their corpses were thrown in the land fill like garbage. I had everyone's attention. I involved the crowd by looking around and saying, "I believe we are all animal lovers here – am I right?" Heads nodded vigorously and enthusiastically. Then I asked, "Please raise your hand if you own a pet or have animals of some sort." Every single hand went up. I nodded and then said, "Please raise your hand if you are against the mass slaughter of dogs and cats which is taking place at the Louisa shelter. Would you want your pets killed and thrown in the land fill like garbage?" Every hand went up and everyone was becoming animated with emotion.

Then I said, "Do you feel these gentlemen on the Louisa County Board of Supervisors should make the necessary changes which I have outlined in order to protect, save and care for our animals?" Once again, every single hand went up and the crowd was becoming quite agitated and angry with the County Supervisors. Several people stood up and yelled nasty things at them. The Supervisors were all cringing under their podiums.

Then I flat out asked the Supervisors what they were planning to do regarding the horrific situation at their animal shelter. The Supervisors were afraid to speak, but I kept pushing them. I said, "These people would like to know what you are going to do right now – am I right everyone?" Now people were on their feet and really aggravated with the Supervisors.

One Supervisor finally spoke up in a painfully timid voice and stated that they did not have the money to make the necessary changes at the animal shelter. I was prepared for this and had done my homework. I was just getting started. I said, "Really! That is quite interesting as I know that at least six of you have recently purchased brand new cars, trucks or SUVs. One of you just bought a boat and a few of you have just returned from a fancy vacation."

Then I turned to the crowd and asked, "How many of you have recently bought a brand-new vehicle or a boat or gone on an expensive vacation?" Not one hand went up and the crowd was now becoming quite outraged and motivated. Then I asked the crowd, "Do you think that perhaps the reason these Supervisors have no money to help our animals, is because they are spending it all on themselves? Remember that it's our hard-earned taxpayer dollars funding these men."

Now the crowd was up on their feet again and extremely rowdy, yelling at the Supervisors in loud, angry voices and shaking their fists. Finally one Supervisor said that they would meet with me and form a plan to improve the shelter and save the animals. I stated that we needed to do it sooner rather than later, as only more animals were going to be slaughtered and thrown out like trash.

The crowd were standing and demanding answers. They were now extremely angry with these pompous, fat, entitled Supervisors who had used their tax money to buy luxuries for themselves and allowed the horrid, lethal conditions at the animal shelter. The crowd was turning into an outraged mob.

I said to the Supervisors, "You think about this issue gentleman, because I will be at every town hall from now until eternity, or until this problem is resolved. The blood of every animal killed at the Louisa Shelter is on your hands." The crowd was on their feet applauding me and yelling ferociously at the Supervisors, shaking their fists like madmen. We now had an extremely angry mob. The Supervisors said the only thing that they could say in order to get out of the auditorium alive. They said that they would meet with me right now. The town hall was adjourned.

I went in a back-conference room with the Supervisors to discuss my litany of necessary, immediate changes for the shelter. I had the documentation to back up these demands in my briefcase. I stood at the head of the conference table with my briefcase open and told them all to have a seat. It was a relatively short meeting.

They were clearly shaken and said, "We will give you anything that you want for the animal shelter – anything. Just tell us what you want for the shelter. It will be there. Tell us what you want us to do. But please, please do not ever come back to another Town Hall meeting."

I left them each with a list of my demands and took each of their business cards. I told them that I would be in touch. I also told them that if things went really well, I may not need to come back to another Town Hall event - but that would all depend on how well the shelter animals of Louisa do from now on. With that I said, "Have a good evening Gentlemen". I turned on my heel and left them there still quite shaken. It had been a productive meeting and the animals of Louisa had a strong voice that night. In fact they had many strong voices.

I would like to end this chapter with the fact that my efforts and those of the Animal Haven volunteers - combined with the press and the public - forced both Albemarle and Louisa Counties in Virginia to become NO KILL counties. Many wonderful people played a role in saving these beautiful lives. I consider this movement to be my greatest accomplishment.

This world belongs equally to all of us. That includes the animals. It is their world too and humans should never forget that.

HELPING HUNTING DOGS

My Old Beagle – Marietta from Louisa

Another "big elephant in the room" if you will, was the problem of the hunters. There was a large contingent of local hunters. Each hunter owned packs of hounds and beagles for their hunting expeditions. These packs of dogs ran free over the countryside, breeding any dog in their sight – thus producing more homeless animals.

The gentlemen who owned these dogs were generally of a lower income bracket and perhaps had less opportunities for a good education than most – with some exceptions. Unfortunately wealthy and well-educated people sometimes hunt too. The only difference is that the lower income hunters are literally hunting for food.

If they could kill a deer, it would give them food for their family for the entire winter. The wealthy just killed for the fun of killing, which I find inherently sick and abhorrent.

The problem was that all of these loose unaltered hounds and beagles running around the countryside would breed everything they could and then end up at the local animal shelters – as would their puppies. The hunters were afraid to go in the Albemarle SPCA and claim their dogs, because Mike had treated them so badly in the past. So the unclaimed hounds and beagles were euthanized on mass, as were their litters of pups. It had to be stopped.

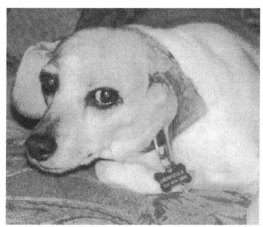

A Hound - Living the Good Life at Showstock

For the record, hounds and beagles can be very loving, sweet, intelligent household pets and were extremely popular in Northern Virginia, as well as up in New England. They are generally good with kids, cats and other dogs. Hounds and beagles can be wonderful, quiet, mellow pets and I adopted truckloads of them to good homes in Northern Virginia. I called the hounds "English Foxhounds" and the adopters went crazy and had to have them. We even flew some to Massachusetts with great success. They loved them. I kept the extremely old ones myself and I adored them. They were a joy.

As much as I abhor hunting and the killing of any animal, I knew that I was not going to be able to stop it. So I did the next best thing in the interest of improving the lives of the hunting dogs. I befriended the local hunters and gave the reputable ones spayed and neutered hounds to hunt, with the promise that the dogs would get the best of care.

One of my neutered dogs in particular turned out to be an outstanding hunting dog and became quite famous in the local venue. He was named "Mike" and I had given him to Kenny Wheeler Jr.

After "Mike's" terrific success, I was able to convince the other hunters that good hunting dogs can be spayed and neutered. I explained that these dogs would not only hunt well, but quite often perform even better than unaltered dogs because they had no distractions to pull them off of the scent. These hunters had been taught throughout the generations that a spayed or neutered dog would not hunt – but I changed that belief, at least locally. This took one hell of a sales job on my part but I succeeded, with the help of the dog "Mike" and some other wonderful hounds and beagles.

So I set up "Hunter's Day" at Showstock Stables. I invited all of the local hunters to bring their dogs and get them checked by a veterinarian for free, as well as acquire a free spay or neuter certificate from the SPCA.

I had refreshments and sandwiches for the hunters and they already liked me, so they came in droves with all of their dogs. My place was overrun by hunting trucks and a ton of barking hunting dogs – hounds and beagles were everywhere. I organized with Beth from the SPCA and a superb veterinarian to meet with all of the local hunters and their dogs at my farm in Keswick. The wonderful Dr. Donnie Peppard showed up with his truck full of supplies. Beth showed up with FREE spay and neuter certificates from the SPCA for the hunter's dogs. I set Beth up in the air-conditioned client's lounge at Showstock, with a desk and a good area to do her work.

Dr. Donnie and I examined each dog individually. I bathed every single dog with flea and tick soap and dip. I cleaned and treated every single dogs' ears and eyes. Dr. Donnie vaccinated and wormed the dogs, while checking them over for good health and condition. Donnie took the time to speak with each man regarding each of his dogs' needs. God Bless Dr. Donnie Peppard – a Saint of a Man.

Beth gave each hunter a FREE spay/neuter certificate so they could have their animals fixed free of cost by the SPCA. She was fabulous with these guys and made them very comfortable about working with the SPCA. Beth gave them her work number and told them to call her if they were missing a dog or having any problems. God Bless Beth too. Another Saint.

I became the hunter's "Go to Girl" if there were any minor problems with their dogs. I could personally tend to vaccinations, worming, very small lacerations, ear mites, sarcoptic mange or flea/tick problems, but I also knew when we needed a real vet and would organize all of that. Any additional vet work on these hounds and beagles was done at Animal Haven prices, because these were mostly lower income citizens. I had made this a community effort to improve the lives of the area's hounds and beagles.

Earlier I had mentioned that I kept the very old hounds and beagles for myself because their hunting days were behind them. There were too many dogs to write about, but I would like to speak of "Marietta", an eighteen-year-old beagle out of the Louisa Shelter. Given her age, Marietta automatically became one of my dogs. However I had not expected how much she would touch my heart.

Marietta was the Queen of Showstock and ran the show. She kept all of the other dogs calm and behaving well, which was a big job for a little old lady. It was obvious that Marietta had given birth to numerous litters of puppies in her day, but she was now spayed and all of that was behind her.

So Marietta started on her very own fitness regime. Every morning Marietta would walk across the field to the little country Cismont Store next door. She would nose open the door, peruse the various edible options on the bottom shelves, take what she pleased and carry it out of the store. This was a seven day a week event, each and every morning. Marietta was now hunting treats instead of prey.

The store owner called me initially to make me aware of what was going on. He said that everyone loved Marietta and looked forward to seeing her each morning, but she was eating into his inventory. I told him that it was not a problem. I gave him my credit card number and told him to "run a tab" for Marietta and I would pay it. I suggested that he just regard Marietta as another loyal, happy and satisfied customer.

And so it was. Every morning Marietta would come back with her chips or cookies - or sometimes a bacon, egg and cheese biscuit. I think she had a little help with the latter entrée, but if Marietta was happy, I was happy.

Marietta was probably the only beagle in Virginia with her very own charge account and she made good use of it.

WHAT DOES IT ALL MEAN?

Jessamy feeding the orphaned deer

I believe that I'm not alone when reflecting on life's experiences, to ask the unanswerable question, "What does it all mean?" I won't even pretend to have the answers, but I do have a few thoughts – some of which may have some merit. We find ourselves in this crazy world with no clear, definitive understanding as to exactly what the hell we're supposed to do. Speaking for myself, I believe that we are destined to find our own path – however rocky that path may be. I believe that one must follow their heart. For me, my heart made that path extremely clear. I wanted a life with horses and animals – anything else would be intolerable.

The horses and the animals are from where my strength lies. I have had a good degree of success in the horse business and I owe all of it to the horses themselves. I am grateful to each and every horse I have ever known and ridden, for the valuable lessons which they have taught me. These lessons have helped me survive in life – through the good and the bad.

I've been through my share of heartbreaking tragedies and life blows. I have often stopped and asked "Why?" I don't know why. I have somehow figured out in my own mind that the world is half good and half evil. Animals fill the greater part of that good. It is extremely difficult to find a truly evil animal. I have never met one. But it is not difficult to find truly evil people – they are plastered across our newspapers and television screens every day. In fact we bump into some of them regularly without even realizing it. Unknowingly we may even trust them. Why is that?

One reason why animals are so pure is that they do not care about money or luxuries or expensive possessions. Their love is based on their personal interactions with other animals and with humans. If those interactions are good, their love is unconditional. I don't know if it's possible for a human to give unconditional love, but I try to do so with all animals. I follow their lead.

I can honestly say that animals have made my life whole and have never caused me harm – grief yes, when they were gone - but never harm. I am unable to give that blanket statement regarding humans.

**Peanut - a miniature donkey I recently saved
From A Kill Pen in Pennsylvania**

The best that I can do is say that there are some wonderful, kind hearted, good to the soul people in the world. Ironically I met several of these wonderful people through the horses and animals – one way or another.

My personal belief is that one should be wary of anyone who does not like animals or causes them harm. In my opinion there is something intrinsically wrong with these people. I believe that at the very least, people who don't care for animals will inherently hurt you in some way. In the worst case they can be devastatingly destructive to your life. I would not trust someone who has no feelings for animals, because I believe there is an evil component to such people. Be very careful when dealing with these people. The truly devastating blows which I have received in my life have inevitably come from such heartless people. It is difficult to recover.

I was hoping to accomplish a few things with this book. First, I wanted to show how a life of one who has followed their heart and shared that life with horses and animals, could be exciting, rewarding and even profitable – although profit should not be the number one motive. Profit should only come as a result of improving the lives of animals and preparing them for a world where they may happily excel – whatever that may be.

Secondly, I am hoping to raise people's appreciation of their animals and perhaps even their understanding of them. Animals give us so much every day, we should reciprocate with love, good care, protection and providing a good life for them. We are constantly rewarded with their unconditional love.

Thirdly, I wanted to point out how much we can and do learn from animals. I believe animals are much wiser than humans in some dimensions, such as the understanding of life and death. When animals are prepared to die of natural causes such as old age, they often quietly go off alone and allow the passage. There is no fear or panic – just a level of understanding and acceptance regarding death, which humans have yet to achieve. I often wonder, what do they know that we do not?

Animals speak all the time. They speak with their eyes, their souls, their mannerisms and often their voice. The problem is that humans generally don't pay attention and listen. It's not the horse's or the animal's responsibility to understand us. It is our responsibility to understand them.

We all need to remember, it's the animal's world too – just as much as it is ours. Maybe more so, because they don't do as much harm to the planet or to each other as humans do.

People have often praised me for saving animals, but the truth is that the horses and animals have saved me and kept me going – right up to this very day.

Open your heart.

Save a life and see how that life can save you.

That is From Where My Strength Lies.

That is why I became a Horse Whisperer.

Some of the Wonderful Horses I have developed and loved

ACKNOWLEDGEMENTS

As many of the photographs used in this book are older and do not have a photo credit printed on the actual photo, I shall list all of the horse show photographers which I am able to remember. If I have missed anyone, it is because there were no photo credits available on the photo. Thank you to all of the photographers for their beautiful work. My apologies to anyone who may have been omitted by accident.

I have also listed all of the credits I was able to find for the photos from "The Troubles" in Crossmaglen, Northern Ireland during the 1970s.

<u>The Photographers from Northern Ireland and the UK - Credits</u>:

Pinterest.com, belfasttelegraph.co.uk, rte.ie, wikiwand.com, flashback.com, pressreader.com, gettyimages', Imperial War Museum, alamy.com

<u>The Photographers from the Horse Shows – Credits</u>:

James Parker

Pennington

Darkroom on Wheels

The Bud Brothers

Liz Callar

Bud Smith

Again, I apologize to anyone who may have been missed, but I thank every one of you for your fabulous work. It enables all of us to enjoy our wonderful memories.

I would also like to express my sincere gratitude to Thomas Bendixen for his patience in the formatting and editing of this book, as well as the navigation of Amazon.com.

There are way too many people to name who have inspired me to write this book and to whom I am extremely grateful. I can start with the Wheeler family, Helen Bilby, Robert Crandall, Andrea DeMarco, Albert D'Ambrosio, Hallie McEvoy, Bobbie Reber and Mary Donner, but there are so many more. I am grateful to everyone who has inspired me and shown interest and support for my work – whether it be with the horses, animals or my book.

Thank you and God Bless to ALL my friends and to the horses and animals who make us what we are. We owe them everything.

Made in the USA
Middletown, DE
25 September 2019